Childhood in Contemporary Performance of Shakespeare

RELATED TITLES

Early Modern Theatre and the Figure of Disability
Genevieve Love
ISBN 978-1-350-01720-7

Imagining Cleopatra: Performing Gender and Power in Early Modern England
Yasmin Arshad
ISBN 978-1-350-05896-5

Performing Shakespeare's Women
Paige Martin Reynolds
ISBN 978-1-350-00259-3

Shakespeare's Body Language: Shaming Gestures and Gender Politics on the Renaissance Stage
Miranda Fay Thomas
ISBN 978-1-350-03547-8

Shakespearean Character: Language in Performance
Jelena Marelj
ISBN 978-1-350-06138-5

Shakespeare and the Politics of Nostalgia: Negotiating the Memory of Elizabeth I on the Jacobean Stage
Yuichi Tsukada
ISBN 978-1-350-06722-6

Childhood in Contemporary Performance of Shakespeare

Gemma Miller

THE ARDEN SHAKESPEARE
LONDON • NEW YORK • OXFORD • NEW DELHI • SYDNEY

THE ARDEN SHAKESPEARE
Bloomsbury Publishing Plc
50 Bedford Square, London, WC1B 3DP, UK
1385 Broadway, New York, NY 10018, USA
29 Earlsfort Terrace, Dublin 2, Ireland

BLOOMSBURY, THE ARDEN SHAKESPEARE and the Arden Shakespeare logo are trademarks of Bloomsbury Publishing Plc

First published in Great Britain 2020
This paperback edition published in 2021

Copyright © Gemma Miller, 2020

Gemma Miller has asserted her right under the Copyright, Designs and Patents Act, 1988, to be identified as author of this work.

For legal purposes the Acknowledgements on pp. x–xi constitute an extension of this copyright page.

Cover design: Charlotte Daniels
Cover image © Arno Declair Photography

All rights reserved. No part of this publication may be reproduced or transmitted in any form or by any means, electronic or mechanical, including photocopying, recording, or any information storage or retrieval system, without prior permission in writing from the publishers.

Bloomsbury Publishing Plc does not have any control over, or responsibility for, any third-party websites referred to or in this book. All internet addresses given in this book were correct at the time of going to press. The author and publisher regret any inconvenience caused if addresses have changed or sites have ceased to exist, but can accept no responsibility for any such changes.

A catalogue record for this book is available from the British Library.

A catalog record for this book is available from the Library of Congress.

ISBN: HB: 978-1-3501-3314-3
PB: 978-1-3502-3947-0
ePDF: 978-1-3501-3316-7
eBook: 978-1-3501-3315-0

Typeset by Integra Software Services Pvt. Ltd.

To find out more about our authors and books visit www.bloomsbury.com and sign up for our newsletters.

To Tony Burnett

CONTENTS

List of Figures viii
Acknowledgements x
Notes on the Text xii
List of Abbreviations xiii

Introduction
   Simulacrum and Surrogation: The Children of Christopher Wheeldon's *The Winter's Tale* (2014/16) 1

1 From the Facsimile Page to the Plastic Princes: The Effacement of Childhood in *Richard III* 23

2 'Fair is foul and foul is fair': The Janus-Faced Child in *Macbeth* 57

3 'Behold the child': The Burden of Futurity in *Titus Andronicus* 93

4 'No age': Disappearing Childhood in *The Winter's Tale* 135

Conclusion
   Performing Childhood: Shakespeare and Beyond 175

Notes 179
References 189
Index 217

LIST OF FIGURES

1. Edward Watson as Leontes and Lauren Cuthbertson as Hermione, in *The Winter's Tale*, dir. Christopher Wheeldon, 10 April 2014 2
2. Gary Avis as Father Shepherd, in *The Winter's Tale*, dir. Christopher Wheeldon, 10 April 2014 4
3. Henry Goodman as Richard and David Jowett as the page, in *Richard III*, dir. Sean Holmes, 2003 35
4. Laurenz Laufenberg as Rivers, Christoph Gawenda as Clarence, Dorset and Stanley, Jenny König as Lady Anne, Eva Meckbach as Elizabeth, Lars Eidinger as Richard and Thomas Bading as Lord Mayor of London, in *Richard III*, a production of Schaubühne Berlin, dir. Thomas Ostermeier, 2015 41
5. James McAvoy as Macbeth and Claire Foy as Lady Macbeth, in *Macbeth*, dir. Jamie Lloyd, 2012 66
6. Unidentified actor as witch, in *Macbeth*, dir. Michael Boyd, 2011 72
7. Seylan Baxter, Lynn Kennedy, Kayla Fallon and Anber Rissmann as the witches, in *Macbeth*, dir. Justin Kurzel, 2015 85
8. Marion Cotillard as Lady Macbeth, in *Macbeth*, dir. Justin Kurzel, 2015 87

9   Scot Greenan as boy-soldier in *Macbeth*, dir. Justin Kurzel, 2015   89
10 Edward Hardwicke as Marcus, Paul Davies Prowles as Young Lucius, Trevor Peacock as Titus and unidentified male in *Titus Andronicus*, dir. Jane Howell, 1985   115
11 Paul Davies Prowles as Young Lucius, in *Titus Andronicus*, dir. Jane Howell, 1985   117
12 Osheen Jones as Young Lucius in *Titus*, dir. Julie Taymor, 1999   121
13 Osheen Jones as Young Lucius in *Titus*, dir. Julie Taymor, 1999   123
14 Unidentified actor as Aaron's baby in *Titus*, dir. Julie Taymor, 1999   129
15 Alex Jennings as Leontes and Liam Hess as Mamillius, in *The Winter's Tale*, dir. Nicholas Hytner, 2001   148
16 Pierre Atri as Mamillius and Judi Dench as Paulina, in *The Winter's Tale*, dir. Kenneth Branagh and Rob Ashford, 2015/16   159

ACKNOWLEDGEMENTS

I am grateful to Lara Bateman, Mark Dudgeon and everybody at the Arden Shakespeare for agreeing to publish this book and for providing support and guidance throughout. The feedback from the three anonymous reviewers for Arden was encouraging and perceptive, and my book is undoubtedly a more polished version of its original incarnation as a result of their suggestions. I would like to thank Carol Chillington Rutter, whose article 'Remind Me: How Many Children Had Lady Macbeth?' set me on this interesting journey into Shakespeare's children, and Lucy Munro, my PhD supervisor at King's College London, whose support over the past five years has been invaluable. She has helped me to develop my ideas into a focused study and provided guidance and encouragement throughout, never allowing me to lose faith in the value of my project. I am also grateful to Gordon McMullan, whose timely interventions at key stages in my research have been vital to keeping my project on track.

I am extremely grateful to my MA supervisor at Birkbeck, Gillian Woods, for encouraging me to undertake this project and giving me the confidence to apply for PhD funding. Without the generous grant from the London Arts and Humanities Partnership, I would not have been able to dedicate the three years to this project. Many thanks to Valeria Faruggia, Stephen Colvin and everybody at LAHP for their support and encouragement. I am grateful to the Shakespeare Birthplace Trust, The National Theatre Archives and the Glasgow University Archives for allowing me to access their material, which has been essential for my research, and to Michael Boyd, Edward Stambollouian, Stuart Delves and Nick Morrison for generously sharing insights into the artistic process behind their productions. A special thank you is due to Ithaca College London Centre and the Society for Theatre Research for kindly sponsoring my images, and to all the photographers, theatres, film production companies and image archivists for allowing me to reproduce their images in this book. Finally, I dedicate this book to my friends and family, particularly Tony and Kate Burnett, and Howard, my husband, without whom I would not have been able to start, let alone finish, this project.

NOTES ON THE TEXT

All early modern primary sources can be found on *Early English Books Online* (*EEBO*) unless otherwise stated.

Theatre reviews and newspaper articles are all listed under secondary sources in the references.

All references to Shakespeare's plays and sonnets are taken from the Arden Third Series unless otherwise stated.

LIST OF ABBREVIATIONS

EEBO *Early English Books Online*

OED *Oxford English Dictionary Online*

RSC Royal Shakespeare Company, Stratford-upon-Avon

SBT Shakespeare Birthplace Trust, Stratford-upon-Avon

Introduction

Simulacrum and Surrogation: The Children of Christopher Wheeldon's *The Winter's Tale* (2014/16)

When the statue was unveiled in the final act of Christopher Wheeldon's balletic adaptation of Shakespeare's *The Winter's Tale*, it was revealed to be a double statue: both Hermione and Mamillius had apparently been immortalized in stone. However, the double statue did not equal a double resurrection. Almost immediately Hermione began to descend from the plinth, leaving Mamillius frozen in time, his right arm bent stiffly across his body and his face fixed in a wide-eyed expression of horror. It was a disconcertingly un-lifelike representation that did not appear designed to evoke the face of the young dancer Joe Parker who had played Mamillius in the first act. Hermione and Leontes danced their final *pas de deux* in front of the statue, their passionate and soberly joyful movements throwing his rigid, lifeless pose into high relief (see Figure 1). At one point, Leontes returned to the statue and reached out his hand but was gently led away by Paulina. There was to be no second miracle in Wheeldon's bleak interpretation of Shakespeare's notoriously ambiguous ending. As the reunited family embraced, Mamillius's

FIGURE 1 *Edward Watson as Leontes and Lauren Cuthbertson as Hermione, in* The Winter's Tale, *dir. Christopher Wheeldon, 10 April 2014. Courtesy Johan Persson/ArenaPAL.*

statue loomed over them like a spectral interloper, his conspicuous absence from the text turned into a conspicuous and overdetermined presence in petrified form. In her insightful analysis of Wheeldon's ballet, Judith Buchanan argues that by bringing the boy's statue on stage in this way, Wheeldon flirted with the possible resurrection of Mamillius and deepened the tragedy by 'toying with, and then decisively eschewing, this possibility' (Buchanan 2017: 127). However, the statue of Mamillius was so self-evidently *not* human that there could be no question of its animation. And this was the point: the replacement of the boy Mamillius with a statuary surrogate drew attention to his absence by the manifest failure of that very surrogation. The statue's stiffly formal stance, grey death-like pallor and rigid, horror-stricken expression left the audience in no doubt of its artificiality. It was a simulacrum that seemed designed to evoke memories of what it was so clearly failing to simulate – the face and body of a lively and vibrant young boy.

Wheeldon's production of *The Winter's Tale* was significant for a number of reasons. It was the first ever full-length balletic adaptation of the play and the first Shakespearean ballet to premiere at the Royal Opera House in fifty years.[1] It was hailed as 'the finest and most important, new full-evening ballet in recent memory' (Monahan 2016) by the *Telegraph* dance reviewer and was revived in April 2016 for a ten-week run. It was also staged by the National Ballet of Canada in Toronto in December 2016 and premiered in Australia in 2017. The performance was broadcast by live relay into over one thousand cinemas worldwide on 28 April 2014 followed by 250 'encore' screenings and a DVD released in early 2015. It was a commercial and critical success, praised in particular for its 'freshness' (Crompton 2014), 'extraordinarily inventive and resonant designs', 'spectacular video projections' and 'scintillating score' (Norman 2016). I saw this ballet live during its revival in 2016 and subsequently at an 'encore' cinematic screening and on DVD. What struck me as particularly significant about Wheeldon's adaptation, however, was less the choreography, music and design (although these were, to my untutored eyes, rightly hailed as breathtaking) than the striking and unconventional resurrection of Mamillius in the form of a horror-stricken statue.

In the opening sequence of this ballet, the dancer playing Mamillius briefly appeared as a young version of Leontes playing with his boyhood friend Polixenes. The two children then disappeared into the crowd and their adult selves emerged, danced by Edward Watson (Leontes) and Federico Bonelli (Polixenes), dressed in the same costumes as their miniature doubles. When Leontes looked at Mamillius, he was thus seeing not merely his likeness but his own childhood brought back to haunt him, and the statue represented the death not only of his son but also of his own infantile self. Mamillius's statuary surrogate was not the only eerily anti-illusionistic representation of childhood on display in this production. The animatronic baby Perdita, abandoned on the shores of Bohemia in her bassinet at the end of the first act, was also self-evidently artificial. As with the waxy pallor and fixed, terrified glare of Mamillius's statue, the jerky robotic movements of the mechanical baby seemed designed to foreground rather than conceal its uncanny, un-human and decidedly un-lifelike qualities. The close camera shots in the livecast and DVD recording made this artificiality even more apparent. What might have seemed momentarily 'real', and therefore slightly disconcerting, for the theatre audience was manifestly not so for those watching in the cinema. For a production whose sumptuous set, designed by

FIGURE 2 *Gary Avis as Father Shepherd, in* The Winter's Tale, *dir. Christopher Wheeldon, 10 April 2014. Courtesy Johan Persson/ArenaPAL.*

Bob Crowley, suggested that no expense had been spared, it was particularly striking that the two children should be represented in such crude and unrealistic forms. By drawing attention to Mamillius's statue and the robotic baby in this way, Wheeldon seemed to be deliberately subverting the child as object of the gaze and bringing the ontology of childhood itself into question.

The manifestation of childhood in Wheeldon's production was symptomatic of a move in contemporary performance of Shakespeare towards a de-idealization and demystification of ideas about childhood. The reincarnation of Mamillius as a statue was a novel way of staging the return of the dead child. However, as I demonstrate in Chapter 4, it was just one technique among many that directors have employed in recent years to remind audiences that at the end of *The Winter's Tale*, in the words of Stanley Cavell, 'a dead five- or six-year-old boy remains unaccounted for' (2003: 193). Wheeldon's double statue not only problematized the happy ending but also brought into focus questions about the nature of childhood and its relation to authority, agency, temporality and the gaze. Moreover, the substitution of the body of the child for an artificial surrogate also foregrounded what childhood scholars have identified as a peculiarly postmodern crisis: the crisis of 'disappearing childhood' (Postman [1982] 1994: 98).[2] I expand upon these tropes throughout this book as I demonstrate, through the close analysis of a range of contemporary Shakespearean productions, how the dramatization of his children in recent years – on the stage, on film, in television adaptations and in simulcast and 'encore' screenings – has provided a lens through which to view changing ideas about childhood and the rhetoric surrounding it more generally. Shakespeare's children have quite simply become increasingly central to our understanding of his plays in performance.

Child characters feature more numerously and prominently in the Shakespearean canon than in that of any other early modern playwright (Campana 2011: 1); how they are reflected, refracted and reinterpreted in performance thus provides valuable insights into modern concerns about how we see not only our pasts but also, and perhaps more importantly, our futures.[3] As a group, Shakespeare's children have all too frequently been treated as supernumeraries, with little dramatic function beyond that of foil for the adult protagonists. Marjorie Garber, for whom Shakespeare's 'pert and malapert' children are a source of disquiet, has commented that 'we are relieved when these terrible infants leave the stage' (1997: 30). Garber's rather dismissive treatment of the child roles in Shakespeare is characteristic of a homogenizing approach that denies the nuanced, individuated and often contradictory nature of these characters and their thematic and dramatic centrality. More significantly, it does not address the affective power of the child in performance, whose stage presence (and absence) invariably exceeds his/her textual significance, a phenomenon which is increasingly evident in contemporary productions. Far from rushing 'these terrible infants' off the stage, directors are increasingly foregrounding the children of Shakespeare's plays through interpolated frame-sequences, strategic doubling of roles, substitutions and ghostly reincarnations. I argue that this is no coincidence, but is rather a response to a conspicuous change in attitudes towards childhood and the ways in which society defines, controls and responds to its children.

Childhood scholars, historians, sociologists and media commentators have identified the 1990s as a time of seismic change in attitudes towards childhood in Western society. The Wheeldon ballet synthesized many of the dramatic devices that have become increasingly commonplace in representations of the Shakespearean child, both on stage and on screen, and is axiomatic of the ways in which perceptions about and manifestations of childhood have shifted. Shakespeare's plays continue to be performed more widely around the globe than those of any other playwright, and thus as a barometer of social anxieties, his plays in performance can provide vital historical information about the pressing concerns of each generation. The plays avoid overly specific topicality in their treatment of trans-historical themes such as ageing, the life-course and intergenerational relationships, and, unlike the restrictive style of realist drama, they are both generically and stylistically fluid and replete with inconsistencies, making them particularly suited to adaptation to later contexts and tastes and to reflect, refract and contribute to contemporary debates. To quote Marjorie Garber again, 'Shakespeare is not only modern but postmodern: a simulacrum, a replicant, a montage' (2008: xvii). As Shakespeare frequently looked to classical antiquity for a paradigm to reflect early modern society, the current generation of directors is increasingly turning to Shakespeare to reflect current social concerns, most notably relating to conceptualizations of childhood.

The children of Shakespeare, as I argue throughout this book, are particularly ambiguous characters. They are frequently on stage for extended periods, and the details of their disappearance are often either unexplained, relayed in brief second-hand reports or entirely elided. The plays therefore invite directors to place their own particular interpretation on these characters, an invitation that they have accepted with increasing inventiveness in recent years. It is all the more surprising, therefore, that this is a subject that is yet to receive sustained critical attention and remains, as Robert Shaughnessy has identified, an 'underdeveloped area of scholarly investigation' (2007: 2). By analysing the performance of Shakespeare's children in the context of what experts have identified as a postmodern crisis in childhood, I argue that the 'terrible infants' of Shakespeare are far from mere supernumeraries, but rather key to unlocking the meanings of the plays and, through their manifestation in performance, vital indicators of social concerns.

'Children of divers kind': Shakespeare's child characters

Childhood is inextricably linked to time: the past, the future and the passing of time from the one to the other; it is thus a concept in which society has a strong political and financial investment. Although parent–child relations underlie the central narrative and symbolic structure in many of Shakespeare's plays, my study limits the definition of 'child' to a life-stage ('childhood' in opposition and contradistinction to 'adulthood') rather than a position in the family ('child' in relation to 'parent') and incorporates not just the child characters but memories of and nostalgia for childhood, as manifested in the adult characters and metaphors of childhood. Issues related to maternity, pregnancy and birthing; the gendering and eroticization of childhood; substitution, surrogation and doubling; and the uncanny nature of the child are all aspects I explore in my analyses. The 'child', for the purposes of this study, is not constrained by specific age parameters (the play texts are often unspecific about the age of the children) and includes babies and infants, as well as lost, dead, remembered and imagined children. As this book makes evident, childhood is far from a stable concept and there are multiple and varied interpretations and manifestations of childhood in the productions I discuss.

James R. Kincaid has controversially asserted that 'a child is, not in itself, anything. Any image, body, or being we can hollow out, purify, exalt, abuse, and locate sneakily in a field of desire will do for us as a "child"' (1992: 5). This is an argument which certainly resonates with my own critical approach and provides a theoretical framework for analysing particular representations of childhood both in performance and in the texts themselves. However, it is too narrow for the wider purposes of this study. I do not concentrate specifically on the child as a 'field of desire' but rather as a blank canvas onto which multiple social, cultural and historical concerns are projected, whether those concerns reflect desires, fears, anxieties or hopes. I argue that each child in each play and in each performance – literal and metaphorical; living and dead; real, imagined, remembered and forgotten – is an amalgam of various ideas about childhood. The points at which these ideas intersect are particularly revealing in terms of the society and context they reflect. The question I address can therefore be summarized as follows: what do these children, as symbols of our past, our present and our future, tell us about the contexts in which they are performed and, conversely, what can those performances teach us about the significance of Shakespeare's children?

Over the past decade, groundbreaking work on childhood in Shakespeare has been produced by scholars including Carol Chillington Rutter, Kate Chedgzoy, Suzanne Greenhalgh and Robert Shaughnessy, Jennifer Higginbotham, Deanne Williams, Charlotte Scott, Michael Witmore and Katie Knowles. However, although some attention has been given to the place of the child characters on the contemporary stage, particularly in the work of Rutter and Knowles, the primary focus of this body of work has been historicist in nature, concentrating on conceptualizations of childhood and how children were dramatized in the early modern period. Rutter, Higginbotham, Knowles and Williams focus specifically on the gendering of childhood, while Witmore's study explores the role of the child in fiction-making. Chedgzoy, Greenhalgh and Shaughnessy's edited collection *Shakespeare and Childhood* pays some attention to performance, but it adopts a wide-ranging and diachronic approach, tracking the afterlives of Shakespeare's children through the centuries rather than concentrating on contemporary adaptations.

In order to address this gap within the arena of Shakespeare and childhood, and to continue the conversation started by the works outlined above, this book explores the ways in which performing childhood in Shakespeare's plays can reveal often uncomfortable truths about conceptualizations of childhood. Where contemporary productions evoke different historical periods, such as Julie Taymor's references to 1930s Fascism in her 1999 film *Titus* and Kenneth Branagh/Rob Ashford's 2015/16 Victorianized stage production of *The Winter's Tale*, a complex form of cultural and temporal palimpsesis occurs. In these instances I explore the particular effects such practices have upon the images of childhood they produce and reflect. My analysis ranges across the different mediums of film (including simulcasts, 'encore' screenings and DVD releases), television and theatre, and incorporates both independent and publicly funded productions. This broad perspective is intended to provide a study that is not overly reliant on one medium, methodology or ideological perspective. I focus primarily on productions in English, staged in the UK, although I also consider some material drawn from outside this frame, such as American films and foreign-language productions. Where possible, I draw on my own viewing experience, incorporating what Clifford Geertz calls 'thick descriptions' (1973: 9) based on semiotic and phenomenological approaches.[4] These descriptions are supported by analyses of sources including promptbooks, director and actor accounts, critical reviews and academic studies in order to provide a multi-perspectival reading that is more multifaceted and less narrowly subjective than one single spectator's impression. I limit my analysis primarily to productions staged in the UK. This is partly for pragmatic reasons relating to availability and accessibility of materials. However I also felt that, were I to extend the scope to incorporate other cultures, the range would be too broad to permit close analysis within the parameters of this book. Most of the productions were filmed or staged in the past three decades. Where I do discuss earlier examples, these are included either because they significantly changed the direction of the plays' performance history, such as Roman Polanski's *Macbeth* (1971), or because they provide a useful point of contrast for more recent adaptations, as in the case of Deborah Warner's *Titus Andronicus* (1987).

I incorporate analyses of the child as an embodied presence, a rhetorical construct and a symbol of idealized pasts and projected futures. I explore the semiotic and phenomenological effects of both the child actor (or child surrogate) and the child character, and the slippage between the two categories and the disjunction between words and embodied presence. I consider how directors rewrite the text through the reordering of temporal sequence, the doubling of key characters, the enlarging or effacement of the role of the child and the multiple ways in which they literalize metaphors of childhood. Although the focus of this book is on the child in contemporary performance rather than through history, I conduct close textual analyses of the plays and source materials in order to uncover the origins of the child characters' conception, and thus provide context for their reincarnation in contemporary stage and film productions. And I argue that analysing the performances of childhood in Shakespeare, in their varied and diverse forms, not only facilitates fresh insights into the plays themselves but also enables an appreciation of the wider social context of those performances.

I draw upon a broad range of theoretical studies from multiple disciplines. Performance theorists such as Bert O. States and Nicholas Ridout have produced important works on the phenomenology of theatre, and, while they have acknowledged to some extent what Ridout terms the 'affecting surplus' (2006: 68) of the child on stage, the child has not formed a central part of either scholar's thesis. As Ridout himself observes, the subject of childhood in performance 'is a topic in its own right, and awaits a full study' (2006: 98–9). I take their interpretive paradigms (and Ridout's critical challenge) as a starting point and, referring to theorizations of gender, sexuality and subjectivity by writers such as Lee Edelman, Kathryn Bond Stockton, Laura Mulvey, James R. Kincaid and Anne Higonnet, I explore the performing child as it relates to the 'gaze' of the adult spectator and the fetishistic nature of viewing.[5] The work of these scholars provides a useful critical entry point into exploring representations of childhood, especially in relation to the darker side of childhood innocence and what Kincaid calls the 'alluring child' (1998: 20): a complex and self-contradictory amalgam of innocence, precocity and eroticism that, although originating in the Victorian period, is also a curiously postmodern imposition. Although many contemporary directors now use the Shakespearean child in performance as a means to interrogate received notions about childhood, the 'alluring child' is still evident in some adaptations, as this book demonstrates.

Three key writers who have made significant contributions to childhood and its literary and cultural formations, and who provide crucial critical frameworks for my work, are James R. Kincaid, Lee Edelman and Kathryn Bond Stockton. According to Kincaid, whose work on the sexualization of children in postmodern Western culture broke new critical grounds, the 'construct' of the child as both corrupted and innocent, desirable and outside the bounds of desire, is repeated endlessly through popular discourse to the extent that it has become a firmly entrenched cultural myth. Maintaining the idea of childhood as a discrete temporal state separate from adulthood is central to maintaining this very myth. Kincaid traces the origins of childhood innocence – a fantasy created by adults that both relies upon and sustains its obverse, the eroticofetishization of childhood – back to the Victorians via Rousseau, Wordsworth 'and a thousand lesser writers, interior decorators, and producers of greeting cards' (1992: 72). However, the extent to which ideals about childhood innocence dominated Victorian attitudes, he maintains, has been vastly overstated and reveals more about twentieth-century needs and anxieties than it does about the Victorians themselves. The result is the postmodern child, which he describes as a 'both radiant and oddly repellant, the object of fawning and not-so-secret resentment' (1998: 53).

While these facts do not erase the Victorian fetishization of childhood 'innocence', as is evident in the literature and art of the period, they do nonetheless provide an instructive corrective. What has entered into popular discourse, then, is a partial snapshot of Victorian culture. The fetishization of the child is, as Kincaid argues, a peculiarly postmodern phenomenon that relies on selective historical memory – a fragmentary and imperfect field through which to interpret the present – in order to perpetuate its own mythology of childhood as at once innocent, desirable and 'other', and to fuel and sustain the narrative of a childhood in 'crisis'.[6] Although there has been a discernable shift away from fetishizing childhood innocence in performance, the fetishization, objectification and exploitation of the child continue to dominate some productions of Shakespeare's plays, as will be seen in my discussion of, in particular, Julie Taymor's *Titus*, Roman Polanski's *Macbeth* and Kenneth Branagh/Rob Ashford's *The Winter's Tale*.

Lee Edelman's polemical study of what he terms 'reproductive futurism' (2004: 3) also explores the fetishization of childhood, drawing, like Kincaid, upon nineteenth-century constructions of childhood as exemplars and precursors of postmodern child-worship. However, where Kincaid considers the child as object of adult desire, Edelman's focus turns towards the child as an emblem of futurity, albeit one in which the child 'must never grow up' (2004: 21) and thus must forever retain its symbolic innocence. Approaching the subject through the lens of queer theory, he argues that representing the child as a means of preserving the present by securing the future is a commonplace so unquestioned as to have become morally unquestionable. 'That Child', he argues, 'remains the perpetual horizon of every acknowledged politics, the fantasmic beneficiary of every political intervention', and thus excludes nonreproductive eros from its formulation (2004: 3). As the antithesis of the future-preserving 'Child', the queer (and queerness) is the only form of resistance, for, as he argues, 'queerness names the side [...] outside the consensus by which all politics confirms the absolute value of reproductive futurism' (2004). For Edelman, then, the 'Child' is an instrumental symbol of the future in the present and therefore embedded in conservative, heteronormative ideologies. Queerness, as a deviance from this ideal, represents a threat to the future functioning of society and is thus marginalized as social deviance. His response is a challenge to political orthodoxies through a queer resistance in the form of what he has termed the 'Sinthomosexual' – a figure who rejects 'the rhetoric of compassion, futurity, and life' (2004: 75) to embrace a 'surplus of jouissance' (2004: 74). Edelman's is a bleak and nihilistic anti-utopianism which inevitably results in 'the undoing of social organization, collective reality, and, inevitably, of life itself' (2004: 13). As a consequence, he has been criticized by fellow queer theorists such as Judith Halberstam (Dinshaw 2007: 194–5) and José Esteban Muñoz (2009: 11) for 'epistemological self-destruction' by failing to offer a viable alternative that, as Halberstam argues, 'works against the grain of the true, the good, and the right but one that nonetheless refuses to make a new orthodoxy out of negativity' (Dinshaw 2007: 194). I argue, moreover, that by proposing a rejection of, rather than an alternative to, the orthodoxy of 'reproductive futurism', Edelman accepts and thus perpetuates the 'cult of the Child'. Rather than suggesting a reconfiguration of attitudes towards childhood, he quite simply accepts them as an inevitability, reinforcing the very heteronormative paradigms he critiques (Edelman 2004: 19). In Chapter 1, I demonstrate how directors such as Sean Holmes and Thomas Ostermeier have rejected the concept of 'reproductive futurism' that Edelman reinscribes through their subversive representations of the child in Shakespeare's *Richard III*. By manifesting the child on stage in non-conventional ways, ways similar to the children of Wheeldon's *The Winter's Tale*, these directors undermined the cult of fetishizing childhood and brought into question the figural associations of childhood and futurity sustained by theorists such as Edelman.

Building upon the work of Kincaid and Edelman, Kathryn Bond Stockton's 2009 monograph, *The Queer Child or Growing Sideways in the Twentieth Century*, explores cultural and literary representations of childhood that do not conform to ideals of continuance and teleological development. She calls this phenomenon 'sideways growth', something 'related but not reducible to the death drive; something that locates energy, pleasure, vitality, and (e)motion in the back-and-forth of connections and extensions that are not reproductive' (2009: 13). Stockton observes that 'the child is precisely who we are not and, in fact, never were. It is the act of adults looking back, it is a ghostly, unreachable fancy' (2009: 5). By constructing a retrospective narrative of childhood as a linear progression from one state of being to the next, while simultaneously 'delaying a temporal approach to a time it is not (namely, adulthood)', Stockton argues that we fetishize childhood and thus enact 'violence' on both adults and children (2009: 15). Stockton concentrates on twentieth-century texts, thus differentiating her study from the nineteenth-century-focused work of her predecessors. Like Kincaid, however, Stockton rejects the idealized image of childhood as a state of imperilled 'innocence'. To truly understand childhood, she concludes, we must disavow childhood 'innocence' and acknowledge instead 'the darkness of the child' (2009: 3). Stockton's work helps to frame my analyses of representations of children that disrupt the narrative of 'straight' temporal development, such as the portrayal of the emotionally stunted Leontes in Nicholas Hytner's *The Winter's Tale* (2001).

Disappearing childhood: A postmodern crisis and Shakespeare

The writings of the scholars discussed above have been key to framing current debates about childhood, Shakespeare and the theatre, and inform my own critical methodologies throughout this book. The overriding concern which connects these scholars in their various approaches to childhood is the question of temporality. Of course, the 'polychronicity' of Shakespeare's plays is a well-rehearsed topic, particularly in works by, for example, Jonathan Gil Harris (2009), Matthew Wagner (2012) and Phyllis Rackin (1986). What my book illuminates, however, is the particular way in which the temporally disruptive children of Shakespeare's plays intersect with the child (or surrogate) in performance and what that point of intersection reveals about our understanding of Shakespeare's children and our attitudes towards childhood. Childhood scholar Hugh Cunningham summarizes this phenomenon as follows:

> In the second half of the twentieth century it was the sense of an erosion or even disappearance of childhood which dominated discussion: children began to claim and be given rights which enabled them to break out of the garden [of protected 'innocence']; some of them, like the killers of James Bulger in Britain, failed spectacularly to live up to the innocence supposedly innate in all children; many more, perhaps all, seemed to be losing their childhood early under the pressures of the twin forces of the media and of mass consumption.
>
> (2005: 172)

According to Cunningham, while, on the one hand, the 'garden' of childhood was being prolonged by the delayed accession of the child from education into the workplace and the concomitant shift from net consumer to net producer, an increase in their rights was also giving them the voice and agency to break free from that very 'garden' of protection. Many sociologists and childhood scholars agree that the conviction of two ten-year-old boys for the torture and murder of toddler James Bulger in 1993 was a particularly significant landmark in terms of changing perceptions of childhood. It not only led to legislative change, but it attracted unprecedented scrutiny across multiple global platforms and provided a touchstone for redefining childhood and its putative innocence.[7] It was also used as an example, however spurious, of the pernicious effects of media – in this case the 'video nasty' horror films – upon the vulnerable infantile mind, although, somewhat ironically, it was the frenzied intervention of the print media (from *The Economist* to *The Sun*) that triggered this 'immediate and ferocious moral panic' and fuelled the ensuing change in public opinion (Cohen 2002: viii–x).

The postmodern sense of a 'childhood in crisis' can thus be considered as not so much a reflection of reality than as a reaction to changes in the agency afforded to and enjoyed by children towards the end of the twentieth century. Having granted children more rights to self-determination and self-expression, and the media through which to express and define themselves, are adults now creating a 'crisis' in order to regain some of the power they have ceded by holding children up to an 'innocent' ideal that never actually existed? In this book, I explore the performance of childhood in four key Shakespeare plays – *Richard III*, *Macbeth*, *Titus Andronicus* and *The Winter's Tale* – within the context of this current crisis in childhood. Although often overlooked by academics, I argue that the children in these plays have a figural and dramatic significance that exceeds the sum of their spoken lines and that directors are beginning to realize this in multiple and various ways. I look at the ways in which the role of the child has been adapted, occluded, substituted and exploited in performance. I examine what these performances reveal about the children in the plays themselves and how they have contributed to the wider debate about childhood. Experimental directors such as Thomas Ostermeier and Sean Holmes have begun to explicitly interrogate the concept of the 'innocent' ideal, while others such as Kenneth Branagh and Rob Ashford have sought to reinforce it through deliberate obfuscation, often with unintended consequences. Whether questioning or evasive, radical or conservative, recent productions have increasingly taken the child as their central dramatic focus, not merely reflecting but actively contributing to the debate about childhood and what it means in a postmodern era of uncertainty and change.

Journalist Libby Brooks observes that childhood remains now, as it has throughout history, 'a disputed territory of memory and meaning' (2006: 4). It is a state, moreover, in which adults believe they have a privileged insight, having once been children themselves. However, the disjunction between the often-idealized memories of a childhood past and the varied lived experiences of a current generation of children means that reality and expectation rarely converge. Thus, childhood inevitably becomes 'a story grown-ups tell themselves' – a story, according to Brooks, that functions to 'explain away personal frailties and to position collective anxieties' (2006: 5). These collective anxieties came into sharper focus in the last few decades of the twentieth century; as historian Hugh Cunningham argues, 'People [...] began to doubt that it was possible to preserve in any integrity the territory mapped out as childhood.' The result, he gloomily concludes, is that 'children themselves become alien creatures, a threat to civilisation rather than its hope and potential salvation' ([1995] 2005: 187). Childhood, a life-stage and a concept which, during the nineteenth century and the first few decades of the twentieth century, was largely reified, idealized, exalted and protected – albeit shadowed, as scholars such as James R. Kincaid and Christine Roth have demonstrated, by a desire to eroticize and objectify – became somehow 'alien' or 'other' than human.[8] Its status as a period of transition from the Lockean and Rousseauean 'innocent' to responsible adult suddenly seemed far less secure.

The role of children as bearers of a bright and optimistic future has thus become gradually less sharply defined over the past few decades, and scholars have begun to look for reasons to explain this trend. What emerged was a remarkable coincidence of events that shaped the critical arena for decades to follow: the release of Neil Postman's *The Disappearance of Childhood* ([1982] 1994), the murder of James Bulger (1993) and the rise of childhood studies as an academic discipline. Postman's book was the first major study about the pernicious effects of technological innovations upon children, arguing that television was the catalyst for the disappearance of childhood through the removal of barriers to adult knowledge and experience. Postman suggests that childhood is a social construct rather than an intrinsic or timeless biological state and that its emergence and disappearance can be linked to specific cultural phenomena. The basis of Postman's thesis is that the rise in childhood coincided with the arrival of a print culture in the seventeenth century and its decline with the invention of electronic media, specifically the television, in the twentieth century. For Postman, the crucial aspect separating childhood and adulthood is the existence of secrets: 'secrets about sexual relations, but also about money, violence, about illness, about death, about social relations' (1993: 49). Access to these secrets, according to Postman, gives children a knowingness that they previously did not have, and that, as a result, childhood as an identifiable life-stage between infancy and adulthood (for Postman, this is specifically the age between seven and seventeen) is 'difficult to sustain and, in fact, irrelevant' (xiii). 'If', he asks, 'the children know the mysteries and the secrets, how shall we tell them apart from anyone else?' (88). This question is one which directors have been addressing with increasing frequency and urgency in their depiction of the Shakespearean child in performance.

As bearers of such complex and contradictory symbolic weight, it is not surprising that children are featuring more prominently in modern productions of Shakespeare, whether in the form of the evil/innocent child motif in *Richard III* and *Macbeth*, as I discuss in Chapters 1 and 2; as both witness and actor in productions of *Titus Andronicus*, as explored in Chapter 3; or as the *puer senex* trope in adaptations of *The Winter's Tale*, as we see in Chapter 4. Through a close analysis of specific examples from four key plays with their own particular investments in childhood, I explore how these dichotomous attitudes to childhood are manifested in performance. I analyse how the child is presented, what that representation means for our understanding of the plays and how that reflects, illuminates and contributes to this unique era of uncertainty. Each chapter concentrates on one Shakespearean play and compares a number of different productions across the mediums of film, television and theatre. I have chosen to restrict my analysis to just four plays to provide depth of analysis rather than a broad (and potentially shallow) overview of a greater number of plays. It will not go unnoticed that, apart from the page in *Richard III*, the children in all of the plays I discuss are victims of adult tyranny. This is not to say that Shakespeare only wrote tragic child roles; Moth, the pageboy in *Love's Labour's Lost*, or William Page in *The Merry Wives of Windsor*, for instance, has far happier outcomes. But, as Charlotte Scott has observed, apart from William, 'There are no young children in Shakespeare's comedies' (2018: 103). Even taking into account the pageboys, there are just eleven speaking roles for children with a total of 233 lines (Lawhorn 2007: 237–47), and none of these children are of central dramatic or narrative significance. The children of *Macbeth*, *The Winter's Tale*, *Richard III* and *Titus Andronicus*, by contrast, are not merely commentators on the dramatic action but pivotal figures in the central conflict around which the plays revolve. It is no coincidence perhaps that these particular plays have been adapted for stage and film more frequently in the past four decades than either *Love's Labour's Lost* or *The Merry Wives of Windsor*.

The first chapter, 'From the Facsimile Page to the Plastic Princes: The Effacement of Childhood in *Richard III*', addresses the play with the largest number of speaking roles for children with singularly unique and vital afterlives. It considers two stage productions of *Richard III* that are symptomatic of a trend towards de-idealizing childhood in performance. In Sean Holmes's 2003 production, the young pageboy, who was styled as a miniature facsimile of Richard, was knowing, precocious and the antithesis of Edelman's 'sacred child' (2004: 19). Far from a guardian of futurity, this young boy began as a dramatic manifestation of the child as a 'reproductive medium' and developed into an infanticidal agent with political aspirations of his own (Witmore 2007: 174). Thomas Ostermeier (2015) undermined the romanticized idealization of childhood through unconventional casting choices. By replacing his boy-princes with puppets, Ostermeier refused to put the body of the child on display, thus exposing and rejecting sentimentalized images of children and highlighting the way in which 'childhood' is appropriated and propagated as an emblem of both purity and futurity. By using *Richard III* as a means to interrogate received notions about childhood in this way, Holmes and Ostermeier broke with a long performance tradition of fetishizing childhood innocence to establish new ways of thinking about the child in performance.

Chapter 2, '"Fair is foul and foul is fair": The Janus-Faced Child in *Macbeth*', looks at the ways in which the multiple and diverse manifestations of childhood in *Macbeth* have been represented in performance over the past four decades. Beginning with the question of the Macbeth baby, I analyse a production by Jamie Lloyd (2013), whose dystopian adaptation placed childlessness at its centre. The mysterious Macbeth baby in Lloyd's adaptation was symbolic of not just the 'rooted sorrow' (5.3.41) of one couple but the tragic emblem of a whole society facing an existential crisis.

Next I consider three productions by Michael Boyd (1985, 1993 and 2011) which all featured child actors doubling as the Macduff children and the weird sisters. I look in particular at questions of ontological indeterminacy and temporal disruption arising from the conflation of the human with the supernatural in the figure of the child. Finally, I compare two filmed productions of *Macbeth* by Roman Polanski (1971) and Justin Kurzel (2015) and explore how their contrasting attitudes towards the child reflect a more general shift in thinking about childhood over the four decades between their respective release dates. Although, as we shall see, these six adaptations take different approaches to staging the children of *Macbeth*, they demonstrate the child characters' powerful dramatic potential for turning a mirror on society and showing us our reflection – a reflection that is, in all six cases, barren, bleak and devoid of hope.

Chapter 3, '"Behold the child": The Burden of Futurity in *Titus Andronicus*', picks up the theme of the child as emblem of futurity and considers how three productions have attempted to resolve the play's ambiguous ending and account for the two children in performance. Firstly, I consider Deborah Warner's 1987 stage production which cast a young adult actor rather than a child in the part of Young Lucius and subsumed him into his grandfather's narrative of revenge. Although questions about childhood and agency were raised by Warner's use of a self-evidently artificial baby (as stand-in for Aaron's son), these were questions that the production avoided addressing directly. Unlike Wheeldon's statue of Mamillius, which was particularly striking because it contrasted with an earlier manifestation of the boy as a vibrant young dancer, Warner's prop-baby had no such point of comparison. Her *Titus Andronicus* was a star vehicle for the actor Brian Cox who played Titus, and the 'children', who were ineffectual and inconsequential supporting roles, were kept firmly in the margins. I use Warner's production as a point of contrast for two filmed adaptations by Jane Howell (1985) and Julie Taymor (1999). Far from marginalizing the child, both Howell and Taymor chose to present their films through the eyes of Young Lucius and attempted to resolve the play's ambiguities by gesturing towards a future in their closing sequences. However, in spite of their different ideological and aesthetic approaches, I argue that the ultimate effects of these two films' endings, particularly in terms of how they relate to questions of childhood and futurity, are far more similar than initially appears or were apparently intended.

Chapter 4, '"No age": Disappearing Childhood in *The Winter's Tale*', considers the question of childhood – and its disappearance – in relation to the character of Mamillius. How productions account for the death of this young boy and his absence from the final scene of reconciliation and redemption has profound implications for the overall tone of the play in performance, as we have already seen in the case of Wheeldon's adaptation. The first production I consider, by Nicholas Hytner (2001), foregrounded the death of Mamillius and turned his absence into an overdetermined presence that problematized the redemption of Leontes and his happy ending. Like the lifeless statue in Wheeldon's ballet, his Mamillius haunted the play throughout, ensuring that his audience could not forget that, in Shakespeare's text at least, 'a dead five- or six-year-old boy remains unaccounted for' (Cavell 2003: 193). Finally, I consider Kenneth Branagh and Rob Ashford's 2015/16 production which re-imagined Mamillius as a sentimentalized Victorian 'wise child' created to save his sister and reverse the moral degeneration of his father. For Branagh and Ashford, the tragedy of Mamillius was obviated by locating the tale in a Victorian setting and thus enabling a representation of childhood that was reactionary, nostalgic and, on the surface at least, an evasion of twenty-first-century cultural and social realities. However, I argue that beneath the surface of their romanticized interpretation lay a submerged tale of loss whose silence spoke volumes not only about the 'dead five- or six-year-old boy' but about a society facing a crisis.

Like the Janus-faced children of *Macbeth*, the doomed young princes and precocious page in *Richard III* and the ambiguous children of *Titus Andronicus*, Mamillius is a character who disrupts notions of the child as emblem of futurity. His death presides over the final scene of reconciliation like Banquo at the feast, threatening to disrupt the 'happy ending' with his conspicuous absence. The different ways in which Hytner and Branagh/Ashford managed this final sequence were axiomatic of the anxieties and debates about childhood that I address in the first three chapters. The child in Shakespeare, as I argue throughout this book, is a site of conflicting hopes, desires, fears and doubts. The ways in which directors have approached the question of how to represent the child in performance reveal as much about these under-analysed characters in Shakespeare's plays as they do about the contexts in which they are performed and received. In the past three decades that context has, as Postman, Cunningham, Rutter and many others have argued, been one of increasing uncertainty. The children of Shakespeare have the capacity to not only reflect but contribute to the debate about what childhood represents for a postmodern audience, as directors are realizing through increasingly innovative means. This book illuminates how these children have been manifested in performance and what those performances tell us about the children of Shakespeare and, perhaps more importantly, what they tell us about how we conceptualize childhood today.

1

From the Facsimile Page to the Plastic Princes: The Effacement of Childhood in *Richard III*

Richard III features more speaking roles for children than any other Shakespeare play: Prince Edward; Richard Duke of York; Boy and Daughter, children of George, Duke of Clarence; and Page. However, it is common practice for directors to cut the roles of Clarence's children and the page or re-imagine the page as an adult messenger or aide, thus focusing dramatic attention exclusively on the child-princes, Edward and Richard. Such is the impact of these two young princes that they have provided inspiration for numerous manifestations, adaptations and reinterpretations in the genres of art, theatre and film across the centuries. In terms of cultural purchase, they are arguably as iconic an image of Shakespeare's dramaturgy as Richard himself. However, although Shakespeare's representation of the two boys is nuanced and ambiguous, juxtaposing the precocity and verbosity of the princes with the idealized rhetoric of the adults who mourn their deaths, the tendency in visual, theatrical and cinematic representation has been towards smoothing over such ambiguities to present the boys as icons of innocence and vulnerability. This tendency was particularly prevalent in the nineteenth century, when artists such as James Northcote and intellectuals like William Hazlitt immortalized these child-victims as, in the words of Meolwyn Merchant, 'mawkishly sentimental' symbols of pathos (1959: 75). Colley Cibber's 1700 adaptation was still in common use during this period, and his depiction of the two princes as vulnerable innocents reflected an ongoing desire within nineteenth-century culture to draw boundaries around childhood and preserve its privileged status as a time of innocent charm.[1]

In both the eighteenth and nineteenth centuries it was common practice for the parts of all of Shakespeare's boy-characters, particularly the two princes of *Richard III*, to be played by women. The reasons for this practice of cross-casting were largely pragmatic. As part of the process of protecting and extending the rights of children, legislation affecting the employment of child performers had become increasingly restrictive during the nineteenth century, resulting in more adult women taking the parts of children on stage. Even when a child actor was employed, it was just as likely that a young girl would play the role as a young boy. Gender, it seems, was as much if not more of a factor influencing casting choices as age. It can be argued that it is easier for an audience to accept a woman than a man impersonating a child. Women generally have a smaller frame, higher-pitched voice and smoother skin than men, but this is certainly not always the case. Stephen Orgel argues, in relation to the early modern practice of boys playing female roles, that 'it is important to bear in mind how time-bound the notion of what "women" look like is', and in fact, 'boys do not look any more like women than men do' (1996: 69). The same argument can be applied to the substitution of women for boys in the Victorian theatre. What was it that made children interchangeable with women in the performance of Shakespeare's boys? 'In an era of increasing sentimentality', as Laurence Senelick explains, '[girls] were better than boys at evoking pathos. More tears might be shed over a waif portrayed by a woman (a victim by definition) than over a gangling youth, and the pathetic element was a satisfactory substitute for verisimilitude in male impersonation' (2000: 267–8). The substitution worked, in other words, because of the coincidence between the political, social and literary constructions of women and children as subordinated groups. The dominant representation of childhood during the nineteenth century, as Carolyn Steedman has argued, was feminine or at least endowed with 'a feminised set of qualities' (1995: 8). With the move from sentimentalism to a more realist style of theatre in the twentieth century, the parts have routinely been played by young prepubescent boys. But the emphasis on sentimentality still prevails in many quarters and far from casting Senelick's 'gangling youth[s]' to play the princes, directors have tended to use young boys to evoke pathos and to stage what Bridget Escolme has termed 'the political dramaturgy of grief' (2014: 184).

Demonstrations of grief in Shakespeare's plays can be disempowering and are often both posited against action and gendered female. But, as Escolme explains, these demonstrations of grief can also be, somewhat paradoxically, politically empowering (2014: 190). This can be seen, for instance, in the chorus of mourning women in *Richard III* who intercept Richard and precipitate his tragic downfall, a scene which has no historical precedent (Smith 2019: 38). The power of collective grieving, specifically in relation to iconic images of dead or doomed children, has been particularly compelling in recent years. The case of James Bulger and the poignant CCTV images is one such example of public demonstrations of grief leading to legislative change, as outlined in the Introduction. More recently, the public response to the photograph of the dead three-year-old Syrian boy, Alan Kurdi, washed up on the beach of Turkey in 2015, resulted in the Canadian government removing some of the legal obstacles to obtaining asylum and significantly increasing their quota of Syrian refugees.[2] And in 2017, the case of Charlie Gard, the terminally ill baby whose parents fought a legal battle with Great Ormond Street Hospital for the right to take their son to America for experimental treatment, was widely covered in the world's press. Media reporting of the plight of the parents, accompanied by emotive images of the baby attached to a ventilator, prompted interventions from Donald Trump and the Pope and resulted in mass demonstrations across the UK. Staff at the hospital even received death threats from outraged members of the public (Gore 2017). The efficacy of the 'political dramaturgy of grief' can still be seen in modern productions of *Richard III*, where the bodies of the dead princes are displayed (and sometimes exploited) in order to turn audience sympathy away from Richard. As recently as the second half of the twentieth century and the opening decades of the twenty-first century, films by Laurence Olivier (1955) and Richard Loncraine (1995) and stage productions by Roxana Silbert (2012), Tim Carroll (2012) and Jamie Lloyd (2014) have portrayed the two princes as helpless victims of Richard's tyranny. By foregrounding the prepubescent bodies of the actors, these productions maximized the impact of the boys' vulnerability by turning them into emotive visual signs of what Judith Butler has termed the 'precariousness' and 'grievability' of life (2009: 1–33).³

In spite of an ongoing tendency towards reifying and aestheticizing the two boys in this way, however, there has been a small but growing countercultural movement towards a de-idealization of the young princes. In this chapter, I analyse the way in which two productions that are symptomatic of this trend, directed by Sean Holmes (2003) and Thomas Ostermeier (2015), have effaced or undermined romanticized images of childhood. Both productions were staged as a stand-alone play rather than part of the first tetralogy (or adaptation thereof). As a result, they were not shaped by the teleology of a historical cycle; instead, they focused on Richard as the starring character in his own historical tragedy, rather than a cog in the wheel of a political history.⁴ The portrayal of Richard played an integral part in framing the representation of childhood – or more specifically, the effacement of childhood – in these two remarkable productions.

Emerging from the shadows: The page as the future-killing anti-child in Sean Holmes's *Richard III* (2003)

Breaking with a long-established convention of cutting, doubling or adapting the child roles in *Richard III*, Holmes's production featured five separate child actors to play the roles of Clarence's son and daughter, the Duke of York, Prince Edward and the pageboy.⁵ It was an adaptation that was heavily invested in childhood: as a symbol, a psychological state and an embodied presence. Where many productions, from Cibber's 1700 adaptation through to twenty-first-century revivals, have either cut the page entirely, cast an adult actor in the role or doubled it with another role such as Catesby, Holmes decided to give his young page centre stage as Richard's miniaturized *doppelgänger*, dressed in a matching outfit and dragging his leg behind him in an imitation of Richard's limping gait. Not only did this often-overlooked figure provide a dramatic counterpoint to the other children, but, as Richard's diminutive alter ego, he also problematized hegemonic ideals of the child as a symbol of futurity. In Act 4, Scene 2, the page introduces Richard to Tyrrel who organizes the execution of the two young princes.[6] In his role as facilitator of infanticide and emblem of Richard's enduring legacy of tyranny, Holmes's pageboy was thus the antithesis of Edelman's future-preserving child. Initially appearing as nothing more than a manifestation of Richard's inner child, Richard's page gradually emerged from the shadows to assert his own autonomy. When he dispassionately removed the sword from the grip of his dead master and presented it to Richmond in the final scene, it was as though we were being given a glimpse into a future that was potentially more terrifying than the reign of Richard himself.

Just as he is often excised from performance or re-imagined as an adult, the page is also overlooked in critical analyses of the children in *Richard III*. Carol Chillington Rutter refers to him as 'the extra' and does not elaborate further on the significance of his role (2007a: xiii). Katie Knowles dedicates a chapter to the 'Pages and Schoolboys' of Shakespeare's plays, but does not include Richard's page in her analysis, choosing to focus almost exclusively on Moth and Falstaff's page (2014: 90–122). Marjorie Garber's summary of Shakespearean child characters makes no reference to any of the pageboys, concentrating instead on just the two princes in *Richard III*, the sons of Macduff and Coriolanus, and Mamillius (1997: 30). Although Catherine Belsey acknowledges Richard's page in her account of Shakespearean child characters, she does not elaborate on his dramatic or symbolic function (2007: 32). That he does not appear to merit the same attention as the pages in *Love's Labour's Lost*, *King Henry IV*, *Part 2* or *Henry V*, or in fact the other four child characters in *Richard III*, is almost certainly a consequence of his relatively small speaking role. Compared to the Duke of York's forty-six lines, young Prince Edward's forty-three lines and the twenty-six combined lines of Clarence's two children, the pageboy's total of only six lines seems paltry. To dismiss him as unworthy of consideration because of the size of his spoken contribution, however, is to underestimate his important dramatic function within the overall representation of childhood in this play. The only childhood scholar to recognize the significance of the pageboy's role is Mark Lawhorn, who observes that, as 'the go-between who brings Richard and Tyrrel together', the page qualifies assumptions about childish innocence and 'raises the vexing question of what structurally, thematically or culturally significant purpose the boy figure might be serving' (2007: 239). The 'vexing question' to which he refers, however, remains tantalizingly unanswered in his analysis. It is a question to which Holmes's 2003 production may provide an answer.

The marginalization of the page is not restricted to the academy but finds its corollary in the theatre, where his role is often cut entirely, as is the case in Ostermeier's 2015 production, as we shall see. In the original Elizabethan production, as Bethany Packard notes, the part of the page 'would likely have been doubled by a child actor playing one of the princes' (2013: 125). Richard Madelaine has similarly argued that 'boy actors seem to have done a little doubling, usually minor female parts with minor male parts such as pages, and these doubled parts were almost certainly given to the less-experienced boys' (2003: 232), while Anthony Hammond surmises that 'the smallest member of the company [played] the pert Duke of York, Clarence's daughter, and the Page' (1981: 63). Evelyn Tribble has also argued that young apprentice boy actors would have been trained in 'scaffolded' or 'shepherded' roles before they were able to progress onto more complex parts. A 'scaffolded' role is defined by Tribble as 'a restricted role' with an inbuilt framework and structure that 'prompts the novice actor's activity', while a 'shepherded' role is one in which the 'boy actor is led onto stage and directed by a more experienced actor playing a parental/guardian role' (2009: 7). Taking into account these studies of early modern playing practices, it is fair to assume that the page was doubled with Clarence's son or daughter, other 'scaffolded' roles whose lines and appearances are minimal. From a staging point of view, therefore, there is no practical necessity to cast a separate actor to play the page. His appearance does not overlap with any of the other children and his age is unspecified, making him suitable for doubling, in fact, with any of the other child characters. From a dramatic perspective, doubling the page with one of the other four children (who are, unlike the page, all victims of Richard's tyranny) would problematize a simplistic representation of childhood as a state of vulnerability and innocence. As intermediary between Richard and Tyrrel, the page is an enabler to the murder of the two princes and therefore an important corrective to the rhetoric of childhood purity that is rehearsed by the female characters in Act 4, Scene 4, and in Tyrrel's famous soliloquy in Act 4, Scene 3. Given that he has such dramatic potential and that there are minimal practical staging and casting obstacles, it is noteworthy, therefore, that he has been cut from many modern productions. In order to understand why this might be, I will consider the dramatic, structural and ideological effects of choosing to *include* the pageboy, beginning by exploring his early modern conception.

Shakespeare's page has his origin in the 'secrete page' of Richard as documented by Edward Hall in *The Union of the Two Noble ... Famelies of Lancastre and Yorks* (1547). The brief passage in which he appears is worth quoting in full because it provides some insight into the way in which Shakespeare reinterpreted the role and the resultant dramatic effects:

> He [Richard] sayde to a secrete page of his: Ah, whom shal a man truste: they that I have brought up my selfe, they that I went woulde mave moost surely served me, even those fayle me, and at my commaundemente wyll do nothynge for me. Syr, quod the page, there lieth one in the palet chamber with out that I dare wel say, to do your grace pleasure the thing were right hard that he would refuse, meaning this by James Tirel, which was a man of goodly personage, and for the giftes of nature worthy to have served a muche better prince, yf he had well served God, and by grace obteyned to have as muche trueth and good wyll, as he had strength and wytt. The man had an high harte and sore longed upward ... which thynge the page had well marked and knowen: wherefore this occasion offered of very speciall friendship spied his tyme to set him forwards, and such wyse to do him good, that all the enemies that he had (except the devil) could never have done him so much hurte and shame.
>
> (Hall 1547: *EEBO*, image 282 of 640)

What becomes apparent when comparing Hall's account of the page and Shakespeare's version is the extent to which the page in *Richard III* is aware of and complicit in the murder of the princes. In Hall's version, Richard does not make explicit the task that he has in mind for Tyrrel ('Ah, whom shal a man truste: they that I have brought up my selfe, they that I went woulde mave moost surely served me, even those fayle me, and at my commaundemente wyll do nothynge for me'), whereas in Shakespeare's text, his murderous intention is quite clear when he asks the page directly, 'Know'st thou not any whom corrupting gold / Would tempt unto a close exploit of death?' (4.2.34–5).

It is not obvious whether Shakespeare intended for the page to overhear Richard's prior dialogue with Buckingham, in which case he would be in no doubt as to the proposed victims of the 'close exploit of death'. In this short exchange with Buckingham, Richard makes three references to 'Young Edward' (4.2.10; 4.2.14; 4.2.16) and at one point explicitly states, 'I wish the bastards dead' (4.2.18). Neither Quarto nor Folio texts note the point at which the page enters, although it is conventional in modern editions to have him enter with Richard at the beginning of the scene, which is when he entered in Holmes's production.[7] Whether he overhears Richard and Buckingham's discussion or not, however, the page's description of Tyrrel as a 'discontented gentleman' for whom 'gold were as good as twenty orators' to 'tempt him to anything' (4.2.36–9) confirms that he understands the mission to be less than honourable and is thus complicit, albeit by proxy, in the murder of the two princes. This is a notable departure from Hall's page, who recommends Tyrrel in good faith as a loyal servant with 'an high harte', ignorant of Richard's intent and the 'hurte and shame' it would cause. This subtle but deliberate reinterpretation of the role of the page by Shakespeare provides a potent counterpoint to the repeated associations of the two murdered princes with purity that resonate throughout the play, particularly in the idealized rhetoric of the adults who mourn their loss. By the time the page appears on stage in Act 4, Scene 2, the play has already introduced a tension between this narrative of childhood innocence and the embodied reality of the living child in the figure of the precocious, disrespectful and 'parlous' (2.4.35) Duke of York, a unique character in Shakespeare's drama because, as Charlotte Scott points out, he provides 'the only instance when a character breaks through another's aside' (2018: 32), with his interjected 'what say you, uncle?' (3.1.80). Shakespeare's reinterpreted role of the page is therefore not an anomaly but a further complicating factor, whose presence reinforces and expands upon the multiple and contradictory versions of childhood on display in this play. To overlook this character and the significance of his brief appearance is, therefore, to obtain only a partial understanding of *Richard III*'s nuanced and multifaceted representations of childhood. Moreover, to choose to exclude him from productions is to present a skewed impression of childhood that does not allow for the darker side that is embodied in the page.

Although the overdetermined presence of Holmes's page can be seen as an extension of Shakespeare's original intention, he also has much in common with the page in the anonymous 1594 play, *The True Tragedie of Richard the Third*. In *The True Tragedie*, the page has a total of 103 lines compared with the six allocated to the page in Shakespeare's play.[8] He fulfils multiple dramatic functions: a choric figure who addresses the audience directly; a witness for the allegorical figure, Report; and a faithful servant to Richard who, like Holmes's page, has a 'very speciall friendship' with his master. In Shakespeare's version, however, he appears in only one scene (Act 4, Scene 2) and his role is limited to that of serving boy, a role which Holmes expanded with considerable consequences for his particular interpretation of both Richard's and the pageboy's characters. In his account of playing Richard in this production, Henry Goodman notes that it was his, not Holmes's, idea to expand the stage presence of Richard's page from his one appearance in the text to a total of seven scenes.[9] The page's role, moreover, was adapted to include a further, symbolic function as the manifestation of Richard as an 'adult-child', to use Postman's terminology ([1982] 1994: 98–119). Goodman describes him as 'a young boy in [Richard's] own image', whose 'frequent, silent presence' as his 'only companion' symbolized not only his isolation but also the traumatic childhood experiences that shaped his character (2007: 200, 214). Goodman's account is written from his own personal perspective and therefore inevitably considers only the ways in which the young pageboy impacted upon *his* role as Richard. What he does not take into account is the additional function of the boy's expanded role as a counterpoint to the other four child-victims represented in this production. From this point of view, the pageboy's foregrounded presence as constant companion to and miniature replica of Richard gave his role a disproportionately large significance within the overall dramatic structure. The boy's complicity in his master's 'plots' and 'inductions dangerous' (1.1.32) hinted at in Shakespeare's text thus became the prevailing image of, rather than merely another perspective on, childhood, to counterbalance and problematize the other representations of childhood on display. The impact of Clarence's children and the two young princes as emblems of imperiled innocence was diluted by the overwhelming presence of the young page, and as a result, Shakespeare's ambivalent presentation of childhood as simultaneously vulnerable *and* threatening became disproportionately skewed towards the latter.

Apart from the silent presence of the page in Act 1, Scenes 1 and 3, the first children to appear on stage in this production, in accordance with Shakespeare's Quarto and Folio texts, were Clarence's son and daughter in Act 2, Scene 2. The lights went up at the beginning of the scene to the pure, soaring melody of a single flute. This refrain was to be repeated in Act 4, Scene 3, before Tyrrel's elegiac account of the murder of the princes. The two children were playing with a large Edwardian rocking horse, framed within the beams of light shining down through the latticed windows above. These signifiers of the nursery evoked idealized images of childhood play, and the centre-stage positioning of the rocking horse coloured the whole scene with a patina of nostalgia. This impression of childhood as a temporally discrete state – a state whose passing is accompanied with regret and whose recollection is imbued with sentimentality – was intensified by the disjunction between actor and role in the character of Clarence's son. From his physical appearance and his strained attempt at falsetto, it was immediately evident that he was no longer a child. In fact, the cast list in the programme confirmed that the actor playing Clarence's son was an adult man, Rob Wynn, who was also doubling as the keeper and as Surrey. Watching this fully grown man push his young sister (played by Daisy Hughes and Isabella James, who were both minors at the time) on the rocking horse and speak in a self-conscious approximation of a childlike pitch was touching rather than comical. Framed within the Merchant Ivory aesthetic of the Edwardian nursery, it was almost as though he were trying to recapture a sense of his own youth by assuming the behaviour and acquiring the accoutrements of this child role. As the adults commenced their choric-style rhetoric of grief, he stood silently by his sister, his hands resting protectively on her shoulders. The children's recriminations ('Ah, aunt! You wept not for our father's death' [2.2.62]) were omitted along with their part in the ritualized rhetorical outpouring of grief, reducing their roles to helpless and almost entirely voiceless witnesses. Like the wooden rocking horse, they were little more than props. Their presence was less a strident defence of their father's memory and more a synecdoche for the lost children of the lamenting mothers.

The lines of the two young princes were similarly reduced and their individuated characters flattened out to appear two-dimensional and colourless. Although the Young Duke of York's repetition of Gloucester's comment that 'small herbs have grace; great weeds do grow apace' (2.4.13) was retained, the ensuing dialogue with the Duchess of York (2.4.23–37) was removed. These lines are significant for a number of reasons and their excision had profound implications for the representation of childhood in this production. Firstly, the Young Duke says that should he have remembered that his uncle had been 'so long a-growing, and so leisurely' (2.4.19), he would have given his 'uncle's grace a flout' (2.4.24) with a 'biting jest' (2.4.30), revealing a precocity and subversive tendency that might prove problematic for Gloucester's authority. Secondly, when challenged by his grandmother to reveal the source of his story, he is revealed to be a liar, problematizing any simplistic representation of the two princes as innocent emblems of purity. And thirdly, the queen intervenes and rebukes him for being 'parlous' and 'shrewd' (2.4.35). Both of these adjectives are associated with cunning and artfulness, the very opposite of the image of idealized childhood innocence the play is later to present in Tyrrel's soliloquy. As Bethany Packard observes, 'York turns Richard's words against him and appropriates his uncle's sharp baby teeth for his own use' (2013: 117). Removing these lines significantly reduced the sharpness of the Young Duke's bite.

Thus, where Shakespeare's texts carefully individualize the two princes, Holmes's production consistently homogenized them. This strategy was particularly apparent in the following scene (Act 3, Scene 1) where the two princes appear on stage together for the only time as living characters. Although Holmes retained the prince's initial questions about the building of the Tower (3.1.68–78), he cut his eulogy to the martial bravery of Julius Caesar (3.1.84–9). This second speech, although only six lines long, is central to the individual characterization of Prince Edward and his function in the drama as a rhetorical and intellectual sparring partner for Richard. The prince here demonstrates a precocious capacity for reasoning, logic and debate – all qualities that would prove problematic for Richard should the prince live long enough to challenge his authority.

The removal of this speech thus neutralizes the threat that Edward poses to Richard and reduces the character, like his brother and the Clarence children, to little more than a cipher. Ultimately, it was Holmes's page, and his capacity for self-serving and unsentimental political pragmatism, that proved to be the greatest threat of all.

The significance of the page became apparent very early on when Henry Goodman's Richard interrupted his opening soliloquy to summon the boy on stage. Having initially appeared dressed in frock coat and top hat like an Edwardian music hall entertainer, Goodman began removing his outer clothing at 'but I, that am not shaped for sportive tricks' (1.1.14) to reveal a twisted and deformed body held together with orthopaedic straps and built-up boots and dressed in a red military-style shirt and black trousers. He paused after 'so lamely' to shout 'Boy!', before continuing 'and unfashionable' (1.1.22), at which point a pageboy appeared through the back curtain and began gathering up Richard's discarded clothing. The boy froze as Richard jabbed viciously with his stick at a barking dog just out of sight behind the upstage left curtain at 'dogs bark at me as I halt by them' (1.1.23). The boy was then dismissed with a curt 'go on', and Richard resumed his soliloquy while the boy disappeared back behind the curtain. It was a brief appearance but quickly established the power relations between the two characters. Silent, acquiescent and, in Richard's mind at least, associated with dogs that need beating into submission, his first appearance gave the impression that this page was Richard's whipping boy. Like his master, he was dressed in a red shirt and black trousers and walked with a discernible limp. In the recording in the Royal Shakespeare Theatre (RSC) archive, the page is played by eleven-year-old David Jowett, whose diminutive stature, blonde hair and angelic looks created an outward image of a vulnerable and innocent child. Moreover, the way in which Richard summoned his page – 'So lamely – Boy! – and unfashionable' – was no accident. In spite of the small pause before 'Boy!', it was clear that the young page was associated in his master's mind with the modifier 'lamely'. What this 'lamely boy' symbolized was thus Richard's own shadowy *doppelgänger*: the 'deformed, unfinished' child-Richard 'sent before [his] time' (1.1.20) and the displaced object of his own self-loathing. If, however, he was to be seen as Richard's whipping boy, it quickly became evident that the whipping was more a metaphorical form of self-flagellation.

THE EFFACEMENT OF CHILDHOOD IN *RICHARD III* 35

FIGURE 3 *Henry Goodman as Richard and David Jowett as the page, in* Richard III, *dir. Sean Holmes, 2003. Photo by Manuel Harlan. Courtesy RSC.*

In his essay 'The Uncanny', Sigmund Freud describes the process by which the *doppelgänger*, which represents for Freud the source of narcissism in childhood, is later manifested in adulthood as an uncanny double that calls forth suppressed memories ([1919] 2003: 141–3). Drawing on Freud's theories, Barbara L. Estrin provides a reading of *Richard III* that, although not cited by either Goodman or Holmes as an influence, provides a useful framework through which to consider the function of the page in this production. Expanding upon the metaphorical 'amorous looking-glass' (1.1.15) and 'shadow' (1.1.26) of Richard's opening soliloquy, Estrin comments as follows: '[Richard's] shadow becomes a child for him, a separate creation he designs for his own purpose. His shadow is his first follower [...] It reacts totally to his whim, reflecting only the image he wants to project' (1985: 111). This certainly seems to echo Goodman's comments on the page being the embodiment of Richard's child self: 'a young boy in [his] own image' (2007: 200). Estrin further describes Richard as 'the scorned child of nature', whose abandonment in childhood represents 'a coveted innocence' (108). She argues that, ultimately, Richard emerges the 'pitiful child' of his own self-fashioning (111). This psychoanalytic reading of what Postman has termed the 'adult-child' ([1982] 1994: 98–119) characterization of Richard finds its corollary in performance in the adult-like knowingness of Holmes's *doppelgänger* pageboy. Where Holmes's presentation of the 'shadow' child diverged from Estrin's reading, however, is in the final scene where the pageboy took Richard's sword and handed it to Richmond. Like his dead master, this boy was an opportunist who was, one can only presume, positioning himself to follow in his footsteps. For Estrin, the focus is entirely on Richard and his regression into a second childhood as he 'absorbs the alienation of the foundling moment and emerges the pitiful child he pretended to be' (ibid.: 116). However, in Holmes's interpretation, it was the adult-like child who came to claim the spotlight, emerging from the shadows to shape his own destiny while gesturing towards a future that was to be a repetition of the past.

The pageboy's presence gradually took on greater significance as the play progressed. In Act 1, Scene 3, for instance, he entered as Richard launched into his soliloquy (1.3.323–37), handed him a shot glass and waited while his master downed it in one swift movement. Unlike his first appearance, where he entered in answer to a summons from Richard, this time he entered of his own volition. His departure, moreover, almost overlapped with the arrival of Clarence's murderers. This laid the groundwork, however subliminally, for his introduction of Tyrrel in Act 4. By the time of the coronation in Act 4, Scene 2 (see Figure 3), he was a central figure in Richard's retinue and his physical appearance, including an exaggerated limp that grew more pronounced as the play progressed, had become like a mirror image of Richard himself. When called upon to recommend a suitable assassin for the young princes, he limped towards Richard, dragging his left leg behind him in an uncanny imitation of his master. He spoke with a bold and confident voice, until asked to reveal the name of the gentleman 'whom corrupting gold / Will tempt unto a close exploit of death' (4.2.34–5). At this point he lowered his voice, leant in conspiratorially towards Richard and said, 'His name, my lord, is Tyrrel' (4.2.40). This change in vocal register indicated that the young boy was fully cognizant of the import of this exchange. Far from the picture of innocence his diminutive size, crippled body and golden blonde hair suggested, he was the epitome of what Anne Higonnet calls the 'knowing child', the child who 'underst[ands] rather more about adults' motives and foibles than their belief in [his]/her innocence allow[s] them to guess' (1998: 207). As though to underscore the complicity of this 'knowing' pageboy in the killing of the princes, he re-entered with Tyrrel in Act 4, Scene 2, and hovered in the background as Richard delivered his murderous instructions. His presence, both in this scene and throughout the play, was a symbol of the self-serving duplicity (the 'motives and foibles' of Higonnet's analysis) writ large in Richard.

Building up to the final moment, the page was almost a constant presence at Richard's side for the remainder of the play: galloping gamely after the king's chariot, delivering written reports of traitorous nobles and observing his battle preparations. However, it was the final scene that was to prove his ultimate unmasking. After Richmond's closing speech in Act 5, Scene 5, the boy limped from the shadows into the spotlight, bent down to retrieve the sword where it had fallen from Richard's lifeless hand and handed it to Richmond without so much as a backwards glance at his old master's dead body.[10] The lights dropped on this frozen image and the audience was left to interpret its significance. On the surface, it was a symbolic representation of regime change, with the sword functioning as metaphor for the transfer of political power and the boy's act a silent commentary on the fickleness of public allegiance. To this extent, it was not a particularly innovative or unusual image with which to indicate the rise and fall of political fortunes. One need only consider the closing shots in Roman Polanski's *Macbeth* (1971), where Ross, the ultimate symbol of political opportunism, hands the crown to a victorious Macduff and Donalbain is seen entering the witches' cave. However, within Holmes's overall conception of childhood, the very fact that this symbolic moment was enacted by the pageboy imbued it with even greater significance. Inextricably connected with Richard from the opening scene, this 'lamely – Boy!' came also to symbolize all that Richard stood for. In his analysis of the uncanny, Freud connects the double in literature with 'a defence against annihilation' and 'an insurance against the extinction of the self' ([1919] 2003: 142). It is a symbol, in other words, of a futurity that is co-extensive with, rather than discrete from, the past and the present. As Richard's *doppelgänger*, therefore, the page embodied the perpetuation of tyranny into a future that transcended Richmond's victory speech. His final prayer for peace, 'Now civil wounds are stopped; peace lives again. / That she may long live here, God say amen' (5.5.40–1), rang hollow as the spirit of Richard returned – alive and well in the figure of the pageboy.

So, to return to Mark Lawhorn's unanswered question – 'the vexing question of what structurally, thematically or culturally significant purpose the boy figure might be serving' (2007: 239) – I will close this section by summarizing the 'significant purpose' of the pageboy and the ways in which Holmes's interpretation of the role informed the overall representation of childhood in his production. I dispute John W. Draper's observation that 'the pages in Shakespeare's earliest plays [...] are so lightly sketched as to constitute mere background' (1939: 477). It is true that the page in *Richard III* is given no context, no history and no character development, and as such, in common with many other supporting characters in this play, is indeed 'lightly sketched'. His only appearance is in Act 4, Scene 2, and it is reasonable to conjecture, as the studies of Madelaine, Packard, Tribble and Hammond outlined above suggest, that the boy actor in Shakespeare's company doubled the role with one of the princes or Clarence's children. The brevity of his appearance may then be attributed to pragmatic reasons related to the experience and capability of the actors available to play the part. However, this does not mean that the page in *Richard III* 'constitute['s] mere background'. There is no dramatic necessity to involve the page as a go-between with Tyrrel. Richard had already hired murderers to dispatch Clarence, and Macbeth, for instance, requires no such introduction to the two assassins hired for the murder of Banquo and Fleance. Moreover, although the page is present in Hall's chronicles, Shakespeare omitted or adapted many elements documented in this work.[11] His decision to retain the page and make him into a 'knowing child', therefore, must surely have been no accident. As the adult-like counterpoint to the 'childish-foolish' (1.3.141) Richard, and the 'knowing' counterpoint to the silenced child-victims, the page fulfils several functions in this play. Structurally, his role as intermediary between Tyrrel and Richard triggers a sequence of events that signal Richard's ultimate demise; thematically and culturally, his precocious 'knowingness' contributes to the ambiguous and multifaceted representations of childhood in this play. Holmes's decision to close his production with this ambiguous child character, however, was not merely a commentary on conceptualizations of childhood but a portentous symbol of an ambiguous future. By appropriating Richard's sword and handing it to Richmond, Holmes's precocious young pageboy brought into question not only the integrity of Richmond's promise of peace but also the very notion of children as the guardians of the future. The page may have looked like the epitome of angelic innocence, but he was in fact the embodiment of Postman's disappeared child in a post-digital age of information overload and blurred child-adult boundaries.

Deconstructing the innocent ideal: The 'fantoccini' princes of Thomas Ostermeier's *Richard III* (2015)

Writing about Tyrrel's sentimentalized description of the deaths of the two princes in Act 4, Scene 3, of *Richard III*, William Hazlitt made the following observations:

> These are some of those wonderful bursts of feeling, done to the life, to the very height of fancy and nature, which our

Shakespeare alone could give. We do not insist on the repetition of these last passages as proper for the stage: we should indeed be loth to trust them in the mouth of almost any actor: but we should wish them to be retained in preference at least to the fantoccini [puppet] exhibition of the young princes.

(1838: 220)

Hazlitt was echoing the attitudes of many of his contemporaries when he suggested that the 'proper' place for Shakespeare's words was on the page and in the mind of the reader, rather than on the stage. Moreover, his dismissive reference to the 'fantoccini princes' is an 'idealized production of adult memory and reverie' (Faulkner 2013: 132) far removed from the embodied reality of a flesh-and-blood child. The other passage Hazlitt singled out for particular praise was 'the farewell apostrophe of the queen to the tower, where her children are shut up from her' (ibid.: 219) in Act 4, Scene 4. As with Tyrrel's soliloquy, Queen Elizabeth's speech apotheosizes the princes, calling them 'tender babes' (4.4.9) and 'gentle lambs' (4.4.22), but again the description is divorced from the physical embodiment of the children. In both instances, the 'fantoccini princes' are conspicuous by their absence, at least in any corporeal sense. At first glance, one could be forgiven for thinking that Thomas Ostermeier had taken artistic inspiration from Hazlitt's sentiments in his 2015 German-language production for the Avignon Festival. Not only did he cut Tyrrel's elegy to innocence lost in its entirety, but he avoided the 'fantoccini exhibition' of child actors by replacing them with *actual* fantoccini stand-ins. His princes were, in other words, not children but puppets. However, the effects of these radical moves were not, as Hazlitt intended, to maintain an image of ineffable childhood purity but to deconstruct and subvert it. Carol Chillington Rutter has observed recent trends in substituting child actors for puppets in stage productions of Shakespeare (2017: 64–86). Ostermeier was not, as her essay demonstrates, particularly radical in his choice to replace child actors with life-size puppets. What was striking about Ostermeier's fantoccini princes was their peculiar appearance. With wax-like pallors, fixed facial expressions and stiff-limbed movements, these puppets were uncannily corpse-like in ways that recalled Wheeldon's statue of the dead child Mamillius from *The Winter's*

FIGURE 4 *Laurenz Laufenberg as Rivers, Christoph Gawenda as Clarence, Dorset and Stanley, Jenny König as Lady Anne, Eva Meckbach as Elizabeth, Lars Eidinger as Richard and Thomas Bading as Lord Mayor of London, in* Richard III, *a production of Schaubühne Berlin, dir. Thomas Ostermeier, 2015. Photo © Arno Declair.*

Tale. The 'wonderful bursts of feeling' (1838: 220) that Hazlitt so admired in the language of Tyrrel's soliloquy, moreover, were replaced with a dumbshow in which the princes' bodies were laid unceremoniously on the floor, their limbs twisted and distorted like victims of some horrific torture. What Hazlitt deemed too sublime to be represented beyond the page was literalized in the most brutal and uncompromising manner on Ostermeier's stage.

Ostermeier's reinterpretation of Shakespeare's young princes was in fact the very opposite of Hazlitt's sentimentalized ideas about children as symbols of 'grievability' (Butler 2009: 45). The absence of an embodied theatrical presence reduced the children to a series of signifiers rather than the 'wonderful bursts of feeling' (1838: 220) expressed in Tyrrel's linguistic 'height[s] of fancy and nature' and, as the only characters not played by human actors (and the only children not cut from the original text), Ostermeier's puppet-princes raised questions relating to subjectivity, agency, alterity and the theatrical exchange more generally. Were they semiotic signifiers of childhood as an abstracted idea that could only be constructed, controlled and maintained by adults? Was their disembodied performance a nihilistic denial of the child as a symbol of futurity? Or was the absence of a body, like the absence of Richard's deformity (symbolized by a removable cushion and surgical boot), a deliberate challenge to the voyeuristic-scopophilic gaze that has become a crucial part of the theatrical pleasure of this play? Through an analysis of the role of the children within the overall context of Ostermeier's deconstructionist aesthetic, I argue that their present-absent, human-not-human, animate-inanimate qualities, and what Rutter calls the puppet's 'obstinate, flagrant "thingness"' (2017: 66), resulted in an ontological indeterminacy that raised important questions about power, agency and the theatrical gaze. I will demonstrate, moreover, that the de-corporealized children were counterbalanced in this production by an insistently corporeal Richard, whose disabilities were demonstrated to be just as much a figment of rhetoric as the pervasive narrative of childhood innocence. In her analysis of puppet theatre, Meike Wagner has argued that the juxtaposition of the 'alienating, othering body of the puppet' with the live body of the human actor results in an ontological blurring in which 'all appearances are transformed into cyborgs – half mediatized technological objects' (2006: 126). This is a particularly useful analysis to apply to Ostermeier's production, which also employed microphones and video projections as a means of problematizing the distinction between the live and the mediatized and the human and the technological. However, I argue that the juxtaposition of the puppet-princes with the artificially constructed 'disabled' body of Richard did something far more specific here. It brought into question the literary, historical and ideological constructions of identity and, in particular, the constructions of childhood that have, as James R. Kincaid has argued, focused on the erotic innocence (and concomitant appeal) of the child's body.

Ostermeier is a director known for his distinctive style. Influenced early in his career by the 'in-your-face' theatre of Mark Ravenhill and Sarah Kane, he developed a radical approach that is confrontational, challenging and highly metatheatrical (McMillan 2016). Originally opening in the Schaubühne theatre, Berlin, in February 2015, his production of *Richard III* became one of the most anticipated and heavily marketed events of the sixty-ninth Avignon Festival in France, before a European tour that included performances in Edinburgh and London. It was, moreover, the only performance to be broadcast as a livecast which remained on the Arte TV website for several months after the festival closed. Ostermeier's sardonic take on the play was, in the words of *Financial Times* reviewer, 'one of the few unqualified successes' of the festival (Cappelle 2015). My analysis is based on this German-language livecast performance which included subtitles in French.

True to his reputation for combining disparate theatrical styles, Ostermeier produced a hybridized blend of expressionism with psychological realism, traditionalism with postmodernist bricolage and comedy with tragedy. The stage of the 700-seat capacity Opera Grand Theatre was bare apart from a backdrop that had clearly been designed to replicate an Elizabethan theatre design. In the centre of the back wall was a tiring-house-style entrance covered by a curtain, in front of which stood a crude scaffold structure with a metal staircase leading up to a gantry extending the full width of the stage. Between scenes, a cyclorama of moving images flickered across the entire back wall and stage floor, intermittently transforming this neo-Elizabethan backdrop into a twenty-first-century projector screen. Above the centre of the stage hung a 1950s microphone with an inbuilt light and camera. Whenever the actors spoke into the microphone, their faces were bathed in a harsh and unforgiving white light, while their images were magnified and projected onto the back wall. The fusion of different historical references – Elizabethan; 1950s; twenty-first century – established an atemporal context, while the use of the digitized image created a symbolic framework of substitution, replication and duplication. This type of intermedial interplay of technology and live theatre is a technique frequently employed by the Wooster Group, notably in their production of *Hamlet* (2006), and has been usefully termed 'cyborg theatre' (Parker-Starbuck 2004: 221). In the case of Ostermeier's *Richard III*, the double image of live and mediatized performance emphasized the semi-cyborg quality of his puppet-children as they hovered uncannily between the human and the not-quite-human. The camera built into the microphone, moreover, emphasized the role of the audience in the actor-spectator relationship, highlighting the act of voyeurism that was central to Ostermeier's treatment of both Richard's deformed body and the bodies of the two children. Less a presentation than an effacement of childhood, these bodies were in fact merely artificial distortions of their originals, evading the voyeuristic theatrical gaze even while drawing attention to it.

The performance opened with distorted synthesizer sounds overlaid with live percussion heralding the arrival of the victorious and celebratory Yorkist courtiers. Actors in black suits and cocktail dresses began pouring in from the back of the auditorium. They were ostentatiously firing glitter cannons and swigging from champagne bottles as they traversed the stage. At the back limped Richard, a reticent and self-conscious loner who looked round in bewilderment at the audience as he passed through. He was wearing black trousers with makeshift braces and a white T-shirt, beneath which a cushion could be seen strapped to his back to signify his 'bunch-backed' hump (1.3.245). Bridget Escolme has noted that early modern theatrical conventions meant that 'clothes were put into theatrical quotation marks in such a way as to emphasize the playfulness and fragility of identity itself' (2013: 120). In this instance, I suggest that Richard's clothing was certainly a form of 'theatrical quotation marks' more in keeping with early modern practices than 'the stage costume of modern production', which are generally 'made for theatrical convenience or to fit a particular design aesthetic' (2013). But Richard's self-conscious display of disability was not merely designed to emphasize 'the playfulness and fragility of identity', although this was certainly a factor, but also to foreground the artificiality of historically and mythically constructed identity. Richard's disability was, in Ostermeier's adaptation, quite literally and self-consciously 'constructed'. He tried to enter into the celebrations, shaking hands awkwardly with his fellow party-goers, but was largely ignored. Grasping the suspended microphone, he began speaking the opening soliloquy in a partial whisper. First in German, then repeated in English (this was the only time the German-language version was translated back into the original Shakespearean text), he itemized his deformities while tears poured down his face and fell in droplets off his chin. Eidinger's Richard was a genuinely tortured social outcast, bustling in the world in the only way he knew to survive. In his account of the early stages of preparation for this production, Ostermeier wrote that he envisaged Richard as a 'very likeable and appealing character' who should never 'lose his credit with the audience' (Boenisch and Ostermeier 2016: 198). Indeed, even as he morphed from social 'other' into merciless killer, Eidinger's Richard never lost the capacity to reach out to the spectators. By stripping back the props that he used to fashion his identity, he revealed the vulnerable human beneath the disguise and implied, in doing so, that we were complicit not only in the constructedness and artificiality of *his* identity but in our own as well.

The first turning point in his character development came with his successful wooing of Lady Anne in the second scene. Bewildered and hurt at her vitriol, he stripped naked, except for his cushion-hump, to place his 'unaccommodated' vulnerability at her mercy. As she pushed the tip of the sword into his chest, he thrust his arms out and flung his head back in a parody of the crucifixion. But this was not an empty gesture, a pose to manipulate Anne into submission; it was clear that this Richard was genuinely prepared to fall on his sword. Anne hesitated for a beat, before eventually capitulating. Evidently surprised at the sudden and auspicious turn of events, Richard began to visibly grow in stature as he understood the transformative effects of rhetoric, not only on Anne but on his audience as well. 'Was ever woman in this humour wooed? / Was ever woman in this humour won?' (1.2.230–1) was delivered with a sense of both disbelief and delight, his words directed for the first time out into the auditorium rather than mumbled in an apologetic undertone. By the time he reappeared in the third scene, dressed in a black suit and white shirt, he was a newly confident and self-aware Richard, ready to grasp any opportunity for advancement that presented itself. However, in order for this metamorphosis to take place, it was first necessary to strip Richard of all his outward trappings of character – the signifiers of his deformity and his concomitant mythological status as a villain defined by those very deformities.

Richard's nakedness was central to Ostermeier's deconstruction of historical myth-making and cultural constructs and provided an interpretive context for the disembodied puppet-children. Just as the corporeal reality of Richard's unimpaired body disavowed the rhetoric of disability and somatic monstrosity by evoking and enacting its artificiality, the dehumanized puppet-princes functioned as a medium to undermine the rhetoric of childhood innocence – a rhetoric that, as Kincaid reminds us, is shadowed by titillation, eroticism and violence (1998: 14). For Kenneth Gross, writing about the inherently uncanny nature of puppets, the 'alien-homely instincts animated by the "living doll"' connect us to our infantile selves, activating fantasies of 'our own lost, *un*fallen knowledge of ourselves and our bodies'. Echoing the words of Kincaid, Higonnet and others, Gross asserts that puppets are 'entities that seek to reorient our ideas of innocence, and thus our ideas of childhood. Their innocence', he concludes, 'becomes more uncanny, and increasingly paradoxical, often haunted by its apparent opposite' (2012: xiv–xv). Ostermeier reinforced the connection with the 'infantile selves' that Gross describes by limiting his use of puppets to the two child characters in this production, all other parts being played by adult actors. The juxtaposition of puppet with human in this way was both alienating and familiar. As Gross explains, 'The word [puppet] derives from the Latin *pupa*, for little girl or doll' (2011: 3). Although its meaning has changed over time, from its usage in Elizabethan rhetoric as both a term endearment and of deprecation, to its current application as a term exclusively used to denote a marionette, the associations of puppet theatre with childhood continue to be maintained.[12] Indeed, as the 2003 Workshop on Science and Technology Communication through Puppetry Communication concluded, puppet theatre is particularly effective for child education and entertainment because 'children are puppeteers themselves from the first time they pick up a shoe, a squeezed-out half orange or a hairbrush and make them move and talk'. Puppets are, the report concludes, the medium through which children naturally 'express thoughts, ideas and feelings' (Sahoo 2003: 976).

When placed in interaction and dialogue with the human characters, however, the un-human, corpse-like essence of Ostermeier's puppets took on a peculiarly alienating aspect. Mieke Wagner makes a similar argument to Gross: 'The puppet is very close to human beings; its features are familiar to ours. However, this familiarity is fragile and endangered – after all the puppet does bear the potential of radical alienation and othering' (2006: 132). This sense of 'radical alienation' was consistent with the deconstruction of Richard's disabled body and the use of digitized images in the production design. Where the children foregrounded the artifice of cultural constructions of childhood with their alienating properties, Richard wore the deformities of his disabled body like a prop, and the juxtaposition of the mediatized and the live created an anti-illusionist aesthetic that foregrounded and subverted the voyeuristic gaze. In the same way that he denied the audience the pleasure of viewing Richard's deformities by presenting a fit, lithe and blatantly 'able' body in its full nakedness, Ostermeier also denied the spectacle of the children's bodies, opting instead to replace them with a simulacrum, or what Gross calls 'substitution, revision, replacement' (2011: 95), that was as artificial and as far removed from real children as Richard's constructed disability was from a real disabled body.

With the emergence of disability studies as a distinct theoretical school over the past two decades, attention has begun to focus on disassociating the rhetoric of disability from the disabled body.[13] While these analyses have focused largely on the textual manifestation of Richard's deformed body, Geoffrey Johns combines disability studies with performance studies to consider the ways in which Richard's 'amorphous body' – amorphous because of the multiple and contradictory ways in which it is defined within the play – 'might be conveyed, logistically and otherwise, to a live playhouse audience' (2015: 41). Johns's approach to performing disability in the theatre is of particular interest here, especially as it relates to the performance of identity and alterity generally and to the corresponding performance of childhood more specifically. Over the past few decades, celebrated performances by star actors from Laurence Olivier to Kevin Spacey have incorporated tics, limps and strapped-up limbs in order to provide the audience with a clear manifestation of Richard's physical deformity. However, as Johns and Williams have argued, to tie Richard down to one specific disability in this way is to elide the inconsistencies that abound in the play as characters try, in a 'frenzy of interpretive fervor', to find meaning in his deformities (Williams 2009: para. 1). Ostermeier's solution was to address the issue of a vanishing, amorphous and ambiguously disabled body by literally separating the body from its disability. His Richard brazenly displayed his deformity as a combination of metatheatrical signifiers which seemed to indicate a physical disability while simultaneously revealing it to be nothing more than a rhetorical, theatrical and historical artefact. His arm, a 'blasted sapling withered up' (3.4.68), was indicated merely by a plaster around the middle finger of his right hand. A cushion strapped to his back gestured towards a 'bunch-backed' hump (1.3.245), while a black leather headband tied under his chin, a surgical boot on his right foot and train-track braces across his top row of teeth suggested more generalized physical impairments.

Eidinger's performance was not merely a performance of Richard but a performance of disability that he was to use to his advantage at key moments in the play and was apparently able to turn on and off at will. It quickly became apparent that his Richard was not defined by his physical appearance but by his complex and, at times, extremely affecting psychological make-up. In this respect, unlike many Richards who have come before him, he frustrated any simplistic attempt to establish a causal link between physical deformity and moral depravity that is, as Garber has noted, 'transmitted not genetically but generically through both historiography and dramaturgy' (2002: 69). In an interview with Joseph Pearson, Ostermeier said that he wanted his production to pose the following questions: 'Have you never wanted to do what Richard is doing? Have you never wanted to commit morally reprehensible acts?' (2015). By humanizing his protagonist in this way, Ostermeier challenged audience preconceptions about theatrical tradition and historical precedent and created a Richard in whom his audience might see themselves reflected. In this context of deconstructing what Hans Robert Jauss has termed the audience's 'horizon of expectations' (1982: 22), the presentation of the de-humanized puppet-princes and the accompanying ontological uncertainty they engendered seemed less of an interpretive leap.

The first appearance of any children on the stage was Act 3, Scene 1, as Ostermeier had not only removed Clarence's children and the pageboy but also cut the earlier appearance of the Duke of York with his mother and grandmother in Act 2, Scene 4. It was therefore somewhat of a delayed *coup-de-théâtre* when the children were revealed, mid-way through the performance, as two life-sized puppets with jointed limbs who were both manipulated and voiced by actors from the troupe. Images of these puppet-children featured prominently in pre-publicity photographs released to the press and on the festival and Arte TV websites. They were marketed as a distinguishing feature of this production and its livecast and would therefore have undoubtedly been uppermost in the minds of the audience members as they watched the play. Deferring their entrance in this way thus raised spectator expectations, ensuring that the princes' eventual appearance achieved maximal impact. Removing the other children also had the effect of focusing attention exclusively on the two princes. As discussed earlier in this chapter, the page plays a pivotal role in complicating the representation of children in this play as naïve innocents. Similarly, the dissenting voices of the Clarence children in Act 2, Scene 2, and the 'parlous' chatter of the Duke of York in Act 2, Scene 4, all contribute to a multiple and heterogeneous portrayal of childhood that is at once antagonistic, complicit, knowing and vulnerable. Ostermeier pared back the play's multiple representations of childhood to just the two princes, thus removing any complicating ambiguities. He also significantly cut the two boys' lines and removed Tyrrel's soliloquy in Act 4, Scene 3, so that the physical presence of these de-corporealized children took on a greater theatrical significance than the rhetoric surrounding them.

Ostermeier was clear from the early stages of his work on this production that he would not exploit the bodies of real children for theatrical effect. In his account of the rehearsal process he asserted:

> The children will be played by puppets that are animated by the actors, who will also lend them their voices. Every single production of *Richard III* has this dreadful moment in it, when real, innocent children are pushed on stage by the director

because she or he is unable to express and represent Richard's brutality otherwise. It is my ambition to convey his monstrosity through the means of theatre and *mise en scène*, and not through casting.

(Boenisch and Ostermeier 2016: 201)

Although Ostermeier's use of the epithet 'real, innocent children' is problematical in itself – it reinforces the narrative of childhood innocence that writers such as Kincaid and Stockton have worked to successfully debunk – the effect of replacing the children with puppets was nonetheless dramatically subversive. By stripping back the language and focusing on the bodies, and replacing these bodies with inanimate puppets, Ostermeier emptied them of their fetishistic appeal and disrupted the voyeuristic-scopophilic gaze. The exploitation of 'real, innocent children' was thus neatly side-stepped. Anne Higonnet notes in her analysis of images of childhood through history that the ideal of childhood innocence is not a function of language but 'an attribute of the child's body' (1998: 8). This bodily ideal, as Kincaid has argued, is shadowed by a darker impulse to objectify, commodify and corrupt. 'By insisting so loudly on the innocence, purity, and asexuality of the child', he explains, 'we have created a subversive echo: experience, corruption, eroticism' (1992: 4–5). It is the very physical attributes of childish innocence – the undeveloped presexual body, the androgynous features, the absence of bodily self-consciousness – that invoke a desire in adults to fetishize and eroticize children. When the body of the child is re-imagined not as a moving, talking individual but as a puppet, this impulse to fetishize is frustrated in a way that is both phenomenologically unsettling and dramatically disruptive.

These puppet-princes thus wore the outward signifiers of childhood but lacked the corporeal presentness of the child's body. What could be 'read' according to the semiotic conventions of theatre could not be correlated with their phenomenological effects. Although children do not form the central focus of his study, as discussed in the Introduction, Bert O. States does make a brief, but nonetheless telling and useful reference to the phenomenological effects of child actors. According to States's analysis, stage images such as clocks, water and children do not always surrender their extra-theatrical nature to the sign/image function but retain a high degree of self-givenness (what States calls '*en soi*') that debunks the theatrical illusion (1985: 29–32). Interestingly, by categorizing children along with inanimate objects that merely *appear* to have a life of their own through mechanized motion or the force of gravity, but in fact have no real capacity for self-determination or ratiocination (like flowing water and ticking clocks), States perhaps inadvertently contributes to the narrative that would deny children any agency of their own. Nicholas Ridout agrees with States's argument about the unassimilability of children to the 'world of the professional actor' but he approaches this from a Marxist perspective, focusing more on the ways in which the child draws attention to the exploitation of actors in the 'bourgeois commercial theatre' (2006: 45). He does not go as far as States in aligning children with insentient objects such as clocks, but he does refer to them (along with animals) as 'minor forms of human adult'(149). Ridout argues that the child on stage, by dint of his/her very unassimilability, creates a heightened awareness in the audience of the division of labour in the theatre (2006: 99, 127). Like the animal on stage who 'means nothing by what it does' because it is not aware that it is in fact performing in a play, the child exposes 'the alienation of the actor and [...] the economic conditions of her [*sic*] presence on the stage' (2006: 101). The alien presence of the child thus, according to Ridout's thesis, points to the alienated state of the performing labour force more generally.

Ridout was not, of course, the first writer to consider the role of the actor within the theatre, particularly as it relates to hierarchies of power. Writing as far back as 1911, Edward Gordon Craig was acutely sensitive to live theatre as a medium for replicating and magnifying the inequities of labour-relations. But unlike Ridout, his objections were not aimed at the exploitation of the actors (by the directors and the audience) but at the revolting actors themselves. As a young director/designer, Craig became frustrated by the ways in which the egoism and unpredictability of actors could take them beyond directorial control and thus threaten the artistic integrity of the production, as he saw it. He proposed a solution to the actor 'problem' that seems as iconoclastic now as it was in the early twentieth century: to replace all live actors with 'the Über-marionette'.[14] Like Hazlitt before him, Craig did not trust the live actor to provide a pure performance of the author's intent. However, this was not because, as Hazlitt contends, they could not possibly do justice to Shakespeare's 'wonderful bursts of feeling' (1838: 220), but because the body of the actor provides an obstacle due its very materiality. Craig explains how 'the nature in man will fight for freedom, and will revolt against being made a slave or medium for the expression of another's thoughts'. As a result, he concludes that the actor is 'by nature utterly useless as a material for an art' ([1911] 2009: 30). His 'Über-marionette', on the other hand, conveys a 'death-like beauty' that does not 'compete with life' but rather 'go[es] beyond it' ((([1911] 2009: 40). Human actors are thus, according to Craig's critical perspective, an impediment to artistic integrity *because* of the qualities that make them human – qualities that mean they will fight against subordination and, by extension, mortality itself. There is some irony in the fact that not only was Craig a successful actor, starting out as a child actor at the age of twelve in Henry Irving's Lyceum Theatre, but that his mother Ellen Terry was an internationally renowned actor who performed from the age of five until her death at the age of eighty-one. Craig's radical proposal for a dehumanization and mechanization of the medium of theatre – a proposal that would have denied his mother and his younger self a career – was intended to be applied wholesale, not merely to child characters. By choosing to replace *only* the children with puppets, Ostermeier's production seemed to be making an observation about subjectivity, subordination and mortality that not only highlighted and disturbed the voyeuristic-scopophilic nature of theatre but raised a number of further troubling questions that were specific to children.

Reading Ridout's and Craig's arguments in the context of the potentially exploitative nature of the theatre exchange, it could be argued that Ostermeier's decision to substitute children for puppets was tantamount to refusing to expose the child actor to the 'slavery' of the labour market. This is a position taken by W. B. Worthen, who makes the case for the use of puppets to create an unmediated relationship with the audience that circumvents the commodification of the actor in the 'social and theatrical exchange' (1994: 4). Ostermeier's comments about directors pushing 'real, innocent children' on stage certainly seem to suggest that this was a factor in his decision-making process. However, the fact that they were not only openly operated by adults (with no attempt at hiding the puppet-masters behind the puppets, see Figure 4) but also were the only characters represented in this way meant that the effect was in fact very different from that originally intended. At one point, Ostermeier had also considered using puppets to represent both

King Edward and the messenger, as he explained in his rehearsal notes: 'Potentially, King Edward will be a puppet, too. We are currently experimenting with a gigantic body for him, with only the head of an actor sticking out on top. For the role of the messenger, if it remains in the play at all, we envisage using a stick puppet the actors will hold up whenever new messages come in' (Boenisch and Ostermeier 2016: 201). These puppets did not make it to the final production and Ostermeier does not explain why they, but not the puppet-princes, were rejected during rehearsals. However, although his refusal to put real children on display appears to be a refusal to exploit their bodies for cynical theatrical gain, replacing them with puppets paradoxically had the opposite effect because it denied the real child (the potential child actor) any agency whatsoever. Rather than liberating the children from the bonds of theatrical servitude, the very visibility of the puppet-masters reinforced their bonded status, suggesting that children are vulnerable to being enfranchised, shaped, moulded and manipulated by the adults who 'protect' them, in both the theatre and beyond. In other words, Ostermeier's desire to protect the 'real, innocent children' actually had the effect of exposing the adult fantasy of childhood as an imperiled and vulnerable state. Secondly, the very fact that these puppets were being voiced by actors doubling as Clarence, Dorset and Rivers, characters who had already been committed to death by Richard, gave the fate of these particular children an uncanny sense of preternatural predestination. Their faces, moreover, were made from shiny, wax-like plastic that created a distinctly deathly pallor and they were moulded into a fixed, bland and eerily lifeless expression, reinforcing the sense that they were already, metaphorically at least, the walking dead. The 'death-like beauty' ([1911] 2009: 40) of Craig's Über-marionette took on a particularly sinister meaning when it was applied exclusively to the children in this play. Like the non-diachronic narrative of Richard's birth, these puppet-children disrupted the linear temporality of official history, revealing it to be a fiction created and sustained by its chroniclers. As Marjorie Garber has noted in her monograph on uncanny causality in Shakespeare, 'The fiction of historical accuracy or "objectivity"' is a 'self-delusive and far from benign assumption that the past can be recaptured without contamination from the present' (1987: 62). By presenting children who were de-corporealized shells rather than flesh-and-blood children,

Ostermeier dramatized this contamination of the present in the past and rejected the linear, cause-and-effect narrative of deterministic historiography.

The puppet-children of the two princes further problematized Craig's ideal of a transcendent 'death-like beauty' ([1911] 2009: 40) in their second appearance in Act 4, Scene 2. When the children's assassin, in this case played by Ratcliffe rather than Tyrrel, returned to report on their deaths, he did not deliver the oft-cited elegy to 'gentle babes [...] girdling one another / Within their alabaster innocent arms' (4.3.9–11), but instead carried their inert bodies onto the stage wrapped in a blanket. He then laid them unceremoniously on the floor and removed the blanket, standing back with a flourish as though he had just pulled off a particularly gruesome magic trick. The image of the distorted puppet 'corpses', and their disassociation from the bodies of real children, functioned as a devaluation of the overblown rhetoric of Tyrrel's eulogy and a challenge to the very notion of childhood innocence that his soliloquy apotheosizes. The 'dead' puppets also problematized Ostermeier's declared desire not to exploit 'real, innocent children' on the stage by removing, and thus exposing, the puppet-masters who pull their strings. He may not have used 'real' children, but his representation of childhood revealed and reinforced, somewhat paradoxically, their bonded status. Moreover, as Meike Wagner argues, although the puppet's features are familiar to those of the human, the familiarity is 'fragile and endangered' because the puppet maintains a potential for 'radical alienation and othering' (2006: 132) and, by dint of its artificiality, becomes an implicit symbol of death – a subversion, in other words, of the 'reproductive futurism' that Edelman both rejects and sustains (2004: 3). Ostermeier's distorted puppet-princes thus not only undermined Tyrrel's eulogy to childhood innocence but gestured towards a fragility that subverted commonplace notions of childhood and futurity.

The final scenes of Ostermeier's production were played almost entirely as the product of an uneasy mind. As Richard lay down for his final night of sleep before the Battle of Bosworth Field, the ghosts appeared at the head of his makeshift bed and spoke their lines into the microphone, their faces projected against the backdrop like disembodied ghoulish visitations. When it came to the turn of two princes, still played by the puppets but now reconnected with their human manipulators, Richard twisted and turned, his face screwed up as though in physical pain. After the ghosts departed, he took the microphone and gave his 'conscience' soliloquy (5.3.177–206) *sotto voce* while still lying curled up, foetus-like, in his bed. Then, taking his cue from the line 'What do I fear? Myself? There's none else by' (5.3.182), he leapt up and began fighting invisible adversaries, furiously thrusting and jabbing at the air with his sword. Eventually exhausted at his efforts, he climbed back onto his bed, hooked his left foot into the loop at the bottom of the microphone cord and was hoisted up into the air. The lights dropped on the pitiful sight of his half-naked body, slowly rotating as he hung like an abandoned marionette. No Richmond arrived to claim victory. No cheering citizens celebrated the arrival of a new era of stability and peace. Just like the fantoccini princes he had destroyed, Richard turned himself, literally and metaphorically, into a state of suspended animation.

In his philosophical study into puppetry and free will, John Gray observes that, according to the scientific materialists, 'human beings *are* marionettes: puppets on genetic strings, which by an accident of evolution have become self-aware' (2015: 10). According to this analysis, there is no such thing as free will, merely an awareness of human limitations and a hope that science will eventually free the human mind from those limitations. The final image of Richard's de-animated body seemed to signify a rejection of such hope, not only for himself but for the whole of mankind. As this final image of Richard's suspended body made apparent, Ostermeier's puppets were thus not merely a commentary on the bondedness of childhood but were symbols of the bonded state of humanity in general. Bleak, uncompromising and utterly nihilistic, the puppet-children of Ostermeier's *Richard III* were not substitutions for the 'fantoccini exhibition' (1838: 220) of precocity against which Hazlitt inveighed, nor were they manifestations of Craig's transcendent 'death-like beauty' ([1911] 2009: 40) but an outright rejection of futurity itself.

Conclusion

As this analysis of the children of *Richard III* has demonstrated, Ostermeier's future-denying fantoccini children represent the culmination in a recent, counter-hegemonic trend towards demystifying idealized narratives of childhood. Both of the productions I have considered in this chapter have taken and expanded upon what Matthew D. Wagner has termed the 'dissonance and thickness of time' that forms such a significant part of *Richard III* (2012: 8). The play's recursive structure and disruptive temporalities undermine fixed adult–child binaries, and the multiple and contradictory manifestations of childhood deny a stable and definitive interpretive stance. Although both Mendes and Ostermeier focused on one particular aspect of the child, using different theatrical devices to present or efface childhood, they share a common interrogatory approach that rejects romantic notions of childhood innocence and raises questions about agency, authority, identity and futurity. By reinterpreting the page as a miniature facsimile of Richard, Holmes deconstructed boundaries of childhood and adulthood and brought into question ideas about temporality and teleology. His page, whom I have called the future-killing anti-child, posed a theatrical challenge to Edelman and others who continue to perpetuate, even while they reject, entrenched adult fantasies of children as guardians of the future. Ostermeier raised similar questions about idealized fantasies of childhood innocence by refusing to put the bodies of children on the stage and thus disrupting the scopophilic gaze. By foregrounding the artifice of childhood in this way, he revealed it to be a rhetorical and social construct – a construct that the multiple afterlives of Shakespeare's play, and its doomed young princes, have traditionally functioned to perpetuate.

2

'Fair is foul and foul is fair': The Janus-Faced Child in *Macbeth*

Moving on from the discussion of the effacement of childhood, this chapter considers the overdetermined presence of the child – alive, dead and hovering indeterminately in-between – in contemporary film and stage versions of *Macbeth*. The all-pervasive trope of the child in *Macbeth* has, certainly for the last few decades, offered the potential for directors to blur the boundaries between innocence and malevolence as the images of 'a naked new-born babe, / Striding the blast' (1.7.21–2) or 'heaven's cherubin, horsed / Upon the sightless couriers of the air' (1.7.22–3) suggest. A play centrally concerned with the image of the child, *Macbeth* therefore provides a particularly apposite discursive framework for interrogating developing narratives of childhood, while simultaneously revealing the tensions inherent therein. With these tensions in mind, this chapter will explore the ways in which modern productions of *Macbeth* have exploited textual ambiguities to construct the child 'other', both literally and figuratively. By comparing film and stage adaptations of *Macbeth*, I chart these changes in attitudes to childhood through the final decades of the twentieth century and the beginning of the twenty-first century. The conclusion I draw is that, as Cunningham and other notable childhood scholars have contended, the current generation's concern for its children and their future derives from an inescapable sense of the ambiguous and 'alien' (Cunningham 2005: 187) nature of childhood itself.

In the first section, I consider the question of the Macbeths' baby, a particularly ambiguous representation of childhood that has garnered much critical commentary and debate over the past eighty years. Beginning with a brief history of the academic and theatrical treatment of this elusive child, I then explore Jamie Lloyd's production (2013), an adaptation that was particularly illuminating in terms of what it revealed about anxieties relating to childlessness, childhood and futurity in modern society. The question 'How many children had Lady Macbeth?' is of increasing concern in revivals of this play, and the mysterious Macbeth baby has come to symbolize not just the 'rooted sorrow' (5.3.41) of one couple but the tragedy of a whole society on the verge of an existential crisis. In the second section, I examine the effects of doubling the Macduff children with the weird sisters through an analysis of Michael Boyd's three stage productions of *Macbeth* (1985, 1993, 2011). I consider in particular questions of ontological indeterminacy and temporal disruption that arise from the conflation of the supernatural with the human in the figure of the child. It was a trope to which Boyd returned again and again, and one which seemed to both intrigue and baffle his reviewers, rendering them, in many instances, uncharacteristically inarticulate. In the final section, I compare two landmark English-language films of *Macbeth* by Roman Polanski (1971) and Justin Kurzel (2015), to explore how the different representations of children in these films – from fetishistic objects to agents of doom – both illuminate and are reflective of changing ideas about children in Western society more generally.

Carol Chillington Rutter has argued that 'as the 1980s moved into the 1990s, *Macbeth* emerged as the Shakespeare play which the British theatre was going to use to think through the nation's current and ongoing cultural crisis in "childness"' (2007a: 172). My comparison of these two filmed productions demonstrates the extent to which Rutter's statement continues to pertain. 'Childness' is a word first used by Polixenes in *The Winter's Tale* (1.2.169) and, according to the *OED*, this is the first ever recorded use of this word. I think it is a particularly pertinent word to apply to *Macbeth* because it points towards its antonym, child*less*ness. Both childness and childlessness are at the heart of *Macbeth*, and the different ways in which Polanski and Kurzel chose to represent these two opposing concepts are, I argue, illustrative of far larger social and cultural shifts. The ambitious scope of this chapter which incorporates theatre and film, hypothetical and actual productions and a broad range of critical writing, illustrates how the children of *Macbeth* have become a source of fascination and objects of scrutiny across the centuries. Children, both real and metaphorical, actual and imagined, are woven through the fabric of this play, and the appetite in directors, writers and audiences for exploring their diverse manifestations shows no signs of diminishing.

'How many children had Lady Macbeth?': Childlessness and Existentialism in Jamie Lloyd's *Macbeth* (2013)

> Just as *Hamlet* deals with the relation of a son to his parents, so *Macbeth* [...] is concerned with the subject of childlessness.
>
> (Freud 1900: 266)

Sigmund Freud was one of the first writers to explicitly state that *Macbeth* is about childlessness, and it is a concern that has preoccupied scholars, directors and actors ever since. The riddle of the Macbeths' child in particular has been the source of lively critical debate for almost a century. Indeed, the question 'How many children had Lady Macbeth?' has become rhetorical shorthand for the perceived opposition between close textual reading and character or performance-based analysis.[1] L.C. Knights first opened up the debate in 1932 with a polemical essay dismissing the then current Bradleyan character-based approach to Shakespeare as 'the most fruitful of irrelevancies' ([1932] 1946: 1–39). Where Bradley focused his analysis on interrogating motivation behind the action of the characters, arguing that prime narrative interest derived 'in action issuing from character, or in character issuing in action' ([1904] 1919: 2), his detractors, notably Knights (1932), F.R. Leavis (1932) and G. Wilson Knight (1949), countered that the plays ought to be considered first and foremost as literary texts. Coinciding with the proliferation and diversification of critical approaches over the past forty years, the question of character analysis has re-emerged as a nexus for critical debate. Moreover, the emergence of childhood studies has further focused attention on this issue, as scholars have argued that along with the 'discovery' of childhood, the notion of motherhood was also invented.[2] Directors have thus begun to question the significance of the Macbeths' missing baby and how it can be translated for a modern audience with its own particular concerns about procreation, childlessness and what it means to be a mother in a post-feminist society. Bradley's once discredited consideration of motive and intent has become a legitimate mode of analysis, and 'How many children had Lady Macbeth?' – far from being an irrelevancy – has proved to be a question worth asking.

One corollary of this expansion in the critical field has been an increasing recognition of the different ways in which actors and scholars approach textual ambiguities. Cleanth Brooks was one of the first writers to identify the child as the 'most powerful symbol' in the play, encompassing the 'larger themes' in a complex interplay of metaphor and character (1947: 37). Although Brooks focused on the metaphorical import of the Macbeths' missing child, writers such as Carol Chillington Rutter and Michael Bristol have more recently begun to give serious consideration to its narrative and dramatic significance – a significance that has also come to form the central focus for many theatre practitioners. Adrian Noble's 1986 production for the RSC was probably the first large-scale stage production in which the absence of a Macbeth heir was foregrounded as the interpretive crux around which the whole tragedy was constructed. Many subsequent productions have since followed suit, a tradition that has culminated most resonantly in Jamie Lloyd's 2013 production for the Trafalgar Transformed season.

In an interview for Rutter's *Clamorous Voices*, Sinead Cusack, who played Lady Macbeth in Noble's production, describes the 'beautiful logic' behind the idea that the Macbeths had had a child and subsequently lost it: 'That sort of loss, the loss of a child, is so huge, so massive, that [...] it can turn the need for a child into an obsessive need for something else' (Rutter 1988: 56). Like Francesca Annis in Roman Polanski's 1971 film, Cusack was a young Lady Macbeth who subverted stereotypes of the evil, domineering wife. However, the motivating factor behind the impassioned incitement of her husband to murder was not, in contrast to Annis's interpretation, the over-reaching ambition of a 'starry-eyed youth' (Williams 2004: 147) but the self-destructive existentialism of a grieving mother. The loss of the Macbeth baby thus became the focal point for this production and images of children dominated its aesthetic. From the monstrous patchwork baby on the poster to the witches' child-apparitions playing blindman's buff with Macbeth, children confronted the Macbeths at every turn, mocking their barrenness with their ubiquitous presence.

Noble's *Macbeth* proved to be a landmark production in terms of the impact it made on both the academic and theatrical communities. Its influence in terms of its focus on the childlessness of the Macbeths can be seen in a number of stage productions that followed. They are too numerous to list in full here, but some notable productions include Philip Franks's 1995 production at the Sheffield Crucible, which featured witches pushing an empty old-fashioned pram that remained on stage as 'a brooding incarnation of a tragedy of childlessness' (O'Connor and Goodland 2007: 710); Gregory Doran's 1999 production for The Swan Theatre, featuring Harriet Walter and Anthony Sher, for whom the 'dead baby' was the 'most crucial' aspect of the play (Sher 2009: 343); Jude Kelly's 1999 production for the West Yorkshire Playhouse, in which Mairead McKinley's Lady Macbeth was revealed 'grief-stricken and bitterly cutting up baby clothes' (Bassett 1999); Andrew Hilton's 2004 production at the Bristol Tobacco Factory, where Lady Macbeth sleepwalked in a room with a 'shrouded cradle and rocking horse' (O'Connor and Goodland 2007: 747); Gemma Bodinetz's 2011 production for the Liverpool Everyman Theatre in which Lady Macbeth's 'incantatory call to be "unsex'd" sound[ed] less like a diabolical ploy than the expression of a despairing hope that an empty throne might compensate for a barren womb' (Hickling 2011); and Daniel Evans's 2012 production for the Sheffield Crucible, which featured a grieving Macbeth rescuing Macduff's baby from the clutches of the murderers and refusing to hand him over until he himself was surrounded by the English forces.

Much critical commentary has been dedicated to analysing the multiple ways in which Noble's production instigated a theatrical obsession with materializing both the real and the symbolic children of Shakespeare's text. Of particular note is the detailed and extensive analysis by Carol Chillington Rutter, who argues that Noble's *Macbeth* 'took a long look at desecrated childhood, perverse parenting, assembling fragments from culture at large into a form that, resonating against the Shakespeare text, interrogated the present' (2007a: 174).³ I will therefore not go over well-trodden territory here with a full analysis of Noble's groundbreaking production, but concentrate instead on Jamie Lloyd's post-millennial re-imagination of the play. Where the barrenness of Noble's Macbeths went some way towards providing, in the words of reviewer Stanley Wells, 'a psychological explanation for their evil' (1989: 170–1), the failure to produce an heir was, for Lloyd's tragic protagonists, a symptom of a far wider social malaise. Quite simply, the inability of the Macbeths to produce an heir signalled the end of the line for not merely one family but a whole generation. The child, the embodiment of Edelman's politics of 'reproductive futurism' (2004: 3), was, in this dystopian production, dying before he/she had even been born.

One writer who saw the point of the missing baby over a decade before the Adrian Noble production and the ensuing spate of childless-themed *Macbeth*s was Marvin Rosenberg. In an essay titled 'Lady Macbeth's Indispensable Child' (1974), he hypothesized about what it might mean to feature a Macbeth baby on stage. For Rosenberg, the only riddle surrounding the Macbeths' child was that its existence should be in doubt: 'Of course Lady Macbeth has at least one child', he confidently asserts, 'Shakespeare begins with a loving pair, and tells us unequivocally – in a play full of equivocation – that they have had a child' (1974: 14). He then describes in vivid detail how he envisages the presence of the baby would work on stage as a literalized motivation for the actions of the protagonists. The baby first appears in Act 1, Scene 5, where he imagines Lady Macbeth reading the letter from her husband while gently rocking her baby in his cot. The presence of the baby would, he suggests, momentarily provide a 'touching domesticity' that emphasizes the 'softer' side of Lady Macbeth (1974: 15). Next he describes with graphic and imaginative precision what happens as the implications of her husband's news sink in:

> The cradle's rocking stops; her terrible prayer to be unsexed, to give up her mother's milk for the juice of anger, shocks the more because voiced in the presence of the babe. And now may be sensed the first sounds of the child, sounds that can orchestrate with the play's scattered animal cries of cat, toad, owl, cricket, and of the child-apparitions in the witches' cave, the ravaged child in Macduff's castle.
>
> (1974)

In Rosenberg's imagined production the 'sounds of the child' provide a constant stimulus to action for Macbeth. They would be a 'tug to his conscience' (1974) when he prevaricates over murdering Duncan as well as an incitement to infanticide when he looks at Fleance, 'whose life', Rosenberg argues, 'seems to threaten the very existence as well as the succession of his child' (1974: 16). Finally, when all hope of securing the crown for his son slips away from him, Macbeth faces his fate, and 'the unmothered, futureless manchild' is abandoned. In the final moments, Rosenberg imagines Macbeth's demise accompanied by the sounds that have dogged him throughout the play: 'A little cry, a final little cry, may herald Macbeth's death knell' (1974: 19).

Although there is no reason why this theoretical production might not work in practice, it is problematic for a number of reasons. Not only does Rosenberg gloss over the equivocation and ambiguities of Shakespeare's text (features he lauded in *The Masks of Macbeth* (1978), to which his essay was subsequently appended), but by literalizing the Macbeth baby he overdetermines the issues of lineage and succession, diminishes the influence of the supernatural, oversimplifies the complex and shifting relationship of the Macbeths and demonizes Lady Macbeth, transforming her into the 'anti-mother' who would 'dash […] the brains out' (1.7.58) of a living (not hypothetical) child. The result would be a version of Shakespeare's play that is neither domestic tragedy, as was the case for Noble (1986) and Doran (1999), or social commentary, like the more recent production by Jamie Lloyd. In Rosenberg's conception of the play, moreover, all ambiguities and character nuances are removed as Macbeth's actions are entirely justified by the need to protect his vulnerable young son whose life depends on the removal of potential threats. Unlike the narrative of the childless couple, a living heir provides Macbeth with a real and unequivocal motive for killing Fleance. An audience might well empathize with the murderous actions of this Macbeth. A father protecting the life of his son is a very different proposition from a man driven to murder by a multitude of potential reasons: an emasculating wife, equivocating spirits, post-traumatic stress disorder, grief and 'vaulting ambition' (1.7.27), to name but a few. By maintaining an element of ambiguity, Shakespeare complicates his characters and denies his audience a simplistic response. Rosenberg, on the other hand, portrays Macbeth as a heroic martyr sacrificing himself for the life of his son. In doing so, he smooths over what he himself calls the 'many, varied, even contrary strains' of the protagonist of Shakespeare's text and demonizes Lady Macbeth as the stereotype of evil absolute (1978: x).

Emma Smith has argued that the propensity of modern productions to subsume Lady Macbeth's behaviour into a digestible narrative of childlessness and bereavement mitigates the ruthless actions of a woman 'that might otherwise be designated transgressively unfeminine' (2013: 156). Rosenberg's Lady Macbeth is not merely 'transgressively unfeminine'; she is a villain without any psychological depth. The grieving mother, on the other hand, offers directors an opportunity to provide Lady Macbeth with a psychologically plausible backstory. The effectiveness of the Lloyd production lay in its capacity to incorporate that narrative of childlessness into a much wider socio-economic context. Rather than representing merely the emotional centre of a domestic tragedy, like many of the productions that had come before it, the sterility of the Macbeth marriage was a symptom of and metonym for the moral, economic and environmental decline of a whole generation. The result was an exciting development in the treatment of the absent Macbeth baby and the wider implications that had for the other children in the play: the murdered Macduff children, the 'birth-strangled babe' (4.1.30) of the witches' cauldron and Fleance, who vanishes without trace. It symbolized, in other words, the widespread eradication of children more generally in a production that, while not to everybody's taste, nonetheless provoked lively critical debate and broke the mould of almost thirty years of domesticated, naturalistic *Macbeths*.

Jamie Lloyd's visual aesthetic depicted a country 'sink[ing] beneath the yoke' (4.3.39) of ecological, economic and political collapse. The theatre had been reconfigured in the round to create an intimate, almost immersive experience, and Soutra Gilmour's stark, post-industrial set comprised of steel trapdoors, concrete flooring, a lone standpipe and a dirty toilet. Lloyd's aim, he declared, was to create a social world that would 'resonate with the here and now' and tap into 'the psychology of our age', a world of the dispossessed struggling to survive in a society 'regressed to its most base animal instincts'. 'What if', he asked, 'all the major fears of our age actually happen?' (Stambollouian 2013). The answer he provided was bleak: the children would completely disappear, taking all hope for the future with them. Expanding upon Shakespeare's metaphorical baby, Lloyd turned one couple's childlessness into a metonym for the sterility of a whole society. On a familial level, the infertility of Lady Macbeth represented the tragedy of a woman denied the maternal role with which her identity was so inextricably linked. On a macro-social level, it signified the loss of futurity itself – a futurity in which Lloyd's desolate Scotland most desperately needed to believe.

From her first entrance, Claire Foy's Lady Macbeth conveyed the brittle fragility and manic restlessness of a psychologically disturbed young woman. Her hair unkempt, her waifish figure clad in shapeless clothing, she strode across the floor in her heavy boots like a child who had raided the dressing-up box. For some reviewers, her relentless pacing and jagged speech conveyed the impression of a nagging and emasculating wife. Using pejorative descriptors such as 'manipulative' (Nathan 2013), 'bossy' and 'morally blind' (Spencer 2013), they mistook her brash exterior for the self-centred rantings of what one reviewer called a 'teenage virago' (Purves 2013). However, detailed business between the couple made it clear that her initial spikiness masked the despair of a grieving mother. This Lady Macbeth was not a 'fiend-like queen' (5.9.35) but a young wife 'driven', in the words of the associate director, 'by a feeling of frustration, rage, jealousy and bitterness for the loss of her child' (Stambollouian 2014). In their first meeting, Macbeth, played by James McAvoy, spread his hand across her stomach. They exchanged a look, and, removing his glove, he repeated the action with his bare hand. However, her stomach was, as one reviewer noted, 'reproachfully flat' (Brown 2013). At this realization, Macbeth's expression turned to one of despair and his wife staggered forward towards him. Before she could fall into his arms, however, he took a step back, coldly announcing: 'We will speak further' (1.5.71). As though steeling herself against his rejection, Lady Macbeth gathered herself with a ramrod-like purpose. Again, their eyes met and his hand stretched out as though to touch her stomach. But this time he paused, pulled it back to his side and walked purposefully off the stage. As the lights fell, her steeliness gave way to despair and her body crumpled like an abandoned rag doll. The sight of her utter physical and psychological dejection perfectly mirrored the devastated wasteland of her surroundings. This was not merely

FIGURE 5 *James McAvoy as Macbeth and Claire Foy as Lady Macbeth, in* Macbeth, *dir. Jamie Lloyd, 2012. Courtesy Johan Persson/ArenaPAL.*

the story of one couple driven to desperation through grief. The Macbeths' tragedy was clearly, in the world of Lloyd's apocalyptic vision, a symptom of a far greater catastrophic decline.

A later, gruesomely ironic replay of this scene brought a reversal in roles for the Macbeths. Lady Macbeth was seated on the edge of a table, alternately comforting and hectoring her agitated husband who had just returned from the scene of Duncan's murder. Standing between her legs, he cried 'Cawdor / Shall sleep no more. Macbeth shall sleep no more' (2.2.43–4) and placed a blood-soaked hand across her stomach, turning her dress into a dripping mass of red. This gesture, which had earlier conveyed a sense of mutual but divisive emotional pain, now created a terrible parody of a miscarriage. The multiple textual manifestations of blood and babies seemed distilled into, and emblematized by, this one horrifying simulation of spontaneously aborted pregnancy.

Children, it seemed, were reluctant to be born into the world of Jamie Lloyd's *Macbeth*. Even the 'bloody child' emanating from the witches' cauldron in Act 4, Scene 1, was not manifested on stage as a child but was represented instead by Macbeth ventriloquizing the apparition's words. Moreover, the unfortunate children who were already alive were being terrorized back into the womb to die, as the scene at the Macduff castle was to symbolically suggest. At the entrance of the murderers, Macduff's young 'fry' (4.2.86), played alternately by a girl and a boy actor in different performances, was pushed by her/his mother into a large chest to hide. Lady Macduff was then pinned down on top of this chest by the three murderers and garrotted with a rope. As the murderers left, Macbeth entered alone. Checking Lady Macduff was no longer breathing, he turned to leave, muttering the first murderer's line, 'he's a traitor' (4.2.84). At this, a childish voice cried out 'thou liest' (4.2.85) from inside the chest. Slowly and deliberately, Macbeth turned, unsheathed his sword, placed his ear to the chest and, after pausing for a beat, thrust his sword deep into its side. The metaphor was clear: Macbeth was killing Macduff's issue, ensconced in her/his womb-like hiding place, as retribution for his own loss. The source of Macbeth's 'rooted sorrow' (5.3.41), in this heavily symbolic production, was his childless marriage; the murders, in the words of the *Independent* reviewer, were a 'hideously doomed and eroticised groping for compensatory intimacy' (Taylor 2013a); and Jamie Lloyd's question – 'What if all the major fears of our age actually happen?' (Stambollouian 2013) – had received its nihilistic answer. The death of childhood quite simply represented the death of society itself.

Ripped out of time: Defying mortality in Michael Boyd's *Macbeth* (1985, 1993 and 2011)

Michael Boyd's 2011 production at the RSC was his third professional experience of directing *Macbeth*. His first two productions were staged at the Tron Theatre in Glasgow during his tenure as the theatre's first artistic director. I am not able to base my analysis of these productions on first-hand experience as I was not present at the original performances and recordings were not made. Documentary evidence and secondary accounts/reviews are also extremely limited.[4] To avoid straying into the territory of the conjectural and the fanciful, I am not, therefore, attempting a detailed study of these performances. However, through an exploration of the material and artistic circumstances of their production and a consideration of some contemporary critical reviews, I provide an interpretive context for my analysis of the 2011 RSC production, which was clearly heavily influenced by choices made in Glasgow two and three decades earlier. The religious iconography, disjointed historical references and revenant, malevolent/innocent children were particularly distinctive aspects of Boyd's original production designs that were to be revisited and further defined for the later RSC revival. The archival evidence I have analysed suggests that these crucial artistic choices were closely related to, if not born out of a response to, the history and architectural design of the Tron Theatre itself. The overall effect that seems to have transported across three decades, and several counties, is one of atemporality: a world thrust out of time into disorder and disarray, in which the past is an intrusive presence and the future an unthinkable prospect. The single unifying principle that symbolized and embodied this sense of disruption was the shape-shifting child.

The Tron was originally built as a Catholic church in the early sixteenth century. It was subsequently reincarnated as a Protestant Kirk when Catholicism was outlawed in Scotland in 1560 and then used as a place of execution, a police meeting house and a workshop before it was eventually converted into a 230-seat theatre in 1980. The Tron Theatre website and publicity material emphasize the unique history of this building. Stories of ghostly visitations, buried corpses and strange conflagrations create a menacing atmosphere that would have provided a fitting context for *Macbeth*, Shakespeare's most thorough exploration of the supernatural. The 1985 *Macbeth* was performed in repertory with *Macbeth Possessed* (1985), a then new play by Stuart Delves which took disrupted temporalities and historical revisions as its central interpretive crux. Delves's play opened with an imagined royal command performance of Shakespeare's *Macbeth* for James VI of Scotland, his wife, Queen Anna and her brother, Christian IV of Denmark. The performance was unexpectedly interrupted at the beginning of Act 2, Scene 3, when the figure knocking at the gate turned out not to be Macduff, but the disgruntled ghosts of 'King Macbeth' and 'Queen Gruoch' resurrected from the dead to 'lash back at the Bard's propaganda piece' with their own revisionary version of history (Programme 1993). The three children, who appeared in Boyd's play doubling as the Macduff children and the witches, had a similarly dual function in Delves's highly metatheatrical drama. They were both terrified 'child actors', whose performance of Shakespeare's *Macbeth* had been interrupted by the ghostly visitation of characters from the past, and supernatural agents of truth in the reclaimed play-within-a-play, sent to show James the 'real' history of his usurping and regicidal ancestors and successors. At one point they entered with the heads of Mary Stuart and Charles I and presented them to a terrified, stammering James. They were followed by 'a line of other children wearing face masks' depicting English monarchs, including 'Charles III' (Delves 1985: 36).[5] On paper, *Macbeth Possessed* reads like a light-hearted, if clumsy, reflection on the nature of theatre and a gentle anti-Jacobean satire. Reviewers were less than generous in their assessment, and Martin Hoyle's critique of Delves's 'protracted and attrociously-written [sic] undergraduate sketch' (Hoyle 1985: 17) is typical of the critical reception this new play received. Negative reviews notwithstanding, its concern with history, temporality and the spirit world would have resonated with Boyd's particularly supernatural interpretation of *Macbeth*. What is striking about these two productions, playing in repertory with the same company of actors, is the way in which they both used the child-figure as the central agent of dramatic disorder and temporal revisions. Of course, it is impossible to say with certainty where the original idea originated. What can be deduced, however, is that either Boyd was influenced by Delves's dual-faced children or (more likely) that Boyd inspired Delves to borrow this conceit. Either way, it was clearly considered central enough to Boyd's dramatic design to be repeated twice more, in 1993 and 2011.

In all three of his productions of *Macbeth*, Boyd doubled his Macduff children with the three witches to create a Janus-faced image of childhood that seemed to foreshadow the real juxtaposition of evil and innocence seen in the mediated James Bulger footage eight years later. I asked him what motivated him to keep returning to the trope of the innocent/malevolent child in his three productions of *Macbeth*, and he responded as follows:

In 1980 ish, as an assistant at the Belgrade Theatre in Coventry, I staged a version of Henry James' *Turn of the Screw*, which centres around two very frightened and seemingly corrupted children, and was struck by the power of contrasting innocence and dark understanding... In the 1985 production [of *Macbeth*], it began as a pragmatic matter of cost, that the witches doubled as the Macduff children, but from the first rehearsals we quickly became convinced that we could make more of this by making the witches in fact the murdered Macduff children ripped not only out of life but of time, and returning to retell their fate and Macbeth's. The audience saw the children simply as dead child victims of war, until they saw them appear in pristine versions of their filthy and bloody costumes as the living children of Lady Macduff, which of course lent that scene even more weight of foreboding than usual. The 1985 and 1993 productions were both staged in the converted church that was the Tron Theatre, and the children were buried under a thin layer of earth and then burst out of their graves to confront Macbeth and Banquo. I had always wanted the children to be more graphically victims of terrible violence, but it was not until the RSC production [of 2011] that I could afford the means to hang them from butchers' hooks, and have them slowly descend, singing the Agnus Dei.

(Boyd 2014)

What is particularly noteworthy about Boyd's response is his focus on the victimhood of his children. Although he talks of 'foreboding', it is a reference to the future fate of the Macduff children rather than their incarnation as witches. For the audience, however, the conceit of doubling the witches with Macduff's 'pretty chickens' (4.3.221) was far more ontologically disturbing and resistant to definition than Boyd intended, and the 'weight of foreboding' was created by the children-as-witches rather than the 'living children of Lady Macduff', as the critical reviews attest. Writing about Boyd's 1985 production, for instance, *Financial Times* reviewer Martin Hoyle observes that his use of children added 'something indefinably sinister', describing them as 'malevolent manikins who greet evil with piercing screams' (1985: 17). Analyses of the 1993 production use similar language to define what, in Boyd's weird children, seems remarkably undefinable. Joyce McMillan, writing for *The Guardian*, for instance, describes the 'weird, blood-smeared children' as 'chilling' (1993), while *The Sunday Times* reviewer describes them as a manifestation of 'amoral innocence', the very distillation of the angel and the demon in one ambiguous figure (Peter 1993: 573). Using a similar vocabulary of hyperbole and antithesis, O'Connor and Goodland describe how the Macduff children 'innocently counterpoint[ed] the evil' with a 'chilling blind man's buff with Macbeth' (2007: 699).[6] Critical reception of the children certainly seemed to focus more on their embodiment of 'innocence and dark understanding', as seen in James's *The Turn of the Screw*, than on their plight as 'victims of terrible violence'.

These were themes that Boyd continued to explore when he returned to *Macbeth* in 2011 as artistic director at the RSC. Unlike the Tron productions, the RSC revival is well documented and I watched a performance live in the theatre and on a DVD archival recording. Drawing on my first-hand experience, I will provide an interpretive framework for comprehending and articulating what seems to have eluded the Tron reviewers quoted above. As the inaugural production in the newly refurbished RSC, Boyd's 2011 *Macbeth* was a fitting blend of the new with the old. Set in a post-Reformation church with desecrated Catholic iconography and crumbling walls, the dominant visual aesthetic was early modern in design. It is surely not overly fanciful to presume that this design choice was influenced by Boyd's earlier experiences of staging *Macbeth* at the Tron Theatre. Indeed, he worked with set designer Tom Piper on both the 1993 and 2011 productions. However, in the 2011 production, the sixteenth-century setting was juxtaposed with a plethora of contemporary references – modern costumes, ethnically diverse casting and a semtex-carrying porter – giving the overall production an added sense of temporal disjunction. Three female cellists were seated in the shadows of a balcony, their dark forms picked out by the light creeping through the shattered stained-glass windows behind them, and the discordant notes of the anachronistic instruments providing an aural corollary to the visual devastation. Into this iconoclastic atmosphere dropped the three 'weird children'. This time, instead of 'burst[ing] out of their graves' (Boyd 2014), they descended like 'spectral dead puppet children' (Purves 2011) from the flies across the front of the thrust stage. They hung suspended from meat-hooks for several seconds, then twitched in choreographed synchronicity before being lowered slowly to the ground. For the brief time that they were hanging, silent and immobile, it was difficult to discern whether they were actors or, as in the case of the children of Ostermeier's *Richard III* and Wheeldon's *The Winter's Tale*, merely surrogates. Their jerky convulsions further intensified the disturbing sense of ontological indeterminacy. Already at odds with the traditional representation of *Macbeth*'s witches as old hags, the styling of the children struck an additional note of dissonance that reinforced the sense that they had indeed been 'ripped [...] out of time' (Boyd 2014). Their Jacobean costumes contrasted with the modern dress of the adult characters; their pure voices, raised in a soaring rendition of 'Agnus Dei', battled with the plangent sounds of the cellos; and their faces were covered in white make-up with a cross branded across their foreheads.

For many reviewers these children-as-witches could only be described in phenomenological terminology: 'startling and harrowing' (Heijes 2012: 104), 'eerie' (Hart 2011), 'horrifyingly disturbing' (Rutter 2012) and, for Charles Spencer 'a truly shocking moment that ma[de] the skin crawl' (2011). It was an image that evoked both 'foul' and 'fair' (1.1.9), child and not-quite-child: a moment of ontological uncertainty that encapsulated not only the epistemological ambiguities of *Macbeth* but also the contradictions of a postmodern world that, as Cunningham has observed, is

FIGURE 6 *Unidentified actor as witch, in* Macbeth, *dir. Michael Boyd, 2011. Photo by Ellie Kurttz. Courtesy RSC.*

both fearful *of* and fearful *for* its children. From the emotive language used by critics, it is clear that, like the Tron reviewers, they responded to these 'weird children' in a visceral manner that was almost primitive. One way of understanding what made this ontologically unstable image particularly disturbing can be found in Freud's notion of the 'uncanny' – the unhomely' (*das Unheimlich*) as a species of 'the homely' (*das Heimlich*) ([1919] 2003: 134). For Freud, the 'Unheimlich' is not simply unnatural but something 'intended to remain secret' that has 'come into the open'. When confronted with this paradoxical conflation of the familiar and the unfamiliar, we experience an inexpressible fear that is ordinarily repressed, or 'locked away', a fear that Freud associates with the pre-rational world of childhood itself ([1919] 2003: 132–4). Applying Freud's theories on the 'uncanny' to the weird children of Boyd's *Macbeth*, it becomes clearer to see why the various critics struggled to rationalize their responses beyond vague descriptives such as 'chilling', 'sinister' and 'eerie'.

The tensions between the familiar and the unfamiliar (child-like innocence and demonic evil) were further sharpened when it was eventually revealed in Act 4, Scene 2, that the 'weird children' were the same actors playing Macduff's 'pretty chickens' (4.3.218). This decision to double the parts was not, however, driven by reasons of pragmatism, as with the smaller-budget Glasgow productions, but a central aspect of Boyd's dramatic design, as is clear from his correspondence with me. The scene at the Macduff castle opened with what appeared to be a picture of domesticity with the three children seated at their mother's feet playing with toys. However, these toys were not conventional signifiers of childhood play but reminders of the duality of the children's roles, as they were in fact the same dolls summoned as apparitions by the three 'weird children' during the cauldron scene and looked disturbingly like voodoo dolls. Voodoo dolls had, of course, been used in this scene before. Trevor Nunn's acclaimed production for the RSC in 1976 featured the witches giving voodoo dolls to a hallucinating Macbeth, and Orson Welles's 1936 stage production and 1948 film adaptation famously featured voodoo dolls that were manipulated by the witches. However, the witches in Nunn's and Welles's *Macbeth*s were adult women, not children. By having the 'weird children' in control of these dolls, Boyd was hinting at a society in which children might be capable of killing children, a notion which the Bulger case had made horrifyingly real. Moreover, by having the same children play Macduff's children *and* the witches, the children-killing-children motif symbolized both a drive towards self-destruction and a perversion of Edelman's ideology of 'reproductive futurism' (2004: 3). As with the miscarried children of Lloyd's production, the fair and foul children of Boyd's 2011 revival seemed designed to indicate a society in which the children were engaged in an existential drive towards extinction.

In a final twist in the interplay between victim and agent, Boyd's two Macduff boys, whose savage slaughter elicited gasps of horror from the audience, lay inert for several moments before standing up and walking offstage. It was a theatrical moment that seemed to invest the bodies of the children with two simultaneous identities that defied simple taxonomy: as Macduff's children, their spirits were entering another world and as the witches, they were defying death via supernatural regeneration. The boys were to re-emerge in the final scene to linger over the body of Macbeth as he lay inert and broken. The sun shone through the restored (un-Reformed) stained-glass windows, and the cellists struck their first harmonious chords of the evening. Boyd's children, who had been 'ripped [...] out of time' (Boyd 2014), returned to dismantle linear chronology all together by reversing the Reformation. Order was restored, but it was an order shadowed by the destabilizing presence of the three uncanny children. Having played the roles of both victim and agent, the 'innocent flower' and 'the serpent' (1.5.65–6), they were now the symbolic embodiment of Scotland's future – a future that, as Coen Heijes noted, promised 'an endlessly repeating cycle of violence, vengeance and murder' (2012: 105). The embodiment of both the past and the future, the victim and the perpetrator, the living and the dead, Boyd's three Janus-faced children encapsulated the dichotomous attitude to childhood that has permeated modern media and popular discourse. Ambiguous to the end, they subverted teleological narratives of progress and dismantled conventional notions of the child as bearer of futurity. If they are our hope for the future, Boyd seemed to be saying, it is a future that threatens to be as chaotic, destructive and self-annihilating as our past.

Boyd's 2011 production was not to be the last word on this subject. A large-scale cinematic version of *Macbeth* had not been released since Roman Polanski's 1971 film and Justin Kurzel was ready to meet the challenge with his 2015 adaptation. In the third and final section of this chapter, I draw comparisons between the two films to illustrate how the treatment of the children of *Macbeth* has altered in the cinema over the past four decades. Whereas Boyd took his dualistic portrayal of children through the doubling of roles to its natural and most shocking conclusion in his 2011 production, Kurzel approached the subject of childhood in *Macbeth* in a far more comprehensive and holistic manner. The result, as will be demonstrated below, was a vision of childhood that is not only as far from Polanski's vulnerable innocents as can possibly be imagined but was even more ambivalent, and therefore disturbing, than Boyd's death-defying revenants.

'Innocent angels' and 'little demons': The two faces of childhood in the films of Polanski (1971) and Kurzel (2015)

In spite of a gap of forty-four years between their respective release dates, there are, at first glance, remarkable similarities between Roman Polanski's 1971 film and the most recent cinematic adaptation of *Macbeth* by Justin Kurzel in 2015. They both take eleventh-century Scotland as their historical setting, although the issues they explore are firmly grounded in the Anglo-American sociocultural context of the 1970s and 2010s respectively. They each have a multinational cast and crew, giving the films a sense of universality that transcends national borders but is nonetheless committed to reflecting a certain kind of historical realism (in each case the multi-nationality did not extend to multi-ethnicity). The brutal realities of war form a constant visual backdrop, locating Macbeth's bloodthirsty reign within a wider context of unremitting violence and self-serving political duplicities. Both directors problematize a Manichean reading of the play as the ultimate triumph of good over evil by casting attractive, sympathetic actors to play the 'butcher' and 'his fiend-like queen' (5.9.35), with particularly fragile Lady Macbeths in the figures of Francesca Annis (1971) and Marion Cotillard (2015). They portray the Macbeths, initially at least, as a loving married couple with visual indications of emotional and physical intimacy that exceed the parameters of

Shakespeare's text. Each film features a chilling coda, moreover, that suggests a continuation of the cycle of violence extending beyond the ending of the play's narrative and certainly beyond the deaths of the protagonists. It is in these codas, however, together with the addition of an opening frame-sequence featuring the burial of the Macbeth baby in Kurzel's adaptation, that the most fundamental ideological difference between the two films is most clearly defined.

Although both films end with the reappearance of a child, Polanski's 'child', Donalbain, is in fact a child only in the generational definition of the word – Duncan's son but clearly no longer a young boy (the actor, Paul Shelley, was in fact twenty-nine when he played Donalbain). When we see him disappearing into the lair of the weird sisters in the final moments of the film, we are left in no doubt that by returning to challenge his brother Malcolm for his murdered father's title, he will set in motion a continuation of the cycle of bloodshed and unrest first instigated by Macbeth. Kurzel's returning child, however, is not an adult but Banquo's equally ambitious and embittered prepubescent son, Fleance, who, through a sequence of parallel scenes created through editing, is shown returning to challenge Macbeth's successor in a far more overtly hostile manner than even the pageboy of Holmes's *Richard III*. Emerging from the blood-red smoke of the battlefield, the boy walks past Macbeth's motionless body and draws a sword from its position where it has been embedded, Excalibur-like, in the rocks. The sequence then cuts to show Malcolm alone and unguarded in his castle. His sword is sheathed, his crown is lying in its case and his contented smile suggests that he is blissfully unaware of the impending danger. The final shot features Fleance running from the battlefield, sword held high above his head, mouth set in grim determination, the sound of his feet pounding rhythmically in time with his breathing. He is back, so this montage suggests, to fulfil the witches' prophecy and seize the crown by as violent and bloody means as Macbeth himself.

Although Kurzel seems to have followed Polanski in eschewing dramatic closure with this nihilistic glimpse into the future, he makes a significant change which has strong implications for the final message of his film. By replacing an adult Donalbain with a young Fleance he raises provocative questions about childhood and political agency, as well as foregrounding the role of children as ambiguous bearers of futurity, both in this film and in the twenty-first-century environment of its release. Far from being the uncomplicated vulnerable innocents of Polanski's dramatic conception, the children in Kurzel's *Macbeth* are polysemous and multivalent. Both victims and perpetrators, slaughtered innocents and death-defying revenants, they are the Janus-faced epitome of the 'foul' behind the 'fair' (1.1.9) that haunts this play and that were such a central feature of Boyd's three productions. This ambiguity is further complicated by Kurzel's opening frame-sequence, which shows the grieving Macbeths burning the body of their dead baby upon a funeral pyre. Unlike Polanski's youthful protagonists, for whom the question of securing the future is less urgent than enjoying the 'ignorant present' (1.5.57), Kurzel's Macbeths (played by Michael Fassbender and Marion Cotillard) are in their late thirties/early forties, and time for securing their future, a future realized in the symbol of the child, is clearly running out.

The movement from representing the child in *Macbeth* as a one-dimensional fetishized object of pathos to a complex and contradictory nexus of hopes, fears and anxieties raises intriguing questions about shifting conceptualizations of childhood more widely. The figure of the child in all its various and multifarious manifestations has taken on an ever greater significance in productions of *Macbeth* since the release of Polanski's film in 1971. That Kurzel has made the child his central organizing principle is therefore the culmination of a trend that has been gathering pace for several decades, as we saw in the first section of this chapter. The result is a complex and contradictory representation of childhood that parallels an increasingly conflicted attitude towards children in society more widely, and represents a general trend away from a sentimentalized depiction of childhood towards one which is, at best, ambivalent and, at worst, depressingly nihilistic.

Polanski's film was released in the immediate aftermath of the swinging sixties, reflecting a decade in which, as Deanne Williams observes, 'the dark side of the combination of boundless individualism and a powerful sense of collective purpose […] characterized the youth culture' on both sides of the Atlantic (2004: 146). 'The sourness of the end of the Free Love era', as one reviewer observed, 'hangs over every scene like the smell of burnt flesh' (Collin 2015). In addition to capturing the 'dark side' of a period which saw the assassinations of Martin Luther King and Robert Kennedy, the 1968 race riots and the horrors of the Vietnam

War, Polanski's film bears disturbing traces of his own personal tragedy of 1969, when three female followers of Charles Manson broke into his house and brutally murdered Sharon Tate, Polanski's partner. She was eight months pregnant with his child at the time, giving the wording used to describe the Macduff's caesarean birth – 'from his mother's womb / Untimely ripped' (5.8.15–16) – a whole new and gruesome meaning. Against this backdrop of horror, it is not surprising that Polanski took the child in *Macbeth* and turned him into an emblem of victimhood. From Fleance, played by a thirteen-year-old Keith Chegwin, to the precocious son of Macduff and his slaughtered siblings, the children in this film are all fair, fragile and vulnerable – the epitome of what James Kincaid has dubbed the 'alluring child'. As is further explored in Chapter 3, this child, which Kincaid describes as 'bleached, bourgeois and androgynous', is a ubiquitous figure in Hollywood mainstream cinema (1998: 20). Unthreatening and one-dimensional, the 'alluring child' is fetishized and idealized for the scopophillic pleasures of its audience. In fact, looking at the film from a twenty-first-century perspective, whose audiences are all-too-familiar with the consequences of sexualizing children, it is striking just how fetishistic the portrayal of childhood is in Polanski's *Macbeth*.[7]

Fleance in this film is never presented as a threat to Macbeth and his crown, in spite of the witches' promise to Banquo. We first see him at the feast held in Duncan's honour at the Macbeth castle. Child-like and charming, he drinks a cheeky sip of wine before cowering in fear when a sudden gust of wind blows the curtains. He then sings a courtly love song to entertain the diners, his sweet, unbroken voice soaring with the purity and piety of an angelic choirboy, while Duncan and his courtiers smile indulgently. From his fair hair, which hangs endearingly across his eyes and curls at his neck, to his underdeveloped body and open, questioning face, he is the image of childish guilelessness. Always shown by the side of his father, he appears younger than his thirteen years and, unlike Kurzel's Fleance, is maintained as an uncomplicated symbol of childhood innocence throughout Polanski's film.

A comparison of the different ways in which the two directors treat the scene after the banquet at Macbeth's castle provides a clear exemplification of their contrasting approaches to representing Fleance. The scene (Act 2, Scene 1) begins with just Banquo and

Fleance on stage. Shakespeare immediately establishes both the time of day and the fact that it is unusually dark in their opening dialogue:

> BANQUO
>   How goes the night, boy?
> FLEANCE
>   The moon is down; I have not heard the clock.
> BANQUO
>   And she goes down at twelve.
> FLEANCE
>   I take 'tis later, sir.
> BANQUO
>   Hold, take my sword. There's husbandry in heaven;
>   Their candles are all out; take thee that, too.
>
>   (2.1.1–5)

Both Polanski and Kurzel represent this opening dialogue as a straightforward conversation between father and son, following the implied stage directions for the setting. It is what happens next that differentiates the two films most starkly and is particularly significant for our understanding of the role of Fleance. In Polanski's film, Banquo switches from spoken speech to voice-over after line five, so that the next four lines are heard by the audience but, and this is crucial, *not* by Fleance:

> A heavy summons lies like lead upon me,
> And yet I would not sleep. Merciful powers,
> Restrain in me the cursed thoughts that nature
> Gives way to in repose.
>
>   (2.1.6–9)

Although it is not made explicit exactly what Banquo means when he mentions 'heavy summons' and 'cursed thoughts', editors have tended to gloss these lines as a reference to his own guilty thoughts.[8] However, the sudden appearance of Macbeth at this point in Polanski's film suggests a direct association between Banquo's insomnia-inducing anxieties and the implied guilt of his host. This is further reinforced when Banquo describes Duncan's 'great largess' (2.1.14) towards both Macbeth's servants and his wife, to whom he sends, via Banquo, a diamond as acknowledgement of her role as a 'most kind hostess' (2.1.16). It is a moment of dramatic irony that connects Banquo's 'cursed thoughts' (2.1.8) with the murderous plans of the Macbeths. His own guiltlessness, in implied contrast to that of Macbeth, is emphasized some twenty lines later when he pointedly insists that he keeps his 'bosom franchised and allegiance clear' (2.1.28). The import of the Banquo-Macbeth exchange in this scene, with its simmering subtext of recriminations and threats, can only be fully appreciated in the context of Banquo's earlier speech, particularly lines 6–9 quoted above. That Polanski chose to film these lines in voice-over suggests that he wanted to keep Fleance ignorant of Banquo's suspicions. Indeed, during the subsequent exchange between Banquo and Macbeth, the boy's behaviour suggests that he is unaware of the underlying tensions. His purity unsullied, Polanski's Fleance can thus be presented as an innocent victim of Macbeth's tyranny and a symbol of pity amid a world of self-serving adults.

Although Kurzel, like Polanski, suggests in this exchange that Banquo's intentions are honourable, he makes a significant change to Banquo's 'heavy summons' speech that is fundamental to our understanding of the role of Fleance in this film. In contrast to Polanski's boy, whose vulnerability and innocence remain unchanged, Kurzel's Fleance undergoes a transformation from young boy to bloodthirsty avenger, and the first signs of this metamorphosis can be seen in this crucial scene. Rather than presenting Banquo's speech in voice-over, Kurzel films it as a direct exchange between father and son. That this is not an artistic but rather a dramatic choice is clear when we consider the extensive use of voice-over elsewhere in Kurzel's film, particularly in the soliloquies. What Kurzel seems to be intending to convey in this exchange by filming it as a conversation is a level of understanding between father and son and an increasingly adult sense of knowingness in the young Fleance. As Kurzel's Banquo articulates his 'heavy summons' and 'cursed thoughts', the camera closes in on the face of Fleance. His expression is inscrutable, but the close-shot focus on his eyes intently watching his father suggests that he is absorbing and processing the import of Banquo's words. Rather than choosing to protect the innocence of his son, Kurzel's Banquo makes this speech tantamount to a warning against the 'cursed thoughts' of a murderous Macbeth. The extent of Fleance's transformation does not become completely clear until the coda when he returns to challenge the throne. However, watching the film with this final scene in mind, it is clear that the seeds of change are sown in this short but crucial exchange.

I have argued that, in contrast to Kurzel's boy, Polanski's Fleance retains his innocence throughout the film. As noted by Katie Knowles, however, Polanski does appear, at first glance, to complicate this image of purity with a dream-sequence showing Fleance stealing the crown from a sleeping Macbeth (2014: 199). This scene occurs directly after Macbeth has watched Banquo and his son leave on their riding expedition, and then given his hired assassins clear instructions to ensure that they do not return. Once the murderers have been dispatched, the camera follows Macbeth as he enters his chamber. He drains his goblet of wine, then walks unsteadily towards the bed, where he removes his crown and lies down. No sooner has he closed his eyes than a gust of wind blows the curtains (a reference to the earlier banqueting scene where a similar gust saw Fleance cowering in fear), and the flame of the fire flickers ominously. Fleance then appears from below the foot of the bed dressed in hunting garb and, knocking away Macbeth's outstretched hand, places the crown on his own head while a smiling Banquo looks on approvingly. Fleance then straddles Macbeth's prone body and takes an arrow from a quiver slung across his back. He points the arrow suggestively at a terrified-looking Macbeth, and Banquo places a hand over his mouth. As Macbeth emerges from his nightmare, the hand over his mouth morphs into Lady Macbeth's hand, as she tries to stifle his screams of terror. For Knowles, the image of Fleance, 'the golden-headed child', parodying Macbeth's murder of Duncan in this manner epitomizes Polanski's practice of problematizing 'conventional assumptions about innocence and guilt, good and evil'. It is quite simply, she argues, the point at which we see 'innocence turning into evil' (2014: 199). Although I agree that it is probably intended to show Fleance as a threat, it is an hallucination originating from the same 'heat-oppressed brain' (2.1.39) that had earlier conjured up the imaginary dagger (which Polanski literalizes in the form of a suspended dagger which Macbeth tries but fails to grasp), and therefore says more about Macbeth's drink-addled and guilt-ridden mind than it does about Fleance himself. The threat, in other words, is a perception made manifest by Macbeth's overactive imagination rather than a reflection of reality.

Far more disturbing than Macbeth's nightmares of a would-be regicidal Fleance is the way in which the image of the child is made the object of a homoerotic dream-sequence. The only way in which this episode complicates the idea of children as symbols of purity is by showing how that symbol can be manipulated and sullied by the adults who control it. It is, I would contend, a highly eroticized scene that is more sexual than sinister – what James Kincaid terms a manifestation of the child as a 'field of desire' (1992: 5) – as a closer analysis of the scene reveals. As Fleance straddles Macbeth, the camera closes in upon his bouncing knees before moving up to his face as he raises one arm to retrieve an arrow from his quiver, his back arching suggestively as he does so. Dressed in an archer's outfit with his golden locks curling at his neck, he looks like the human embodiment of Cupid. The camera then follows the point of the arrow – the source of erotic power in familiar iconography of Cupid – as he places it against Macbeth's naked chest and uses it to pull the bedclothes down towards his groin.[9] It is at this point that Banquo's restraining hand turns into that of Lady Macbeth and the two apparitions disappear. To further reinforce the sexual connotations of this scene, Lady Macbeth gently strokes Macbeth's perspiring face and their lips almost touch as she admonishes him that 'things without all remedy / Should be without regard' (3.2.12–13). Less a premonition of regicide than an erotic dream-sequence, the homoerotic, if not paedophilic, overtones make for uncomfortable viewing. Fleance is less an agent of 'innocence turning into evil' (2014: 199), as Knowles has argued, and more an object of the film-maker's tendency towards scopophilia in this particularly sexualized version of *Macbeth*.

Many commentators have noted the overall voyeuristic texture of Polanski's film, with its concentration of ritualistic violence, dismembered body parts, female nudity and bloody corpses.[10] Much of what has been written focuses on the sexualized nature of Lady Macbeth's sleepwalking scene, with writers repeatedly conflating the vision of a naked and vulnerable Francesca Annis with the erotic image of the film's *Playboy* backers. Deanne Williams, for instance, remarks that her Lady Macbeth 'would be as at home at a party at the Playboy Mansion as she would at a nudist beach' (153), while one American film critic describes her as 'a spot-crazy Playboy bunny' (Polanski 1984: 297.) However, the scopophilic attention to the body of the child has largely passed without remark. One notable exception is Kenneth Rothwell, who, writing about the scene in the Macduff castle, comments with remarkable *sang froid* that watching 'pederasts can feast on the naked body of MacDuff's young son' and that the sequence is 'Polanski, or more accurately Shakespeare, at his best' (1973: 74). From a twenty-first-century perspective, Rothwell's remarks seem worryingly blasé, irresponsible even. However, they reflect a reality that is all-too-clear in this sequence. What Polanski has created is in fact a far more bloody and gruesome spectacle than Shakespeare's text suggests, with the body of the child at its very centre. And as Rothwell's comments highlight, it is a body that epitomizes Kincaid's erotico-fetishized child.

The scene at Macduff's castle opens with a shot of Macduff's son standing naked in a tin bath, wriggling from side to side as his mother pours water over his head. She then wraps him in a white towel and he sits by a blazing fire, the noise of children's voices playing somewhere in the distance. As the two murderers enter the room, the boy jumps up and shelters behind his mother, and the sound of giggling children is ominously replaced with heart-rending screams. The boy runs at one of the men and knees him in the groin. As he turns back to face Lady Macduff, he is stabbed in the back. He then staggers towards his mother, his face twisted in pain as he stutters 'He has killed me, mother' (4.2.86). A piercing scream emanates from another room in the castle. In the back of the shot, the second murderer can be seen slouching in a chair, watching with voyeuristic glee as the boy is wrenched from his mother's arms, and she flies from the room. The camera then follows her as she runs through the corridors of the castle, cutting between point-of-view shots and close shots of her horrified face as she registers the fire and carnage unfolding in each room. We see a maid being raped, a crucifix being burned and hear the howls of terror rising above the plangent discords of the Third Ear Band soundtrack. Then the camera closes in on two of Lady Macduff's butchered children. Bloodied and naked, they lie abandoned, their heads flung back and their small bodies twisted and contorted like broken dolls.

In his autobiography, the director reports how a female member of the film committee objected to the violence of this scene, commenting that it was 'intolerable that "that nice little boy" should have been "savagely murdered"' (1984: 297). In Polanski's defence, it is worth noting that this is one of the only instances in Shakespeare's plays where a child's death is dramatized on stage. In *Henry V*, *Richard III* and *The Winter's Tale*, for example, the deaths of the children are reported after the event, often in elevated language that is detached from the grim realities depicted in this scene at the Macduff castle. However, in his desire to make the violence 'realistic', declaring defiantly that he 'never believed in cop-outs', Polanski turned the body of the child into an object of the voyeuristic cinematic gaze (1984: 297). The children in this scene, in all their naked frailty, are defenceless and vulnerable. They are the 'naked new-born babe[s]' (1.7.21) who emblematize 'pity' but have no power to 'strid[e] the blast' (1.7.22) or 'blow the horrid deed in every eye' (1.7.24). As Bernice Kliman notes in her analysis of this scene, 'Polanski not only keeps the murder of the innocents in view but embellishes them' (1995: 220–1). Shakespeare's bloodiest play, it seems, was not bloody enough for a man who was crafting a cinematic riposte to the horrors – personal and political – of the previous decade. And the figure of the child provided him with the ideal icon of pathos. From Fleance to the murdered Macduff babes, the children in Polanski's *Macbeth* are controlled and manipulated to become depersonalized objects of the cinematic gaze which at times borders on the disturbingly voyeuristic-scopophilic.

The latest big-budget film of *Macbeth* directed by Justin Kurzel, released forty-four years after Polanski's film, takes a strikingly different approach to representing the child. From the opening frame-sequence to the closing montage, Kurzel's film is saturated with children – dead, alive, human and supernatural. He takes the all-pervasive trope of childhood in *Macbeth* and turns it into a visual image that permeates the landscape of his film. Not satisfied with merely doubling his three child actors to reflect the lighter and darker sides of childhood, like Boyd, he creates four new child characters that are not present in Shakespeare's text. These include the ghost of the Macbeth child, two companions to the witches and the figure of the damaged child-soldier who will haunt Macbeth to his death. Filmed on location in the bleak highlands of rural Scotland, the film's costumes, battle sequences and set-design meticulously capture the eleventh-century setting of the play. Yet without in any way compromising the overall feel of period authenticity, it is ideologically and psychologically a *Macbeth* for the twenty-first century, particularly in the multiple and contradictory ways in which it mobilizes the symbol of the child.

The film opens with a close-up on the body of a baby boy lying stiffly on his back, the blue-grey tinge of his skin indicating that he has been dead for some time. The camera pulls back to reveal a crowd of mourners, their faces turned against the bitter winds blowing across the barren landscape. A woman (Lady Macbeth) places a sprig of heather in his chubby fingers and a man (Macbeth) lays tiny rocks across his eyelids, before setting fire to the pyre upon which he has been laid. As the mourners gather to watch the flames flicker into life, the camera pans round and fixes on three women watching motionless from a distance. They loom into focus and begin speaking the opening lines of Act 1, Scene 1 – 'When shall we three meet again?' (1.1.1) – and it becomes instantly clear that these eerie but real, flesh-and-blood women are in fact the three weird sisters. However, they are not alone: a baby lies sleeping in the arms of one of them, as though mocking the loss of the mourners they

FIGURE 7 *Seylan Baxter, Lynn Kennedy, Kayla Fallon and Anber Rissmann as the witches, in* Macbeth, *dir. Justin Kurzel, 2015. Copyright © 2015 Studiocanal S.A./Channel Four Television Corporation.*

are silently observing, and a young pre-teen girl stands by their side, her face inscrutable as she watches the burning funeral pyre (see Figure 7).

Russ McDonald describes *Macbeth* as having a 'reiterative poetic texture' that reverberates 'not just immediately, but memorably, across several scenes' (2006: 44, 47). Although some reviewers have criticized Kurzel's extensive excisions to the original text – Peter Kirwan, for instance, notes that the textual decimation 'removes much of the complexity and equivocation from the narrative' (2015), while Philip Cu Unjieng observes that it is as 'much about spectacle as it is about language and verse' and thus 'it would be incorrect to even call this a cinematic staging of the original play' (2016) – I argue that Kurzel's film takes this 'reiterative poetic texture' and turns it into a reiterative *visual* texture that is constructed entirely around a cluster of child-related symbols. The ritualized slaughter of the Macduff family, for instance, recalls the opening frame-sequence as the mother and three children are tied to stakes and set alight on the heath in front of a watching crowd, including Lady Macbeth. Both the dead Macbeth child and the slain boy-soldier return as ghostly memories – 'false creation[s], / Proceeding from the heat-oppressed brain' (2.1.38–9) – that haunt the Macbeths to their deaths. Macbeth's 'Is this a dagger' soliloquy (2.1.33–64) is a response to a ghostly visitation from the dead boy-soldier who holds the dagger just out of Macbeth's reach. The boy also reappears in Act 4, Scene 1, in the guise of the weird sisters' apparition, telling Macbeth to 'be bloody, bold, and resolute' (4.1.78), and then again in the final sword-fight between Macduff and Macbeth as a silent observer. Like Jon Finch's Macbeth in Polanski's film, Fassbender's Macbeth is haunted by hallucinatory visions of children. However, there is one fundamental difference: Kurzel does not fetishize his children. They are silent witnesses, inscrutable observers and unsentimentalized symbols of loss and despair.

Perhaps one of Kurzel's greatest child-related innovations is realized in the sleepwalking scene, which features Lady Macbeth seated on the floor of the chapel under a flurry of snowflakes, speaking the lines to a point just beyond the camera. The scene is shot in close-up with an almost entirely static camera focused on the face of Lady Macbeth, whose head is draped, Virgin Mary-like, in a cloth headdress. The reference to hagiographic images of Mary, such as the 1476 painting *L'Annunciata* by Antonella Da

Messina, is clear to see. As though to further reinforce the analogy of the grieving mother whose dead child miraculously rises from the dead, the camera switches to a point-of-view shot at 'to bed, to bed, to bed' (5.1.68), and we finally see who she has been addressing throughout: it is the ghost of her dead child. He is sitting upright and looking alert, but his face and neck are covered in ominous-looking red spots which may be suggestive of typhus. There was an epidemic of typhoid fever during the early decades of the seventeenth century, particularly in the Midlands, and it was thus possible that Kurzel was making this connection here. One reviewer has suggested that the spots on the child link him with Lady Macbeth's 'trauma' and her obsessive cleaning (in the sleepwalking scene she rubs her hands, trying to remove the spots of blood), and thus, he argues, indicts her for 'passivity in the face of fate' (Ue 2016: 469). While I concur that a connection is being made here between the spots of Lady Macbeth and the spots on the child, I argue that it is less an indictment of her behaviour than an attempt to justify it. Just like the childless Lady Macbeth of Lloyd's adaptation, this Lady

FIGURE 8 *Marion Cotillard as Lady Macbeth, in* Macbeth, *dir. Justin Kurzel, 2015. Copyright © 2015 Studiocanal S.A./Channel Four Television Corporation.*

Macbeth's guilt is complicated with a backstory of maternal loss that both humanizes and exonerates her actions.

While Lady Macbeth is haunted by memories of her dead baby, Macbeth is tortured by memories of warfare, made manifest in the figure of the ghostly boy-soldier. The battle-scene begins with a shot of Macbeth tying a sword to the wrist of a young boy, played by a fourteen-year-old Scot Greenan, who looks like he is barely strong enough to lift it off the ground, let alone raise it in battle. Macbeth then daubs the boy's face in black warpaint and sends him off to face the enemy in a scene which, as Robbie Collin, writing in the *Telegraph*, remarks, 'is as gut-churning as anything in the Polanski, with limbs severed and throats slit in transfixing slow motion' (2015). What Collin fails to mention, however, is that one of the slit throats belongs to this young soldier, and the full horrors are captured in agonizing slow-motion as the camera lingers voyeuristically on his face contorted in a silent scream. At the end of the 'hurly-burly' (1.1.3) of the battle, we see Macbeth lift the body of the boy and carry him over his shoulder. It is a sequence that recalls the moment in Kenneth Branagh's 1989 film of *Henry V* when Henry carries the body of the pageboy across the battlefield to a rousing chorus of Patrick Doyle's 'Non Nobis'. However, there is no soaring musical accompaniment to Kurzel's citation of this scene, just the squelch of Macbeth's boots in the mud and the dull thump of the boy's body as it is dropped onto a mound of corpses. Later, as the 'Two truths are told' soliloquy (1.3.129–44) is spoken in voice-over, Macbeth places stones over the eyes of the boy-soldier, in an iteration of the opening scene. The loss of this boy-soldier is thus visually allied with the death of the Macbeths' child. However, there is one significant difference: there are no mourners at his funeral. He will, we can only presume, be buried in an anonymous mass grave or burned amid a pile of corpses. This new manifestation of childhood is an addition to Shakespeare's text but nonetheless consistent with the film's overall investment in deglamourizing violence and with its persistent mobilization of the child-figure as a symbol for the larger themes of the film: loss, hopelessness and a past that will not stay buried.

By far the most ambiguous child in this film is Fleance, played by a young Lochlann Harris, who originally auditioned as an extra. One can only assume that this inexperienced actor was cast as Fleance for his natural guilelessness in front of the camera. He has the pretty

FIGURE 9 *Scot Greenan as boy-soldier in* Macbeth, *dir. Justin Kurzel, 2015. Copyright © 2015 Studiocanal S.A./Channel Four Television Corporation.*

features of Polanski's Fleance but lacks his drama-school polish. He is, in other words, 'every child' and all the more worrying for it. He first appears in Act 1, Scene 4, to greet a war-weary Banquo, who envelops him in a loving embrace. Then, like the Fleance in Polanski's film, he is constantly featured at the side of his father, their obviously affectionate father-son relationship constantly mocking the barrenness of the Macbeths. The first sign that this boy might not be a simple portrayal of Shakespeare's Fleance, who does not reappear after Act 3, Scene 3, comes when he is fleeing his father's murderers. As he runs sobbing through the trees, the murderers hot on his heels, he reaches a small clearing and stops short. In front of him is the young girl-companion to the weird sisters. The shot then switches to the murderers, who arrive at the clearing, pause and look around in puzzlement. Both the boy and the girl have disappeared, 'melted as breath into the wind' (1.3.82).

Fleance reappears in the final sequence with the hardened look of a soldier. He is no longer the vulnerable young child but an embittered avenger. As Rutter has argued, the return of Fleance is very much a recent innovation in productions of *Macbeth*, featuring in, among others, Gregory Doran's 1999 RSC production, Dominic Cooke's 2004 RSC revival and John Caird's 2005 production for the Almeida Theatre. 'In today's *Macbeth*, *Macbeth* performed at the turn of the century that has "supped full with horrors"', Rutter observes, 'the child who *survives* – the child Fleance – may be even more disturbing than the children who die' (2007a: 195). What is particularly disquieting about Kurzel's Fleance is the disjunction between the innocent young boy of the first half of the film and the proto-assassin who returns in the final scene. That a child could have the potential to be both innately innocent and innately evil seemed to run counter to all received ideas about the nature of children. In his essay on tragedy and childhood, Peter Hollindale differentiates between tragic and sub-tragic children (2007: 174–91). The former, he argues, are characters with agency while the latter are 'mere ancillary possessions of adult figures' (2007: 177). By closing the film with the startling image of Fleance running, sword aloft, towards an unsuspecting Malcolm, Kurzel transformed him from a sub-tragic to a tragic child, destined to become the protagonist in the next cycle of revenge. Like the young pre-adolescent killers of James Bulger, this boy presents us with a paradox: that those most in need of our protection might also be those from whom protection is most required.

Conclusion

As this brief summary of recent adaptations of *Macbeth* has demonstrated, whether doubling as both innocent victims and demonic witches, functioning as emblems of victimhood or metamorphosing from symbol of pity to avenging revenant, the children of *Macbeth* have been turned from textual ambiguities and a 'reiterative poetic texture' (McDonald 2006: 44) into a visual paradox that is both pitiful and terrifying. Together, they reflect a dichotomous attitude to children that, as Cunningham and many of his contemporaries claim, is particular to postmodernity (2006: 4). If the children are, as we are constantly being told, our future, then in Kurzel's world view it is a future dogged by uncertainty and fear, and Edelman's politics of 'reproductive futurism' (2004: 3) is already beginning to seem outdated.

Where both Kurzel and Boyd presented the child as the source of epistemological and ontological uncertainty – both innocent and evil, alien and familiar – Polanski's representations of childhood are, as we have seen, far less nuanced. A product of his time, and no doubt influenced by his own personal experiences, Polanski exploits associations of childhood with innocence to turn his children into icons of vulnerability and objects of the voyeuristic-scopophilic gaze. Although both Jamie Lloyd's children were also, like Polanski's, emblematic of hopelessness and despair, his production avoided putting the body of the child on display by suggesting, rather than explicitly showing, the violence meted out to them. The 'disappearing' children of his urban dystopia were symptomatic of a society facing an existential crisis, and their violent deaths signalled not just the end of Macbeth's rule but the end of society as we know it. The children of *Macbeth* have a combined speaking part of just twenty lines (in the character of Macduff's son), but the living, dead, metaphorical and hypothetical children of this play have the power to turn a mirror on society and show us our reflection – a reflection that is uncompromisingly bleak. For Polanski and Lloyd, the children represent a future that is perilously under threat by a society ripped apart by violence and neglect, while for Boyd and Kurzel, the message is far more complex and far more terrifying. Not only do they show us a society on the verge of self-destruction, but their children, far from being the guardians of the future, are in fact the agents of its annihilation.

The next chapter expands upon the theme of the child as emblem of futurity through an analysis of one stage and two filmed productions of *Titus Andronicus*. This is a play in which, unlike the ill-fated Macduff children of *Macbeth*, Mamillius in *The Winter's Tale*, the young princes in *Richard III* and Arthur in *King John*, to name but a few, the children do in fact survive. However, theirs is a future that is by no means clear and they are, in ways that recall the metaphoric and absent children of *Macbeth*, ambiguous and polysemous signifiers. How directors account for these children reflects a shift in attitudes towards childhood, its sustainability and its presumed innocence: a presumption that, as we will see, becomes harder to convincingly sustain as we reached the end of the twentieth century.

3

'Behold the child': The Burden of Futurity in *Titus Andronicus*

Titus Andronicus is replete with ambiguities. Paradoxical semantics, disjunctive generic juxtapositions and unresolved questions surrounding authorship and sources make this play notoriously difficult to categorize.[1] Even the closing speeches lack conviction. Marcus rhetorically constructs Rome as a body, whose 'broken limbs' can be healed and made 'into one' (5.3.71), yet he is surrounded by mutilated corpses (the bodies of the recently murdered Lavinia, Tamora, Titus and Saturninus and the pie containing the butchered bodies of Chiron and Demetrius) that seem to mock his metaphor of bodily unity with their vivid corporeal presence. Lucius's final couplet, with its repetition of 'pity', moreover, is a rejection of rather than an appeal for this cathartic emotion when he says of Tamora: 'Her life was beastly and devoid of pity, / And, being dead, let birds on her take pity' (5.3.198–9). That a recently published collection of essays is titled *Titus Out of Joint* is symptomatic of a critical move towards recognizing and celebrating what the editors call the 'inherently dissonant' nature of the play (Stanavage and Hehmeyer 2012: 5). Yet while Stanavage and Hehmeyer's volume explores *Titus Andronicus* as a 'fragmented text' from a range of different perspectives, considering, among other topics, the maimed male body and religious iconoclasm, it fails to acknowledge the most ambiguous and polysemous signifier in this play: the child and his function as a highly problematic icon of futurity. Of course, many aspects of this play's dissonances can be attributed to the influence of Seneca, Thomas Kyd and the revival of the revenge genre in the 1580 and 1590s. Mutilations, feigned insanity, injustice, corruption, multiple deaths, a sense of futility and an unsatisfactory resolution are all characteristics of this genre. However, the ways in which Shakespeare mobilizes the figure of the child as a way of highlighting the genre's inherent contradictions are particularly unique and worthy of closer attention. From symbolic associations of the womb with malevolent maternity and cannibalistic consumption to the 'light-bearing' Young Lucius and the bastard issue of an 'irreligious Moor' (5.3.120), childhood as a regenerative force is continually invoked only to be undermined in an insistent counter-narrative of doubt and obfuscation.

In the final scene, Aaron's baby is held aloft for public display by Marcus, who invites the watching Goths and Romans to 'behold the child' (5.3.118). This is the last reference to the infant, whose existence to this point has been the subject of a series of barters and exchanges, and his fate remains ultimately unresolved. The last appearance of Young Lucius sees him sobbing over his dead grandfather, Titus, choked by tears and unable to speak 'for weeping' (5.3.173). Instructed by Marcus to 'bid him farewell. Commit him to the grave' (5.3.169), the boy instead wills his own death in exchange for the life of his grandfather with the words 'would I were dead, so you did live again!' (5.3.172). These are sentiments normally associated with grieving parents not grieving children and are symptomatic of the play's subversion of 'natural' orders, in both the social and private realms. As successor to the empery and the only Andronicus grandchild, Young Lucius is thus at best a problematic symbol of Rome's future and a powerful manifestation of the very 'pity' that the play invokes only to deny.

Taking these ambiguities as a prism through which to analyse childhood and futurity in *Titus Andronicus*, this chapter will explore different directorial attempts at resolving, or further complicating, these unresolved issues in performance. In order to acknowledge the generically unstable and contextually diverse responses to this play, I concentrate on three productions across the mediums of stage, film and television. In the first section, I consider Deborah Warner's 1987 stage production for the RSC, which was the first recorded full-text performance of this play in the twentieth century and was staged with minimal set and stage properties in the intimate space of the then newly built Swan Theatre.[2] I argue that although Warner did not shy away from displaying the excesses of violence and black humour in the play, hers was a strongly patriarchal representation of Roman society and her marginalized characters (principally Lavinia and Young Lucius) were kept firmly in the margins. The putative 'innocence' of the child in this version was preserved by simply avoiding the question altogether. Not only was her Young Lucius a minor character on the periphery of the action, but he was played by an adolescent male actor as an adolescent character, rather than as a child, while Aaron's son was a self-evident prop rather than a real or simulated baby. Staged before the debate about the changing nature of childhood had fully taken hold, the question of a childhood in crisis was clearly not a question that Warner felt needed to be addressed.

Next I explore two filmed productions of the play: Jane Howell's 1984 BBC Television Shakespeare production and Julie Taymor's 1999 cinematic adaptation, *Titus*. Both directors chose to film the play as though through the eyes of the child. However, the fifteen years between the release of these versions were key in terms of shifting attitudes towards childhood, as we have seen, and the different ways in which the two directors interpret what and how the child sees are symptomatic of this shift. Howell foregrounds the character of Young Lucius, but makes him an unwitting observer of the horrors. By framing the narrative through the eyes of this young witness, I argue that Howell provides a stark warning about the self-destructive nature of revenge while preserving childhood as a blameless, albeit irrevocably tainted, state. The 'innocence' of Young Lucius – a given rather than a question in Howell's interpretation – is only tainted by what he *sees* not by what he *does*. Julie Taymor's *Titus* also uses Young Lucius as a witness with an interpolated opening and closing frame and a considerable enlargement of his role. However, far from being a horrified witness and proxy for the audience, as in Howell's version, this child is implicated in the violence from the start. Filmed at a time when the debate about the future of childhood had already attained widespread cultural and political purchase, Taymor's adaptation addresses the question head-on but is frustratingly non-committal in its conclusions. Drawing upon multimedia filming techniques and intertextual allusions, Taymor's Young Lucius is presented as a child already corrupted by exposure to the very videocentric technology she employs and thus a highly questionable symbol of salvation. Taken together, these stage and film productions demonstrate the ambiguity of the child in the text and the difficulties directors face in resolving those ambiguities in performance. While Warner avoided the issue by casting a young man in the part of Young Lucius and replacing Aaron's baby with a doll, Howell and Taymor turned the ambiguities into a means by which to frame and present their adaptations. The different results reveal a shift in attitudes towards childhood during the fifteen years separating these films: from a residual belief in the innocence of the child towards an ambivalence bordering on despair.

Relegated to the margins: The children of Deborah Warner's *Titus Andronicus* (1987)

Of the three mediums under consideration in this chapter, theatre, film and television, it is widely believed that theatre provides the greatest platform for radical interventions.[3] Although theatre's exclusive claim to interventionism has been refuted by, among others, Philip Auslander, this still remains a critical commonplace. It is true that theatre is a form that has traditionally been used to hold prejudices and preconceptions up for analysis, questioning normative hegemonic paradigms and fostering anti-establishment feeling. However, in the case of *Titus Andronicus*, a play that was not staged without extensive adaptation for 300 years, theatre's experimental status is less certain.[4] Howell's BBC Television adaptation, for instance, filmed two years before Warner's stage production, offers a more subversive account than Warner's. Yet, the very fact of staging *Titus Andronicus* at this time and in this context can be seen as a bold and radical move in itself, particularly as, unlike Howell, Warner's production was not part of a larger project. It is perhaps no coincidence that it was part of the same season as Di Trevis's revival of Middleton's *The Revenger's Tragedy*, also staged in the Swan Theatre to critical acclaim. Like Warner, Trevis was lauded for capturing the 'nasty and hilarious' (Peter 1987) elements of the revenge tragedy genre, setting the tone for a rush of revivals of this previously neglected play.[5]

When later directors such as Lucy Bailey (2006) and Michael Fentiman (2014) came to stage their productions of *Titus Andronicus*, revenge tragedy, with its bloodthirsty excesses and emphasis on the macabre, had already become established as a relevant and vital form for a twenty-first-century audience. Moreover, the rise of playwrights such as Mark Ravenhill and Sarah Kane and 'in-yer-face theatre' in the 1990s had gone some way towards normalizing the staging of shocking and confrontational material. The success of films such as Quentin Tarantino's *Reservoir Dogs*, *True Romance* and *Kill Bill*, not to mention Taymor's *Titus*, had also created an appetite for stylized violence and black humour in the cinema that was crossing over into the theatre. Within this larger cultural context of aestheticizing violence while simultaneously maintaining its capacity to shock, the excesses of *Titus Andronicus* did not seem so out of place on the Globe and RSC stages. As a result, it no longer ranks among the more neglected of Shakespeare's plays and has lost its stigma as a risky venture for a director, although reviewers still sometimes treat it as such.

Undoubtedly, one of the main reasons for *Titus Andronicus*' relatively sparse stage history is a formal and generic structure that resists easy translation into modern theatrical practices as they pertain to 'classic' texts. Steeped in the revenge tradition of the 1590s, the play veers from the tragic to the comic, the grotesque to the poetic, juxtaposing moments of Senecan sensationalism with elevated Ovidian rhetoric. To a modern audience unfamiliar with the mythological allusions and the overt generic instability of *Titus Andronicus*, both of which are, as Jonathan Bate demonstrates, attributable to the play's Ovidianism (1993: 172), the extremes of tragedy and comedy risk inviting inappropriate and unwelcome laughter. Warner managed the tragicomic elements by emphasizing and revelling in their dramatic excesses. Pre-empting inappropriate laughter with slapstick or absurdly grotesque stage business, she permitted viewers, like Titus himself when confronted with the heads of his two dead sons, to laugh in the face of tragedy.[6] This is underscored in the play when Marcus responds to Titus's inappropriate outburst of hysterics with: 'Why dost thou laugh? It fits not with this hour' (3.1.266). At this point, Warner's Brian Cox laughed maniacally for a full ten seconds, prompting reflexive laughter from the audience.[7] An invitation to laugh at 'the supposedly pitiful and wretched' in this way, as Bridget Escolme explains, underscores the role of the audience in the theatrical exchange by creating what she terms 'communities of laughter' (2014: 58–78). It is a dramatic device that announces itself *as* a device, deliberately drawing attention to the artifice of the theatrical experience through exaggeration and excess. But many reviewers were sceptical about the extreme tonal changes. They were almost unanimous in their denunciation of the sanitized display of 'monotonously casual' murder and 'Hammer horror'-style absurdity which, they argued, precluded any empathic emotional response (Hurren 1987). The *Independent*'s Andrew Rissik, for instance, remarked that 'we do not laugh, but we do not cry either'. The use of the inclusive 'we' indicates that Rissik's response to what Cox called the 'get people to laugh, and then kick them' (1987: 188) approach was, in Rissik's judgement at least, shared by his fellow audience members. The effect of this abrupt change in tone seemed to create, and then deconstruct, what Escolme calls the 'communities of laughter'. Warner's production asked its audiences to empathize with Cox's Titus, but his performance did not invite an uncomplicated sympathetic response, particularly in its female members.

For Warner, dramatic focus was clearly centred on Titus and his tragic trajectory, with all other characters, particularly the women and children, relegated to the margins. In *Shakespeare's Violated Bodies*, Pascale Aebischer uses *Titus Andronicus* and the textual aestheticization of Lavinia's dismembered body as a touchstone for exploring stage and film representations of marginalized characters in a number of Shakespeare's plays. In relation to Warner's production, she observes that in spite of Sonia Ritter's 'powerfully assertive performance' of Lavinia and her 'ongoing resistance to attempts to limit her self-expression', the story of her violated body was nonetheless subsumed into the larger narrative of Titus and *his* mental and physical suffering (Aebischer 2004: 45). Reading Brian Cox's self-referential account of his performance, it is difficult to counter Aebischer's assertion that he saw Lavinia as a 'supporting character [...] whose main function was to buttress his own performance of mental and physical pain' (Aebischer 2004: 46). Writing of his decision to kill Lavinia while she is seated on his lap in a position of infantilized vulnerability (he talks of Lavinia throughout this account in terms of her defencelessness, likening her – somewhat tellingly – to 'a little child' and 'a little animal'), Cox describes her death as an instance of 'man's ludicrous journey through life' (Cox 1993: 177). He is not writing here of 'man' in the universal, humanist sense, but, as becomes clear from reading the whole piece, he is referring specifically to one man, the only character who really mattered in this production – Titus himself. This attitude was reflected in many of the critical reviews. Charles Osborne, for instance, placed Brian Cox's 'uncannily [...] moving and funny' performance squarely at the centre of his article, remarking that 'the younger members [of the cast...] are lucky to be engaged by a professional theatre company as prestigious as the RSC'. His critical marginalization of the 'younger' actors here colludes with and reinforces their equivalent marginalization in performance. Other reviews exonerated Titus the tragic hero from any responsibility in the deaths of his own children. One such example is Michael Billington's comment that 'you [...] sense he is a concerned father' (1987). His use of the second-person pronoun here presumes a uniform response that takes no account for audience individuation, least of all for the many women who might have been watching alongside him or reading his review. Michael Coveney's review for the *Financial Times* was even more provocative, noting that Lavinia's death was 'the merciful release of a young girl who has lived too long' (1987) – merciful for Titus, perhaps, but less so for the hapless Lavinia. Seduced by Cox's portrayal of Titus as a man 'more sinned against than sinning', these critics were instrumental in perpetuating the narrative of *Titus Andronicus* as the tragedy of one man. The result was a subordination of all other characters, particularly Lavinia and the two children, to the tragic trajectory of the eponymous hero.

There is some justification for Warner's decision to focus dramatic attention on Titus. From a purely textual point of view, Young Lucius and the bastard child are, like Lavinia, marginalized and manipulated by the adult characters. They are commodified: Aaron's baby is passed from Tamora to Aaron via the nurse, before being taken into captivity by a Goth. He is then passed to Lucius, threatened with hanging and held aloft like a prize by Marcus. They are, moreover, spoken of in possessive terms. Aaron calls his son a 'black slave' (4.2.122), 'my flesh and blood' (4.2.86) and 'the vigor and the picture of my youth' (4.2.110), while both Lucius and Titus refer to Young Lucius as 'my boy' (4.1.110, 114). They are idealized: Young Lucius is referred to as 'tender' (3.2.48, 50) and 'sweet' (5.3.168) and is instructed to 'melt in showers' (5.3.160) at the sight of his dead grandfather, while Lucius constructs an idyllic history of grandfather and son that is at odds with the play's dramatization of their relationship: 'Thy grandsire loved thee well. / Many a time he danced thee on his knee, / Sung thee asleep, his loving breast thy pillow' (5.3.160–2). Aaron, in turn, refers to his baby as a 'beauteous blossom' (4.2.74) and a 'treasure' (4.2.175), offering to lay down his own life to preserve the future of his son. However, in tension with this idealization of childhood innocence is a desire to mould the two boys into miniature warriors: Young Lucius is ordered to carry arms to the court (4.1.114–16) and instructed how to shoot arrows (4.3.64–5), while Aaron vows to turn his son into an avenging soldier with the words, 'I'll [...] bring you up / To be a warrior and command a camp' (4.2.181–2). Both bargaining tools and objects of affection, vulnerable children and warriors-in-training, symbols of futurity and emblems of an idealized past, Young Lucius and the baby are an amalgam of the shifting and contradictory anxieties, fantasies, fears and desires of the adult characters in this play.

The fly-killing episode in Act 3, Scene 2, is a key moment in the play that provides instructive insights into the various productions' investment in the figure of the child and the correlative issue of futurity. Absent from the earlier Quarto editions, this scene made its first appearance in the 1623 First Folio, leading some scholars to question its provenance (Bate 2003: 117–21). In addition to scholarly debate about the origins of this interpolated scene as a whole, there is editorial discrepancy in the interpretation of the line: 'But? How: if that Flie had a father and mother?' Some modern editions – notably the Oxford texts, both single edition and *Complete Works* – have emended it to read: 'How if that fly had a father, brother?' Changing the wording from 'and mother' to 'brother' makes clearer sense of the following lines: 'How would he hang his slender gilded wings / And buzz lamenting doings in the air' (3.2.62–3). As Jonathan Bate remarks in his textual notes, 'Who is "he"? Not the fly which has been swatted, but the father, who is Titus's surrogate' (2003: 120). Two out of the three productions under consideration here follow the more widely accepted 'father and mother' – indeed, Howell cites this as a 'key and crucial line', 'a lynchpin' for her interpretation of the whole play (Fenwick 1986: 17) – but none emend the singular pronoun 'he' of the following line to read 'they'. Howell does not elaborate upon why she found the line so 'key and crucial', but I assume it is because the swatting of the fly is emblematic of the arbitrariness of the violence that permeates this play. In referencing the imagined laments of the dead fly's 'father and mother', Titus not only anthropomorphizes the fly but also implicitly humanizes the ritualistic and cold-blooded violence inflicted on sons, daughters, sisters and brothers throughout *Titus Andronicus*. Given the importance of this line to Howell's understanding of the play, then, it is all the more surprising that she did not change 'he' to 'they'. The disjunction between the plural 'father and mother' of line 61 and the singular pronoun 'he' of line 62 retrospectively removes the maternal subject from the imaginary fly family altogether. It is notable that, of all the productions, it was Warner who chose to emend 'and mother' to 'brother', thereby denying any acknowledgement of the role of maternity in Titus's (and Warner's) androcentric conceptualization of the family. It is a small matter, perhaps, but this textual anomaly is symptomatic of a play that recalls only to dismiss, and finally destroy, not just this mother but *all* mothers (Tamora, the anti-mother who orders the death of her own baby; the midwife and the nurse, the surrogate mothers; and Lavinia, the potential mother) within the family paradigm.

Textual debates notwithstanding, this scene has become an important moment of revelation in performance, displaying in microcosm the play's precarious balance of pity and cruelty, terror and humour, madness and clear-headed sanity. In Shakespeare's text, it is Marcus who explodes in this sudden and unexpected act of aggression. A strong visual and visceral reaction, it throws into high relief his earlier, aestheticized and, for modern audiences at least, alienating Petrarchan response to Lavinia's dismemberment, complicating his characterization as a conciliatory counterbalance to Titus's impetuous excitability. It also acts as dramatic contrast to the exchange between Titus and Young Lucius immediately preceding this outburst, which sees the grandfather exhorting his weeping grandson to desist from self-destructive displays of pity with the words: 'Peace, tender sapling, thou art made of tears, / And tears will quickly melt thy life away' (3.2.50–1). Of the three productions under consideration here, Warner and Howell remained faithful to the text and left these lines to be spoken by Marcus, while Taymor reassigned them to Young Lucius with significant consequences, as we shall see. The identity of the fly-killer is of central significance not least because it proleptically links the perpetrator to Aaron, who declares, 'tut I have done a thousand dreadful things / As willingly as one would kill a fly' (5.1.141–2), and thus dismantles binary oppositions of race, colour and morality. It has also proved in production to be an important precursor of the final scene, in terms of both the play's overall attitude towards childhood and futurity and its movement towards (or away from) dramatic closure.

In Warner's production, the fly-killing scene was clearly designed to give Brian Cox the opportunity to showcase his masterful comic timing as the impetuous and mercurial Titus, with Young Lucius and Lavinia taking subordinated roles. Although it was in fact Marcus who first stabbed the fly, in accordance with Shakespeare's text, he too was relegated to the margins in this scene. Maximizing the tragicomic absurdity of the situation, Brian Cox's Titus displayed what Stanley Wells called an instance of 'masterly acting' (Wells 1989: 180) as he demonstrated the full gamut of emotions from moralistic outrage to manic ferocity. Stuffing bread into his mouth as though to forcibly repress a verbal outpouring of emotion, he leapt across the table, scattering food and cutlery, and viciously stabbed repeatedly at the dead fly with his one good hand. It was a moment of unadulterated rage that, while comedic in its sheer excessiveness, was nonetheless poignant and pathos-ridden. As Billington noted in his review for the *Guardian*, the combination of 'quirky, senescent humour' and 'tremendous bottled danger' (1987) demonstrated in this scene was symptomatic of a production that provoked laughter in the midst of terror. Young Lucius and Lavinia, by contrast, functioned as merely silent observers. Seated on either side of the table and flanking Titus, they looked on as he lamented and cowered as he raged, while Marcus stepped back from the table in horror at the reaction he had provoked in his brother. When Titus leapt across the table, all three characters threw themselves out of his way, like comic stooges to his slapstick routine. That they should be subordinated to Titus's performance in this way was consistent with the production's overall marginalization of the secondary characters, all of whom were destined to be subsumed into the larger narrative of the tragic hero.

Perhaps to avoid the distracting presence of a child on the stage and thus keep focus clearly on her central character, Warner cast an eighteen-year-old actor, Jeremy Gilley, in the role of Young Lucius (presumably one of those 'younger members [...] lucky to be engaged by a professional theatre company as prestigious as the RSC' [Osborne 1987]). Gilley was already an established member of the RSC repertory players and not particularly child-like in his appearance or demeanour. Unlike Rob Wynn, who played Clarence's son in Sean Holmes's *Richard III*, Gilley did not attempt to convey a sense of childishness in his portrayal of the role. As Young Lucius is often referred to by other characters as 'Boy', and indeed all speech prefixes in the Folio and some entry directions in both Quarto and Folio name him as 'Boy' rather than Young Lucius, the character is unlikely to be older than fourteen, which was considered to be the beginning of adolescence in early modern England (Munro 2005a: 39–40). For both spectators and readers, then, the childishness of Young Lucius is constantly reinforced and most modern productions cast an age-appropriate child actor in the role. Although scholars such as David Kathman have argued that the boy-characters in the early modern playing companies were almost certainly played by adolescent apprentices 'no younger than twelve and no older than twenty-one or twenty-two, with a median of around sixteen or seventeen' (2005: 240), acting styles and audience expectations were very different to today.[8] As Catherine Belsey explains, presentation was valued over mimeticism and the child characters were 'not inevitably childish in the modern sense of the term' (2005: 63). Any disjunction between the age of the actor and the age of the character would therefore not have been as unsettling for an early modern audience as it would be today.

Warner's decision to underplay the childishness of Young Lucius in this way was a particularly interesting decision in the light of the RSC's 1986 production of *Macbeth* directed by Adrian Noble which made the young Macduff children central to the dramatic action as discussed in Chapter 2. The exploration of the darker side of childhood in this production of *Macbeth* was far closer to Taymor's dramatic vision than to Warner's, whose Young Lucius might have been more appropriately renamed 'Lucius Junior'. He was not set apart from the other actors by marked age difference indicated by an unbroken voice, childish dress or youthful mannerisms, but appeared to be of a similar age to the late-adolescent Chiron and Demetrius and Lavinia. As a result, his on-stage presence was far less phenomenologically disruptive, as argued by Ridout and States, than if he had been a young child. When lined up with the other archers in Act 4, Scene 3, he blended seamlessly in with the adults, his deep voice, close-shaved head and manly stance marking him out as a warrior-in-waiting rather than an impressionable child. Unlike Taymor, Warner did not reassign the fly-killing episode from Marcus to Young Lucius, preferring instead to keep the boy's presence in this pivotal scene marginal. In fact, the failure of major reviewers to mention either Young Lucius or Aaron's bastard son in their analyses of this production is testament to just how unremarkable the two characters were in Warner's dramatic vision of the play.

Although Warner's promptbook (held at the SBT) states that when Lucius gestures for his son to approach Titus's corpse at 'Come hither, boy' (5.3.159), Young Lucius 'goes to kiss Titus then draws away', he did not in fact recoil (at least not in the archive recording I watched) but silently acquiesced. It is impossible to determine whether this change in stage business was a conscious decision by the director or something that the actor himself adopted, or indeed whether it happened on every performance or merely on the one recorded for the archives. However, what it does show is that *somebody* decided at some point that it was more in keeping with the characterization of Young Lucius to obediently follow rather than undermine the Andronicus revenge ethic. More akin to Young Martius (the 'martial' son of Coriolanus) than the 'light'-bearing Young Lucius, this adolescent soldier did not symbolize an idealistic vision of futurity but rather a future doomed to repeat the mistakes of the past. Indeed, when viewed from a 2019 perspective, Warner's Young Lucius was uncannily proleptic. Watching him on the archival recording, I was struck by the similarities with media images of Jihadi youths posing alongside their Islamic State warrior fathers. Depressingly prophetic though this man-boy proved to be, however, he did not disturb the central focus of this production. On the contrary, he was seamlessly assimilated into a family dynasty of butchers – bloodthirsty, merciless and blindly self-serving.

A different, but no less marginalizing device was used to portray the bastard child of Aaron. Where Warner eschewed the problematics of casting a young child in the part of Young Lucius by presenting him as a young adult, she sidestepped the potentially disruptive issue of the baby and his ambiguous presence in the final scene by self-consciously displaying him as a generic doll. Although the baby is a mute presence on the stage, Shakespeare's deictic language ensures that the audience's attention is constantly drawn towards him ('*this* myself' [4.2.109], '*This* [...] do I prefer, / *This* [...] will I keep safe' [4.2.111–12], '*here's* the base fruit of his burning lust' [5.1.43]) (emphases added)). The baby is, moreover, defined almost entirely in terms of the physical markers of his ethnicity and paternity: 'black' (4.2.122), 'thick-lipped' (4.2.177), 'tawny' (5.1.27) 'the picture of my youth' (4.2.110), 'the issue of an irreligious Moor' (5.3.120). However, in spite of this repeated linguistic insistence on his gendered and racialized presence, Warner's production did not attempt to assimilate the baby into her otherwise illusionistic aesthetic, but rather foregrounded his artificiality with deliberate stage business. Nor did she give her baby a gendered or racialized identity. Before killing the nurse, for instance, Aaron placed the baby, which was wrapped in a blanket with its generic, pink-tinged, plastic face clearly on display, at the front of the apron stage. This very deliberate and self-consciously metatheatrical gesture was later repeated when the second Goth brought the captured baby to Marcus in Act 5, Scene 1 (the promptbook here notes 'Goth puts baby down and unwraps, places centre stage').

As Marcus said 'behold the child' (5.3.118), Lucius raised the doll above his head, its pink synthetic face on full display, then lowered his arm and casually held the baby in one hand as he completed his speech. Even when he walked offstage, he made no attempt to pretend that he was carrying a real baby. In her analysis of Shakespeare's girl-characters, Jennifer Higginbotham notes that there is no evidence that early modern playing companies used real infants on stage. They were represented by 'bundles of blankets or dolls' and anthropomorphized by the actions and words of the players as in the gendering and racializing descriptors quoted above (2013: 104). As she explains, within a theatrical and social environment where costume and props were regularly used to indicate social status, age and gender, these 'inanimate bundles' (2013: 105) would almost certainly not have struck the audience as odd. However, although a blanket baby might have been readily assimilated into the theatrical world of a society in which gender, age and social class were a performance marked by outward signifiers, amid the psychological realism of Deborah Warner's 1987 production the prop-baby, which was so self-evidently a prop, was an anomaly.[9]

The text is frustratingly unclear about the future of Aaron's infant son. Amid the bloodbath of the final scene, he is merely displayed as evidence of the transgressive relationship of Tamora and Aaron: the bastard issue of an 'irreligious Moor' (5.3.120) and his 'ravenous' Goth lover (5.3.194). Lucius's earlier command to 'hang the child' (5.1.51) hovers as an unspoken threat over the life of the infant. For a play that revels in its display of violence and horror, it seems deliberately evasive about the fate of this child. Scholars have read in this ambiguity a subtextual message about the threat of miscegenation and racial contamination. Francesca T. Royster, for instance, comments as follows:

> Aaron has preserved his baby's life and, though he will not live to bring his boy up as a soldier and potential invader, the engendering and birth of Aaron and Tamora's baby raises the possibility that populations with non-Roman 'hues' will invade and inhabit Roman geographic and cultural space.
>
> (2000: 434)[10]

For Warner, such an open-ended conclusion would be inconsistent with her teleological narrative of revenge and retribution. Although, in many ways, the obvious artificiality of the baby bears some similarity to the animatronic baby and the statuary reincarnation of Mamillius in Wheeldon's *The Winter's Tale*, the effects were very different. The eerily unrealistic baby and petrified statue of Mamillius in Wheeldon's ballet were all the more disconcerting because they were set against a vibrant and animated young boy playing Mamillius in Act 1. Moreover, far from being almost incidental to the main action, as was the case with Warner's children, Wheeldon's two incarnations of Mamillius – as a child and as a statue – were central to his adaptation of the play, as we have already seen. By contrast, reducing the baby to a manipulable stand-in so evidently lacking in agency was symptomatic of Warner's overall ideological approach to the text. The Rome of her production was one dominated by patriarchal values: Lavinia was infantilized by a domineering Titus, Young Lucius was re-imagined as a young adult warrior and Aaron's baby was reduced to a prop – an object without agency that 'must physically move or alter in some way as a result of the actor's physical intervention' (Sofer 2003: 12). By drawing attention to the child as a lifeless toy tethered to the actors in this way, Warner not only elided any textual ambiguities about the future of this baby but also neutralized the threats it might pose to her actors, her production and the autonomy of the adult male more generally.

Warner's production avoided the necessity of taking a definite position about the baby and its role in futurity by displaying it as a false icon from its first appearance. Self-evidently plastic and lifeless, it functioned as an empty signifier in which audiences were not encouraged to invest any empathy. Therefore, although her failure to account for the fate of the baby in the final scene might have left some room for indeterminacy had it been presented as though it were a real baby, the fact of its artificiality precluded this as a dramatic necessity. In combination with her presentation of Young Lucius as an adolescent and already a convincing young warrior, rather than an impressionable child, Warner's overall effect was a bleak and deterministic vision of a future in which the past mistakes of her tragic hero were doomed to repetition through his genealogical line; the question of childhood and its place within this overall narrative of historical determinism was quite simply avoided altogether. In the next section, I consider two filmed productions that, far from avoiding the question of how to account for the ambiguous children of this play, expand upon the role of the child and frame the story through his eyes, making Shakespeare's play into a tale both *by* and *about* a young boy.

'What are we doing to the children?': Jane Howell's *Titus Andronicus* (1985)

There were four English-language filmed productions of *Titus Andronicus* in the years 1996 to 2000 alone, making it one of the most popular choices for film adaptation at the turn of the century.[11] As a play that engages with themes of family breakdown, racial violence, female mutilation and sectarian conflict, it is not difficult to see why it was a popular vehicle for reflecting upon the contemporary geopolitical landscape. The two films I have chosen to compare in this chapter, Jane Howell's 1984 BBC Television Shakespeare production and Julie Taymor's 1999 cinematic adaptation, were released fifteen years apart, before and after the debate surrounding the 'crisis of childhood' had taken hold in popular and academic discourse. Of all of the filmed versions of the play, they are, to borrow Pascale Aebischer's terminology, the most 'straight' adaptations among a series of 'slasher-film versions and parodies' (2002: 138). However, they also make for a particularly instructive comparative analysis because they both use the child as a lens through which to view the action but take fundamentally different approaches in terms of ideology and aesthetics.

Jane Howell's film was part of an ambitious project to adapt all thirty-seven of Shakespeare's plays for the BBC.[12] The project was hailed as 'gloriously British, gloriously BBC' by the journalist Henry Fenwick (1978: 25), but it was in fact joint-funded by the American companies Morgan Guaranty Trust and Exxon. The plays in their entirety were screened on both the BBC and the American Public Broadcasting Service (PBS) between 1978 and 1985. The brief for the BBC project was to maintain textual fidelity in order to provide a 'complete and unabridged' audio-visual version of the entire Shakespearean canon for as wide an audience as possible (Willems 1987b: 94). While there are remarkable similarities between Howell's BBC-friendly production and Taymor's highly abridged, surrealist and generically diverse adaptation of the play, particularly in the way the child is used as a framing device, the two directors take vastly different aesthetic and artistic approaches to achieve this framing effect. Howell's use of extended single-take shots, wide-angle lens and sparse, monotonal *mise-en-scènes* all contribute to an overall sense of theatrical artistry. Taymor, by contrast, constructs a postmodernist bricolage of generic hybridity, intertextuality and parodic pastiche, drawing on multiple sources to create a palimpsestic effect that foregrounds not only the constructedness but also the citational aspects of performance.

The treatment of the boy-witness and his role as both dramatic and metadramatic character also differs in fundamental ways. Having foregrounded the image of the child through a stylized opening sequence, Howell then subsumes him into the play as a character within the narrative frame. Expanding upon the role of the Young Lucius of Shakespeare's text, who does not appear until Act 3 and has a total of only forty-four lines, Howell creates a boy-character who features throughout as an observer, his largely silent presence functioning as proxy for the audience at home. This is a technique particularly suited to television, which not only privileges the close-up shots but also, as Neil Taylor has observed, emphasizes the 'casual, domestic, and familial' and thus seems to reflect the viewers' own reality back at them (1994: 87). To this extent, television can be considered a less overtly self-aware medium than film. Projecting directly into the viewer's home, the images on the small screen offer what Margaret Morse calls 'simulations of discourse and fictions of presence that attempt to virtually engage the viewer-auditor with the set' (1998: 19). Taymor's boy, by contrast, plays a more liminal role, slipping between the subject positions of author and object of the gaze throughout the film. It is a far more distancing experience for the viewer, 'inviting our identification' with the boy while simultaneously reinforcing 'a sense of safety or distance in time and space from [...] the events on screen' (1998). As Vicky Lebeau observes, the image of the child as both the subject and the medium of viewing – 'child as object of the gaze; child as voyeur' – is a trope that has long been familiar to the world of cinema (2008: 16). While Howell focuses on the latter, directing her audience to see *through* the eyes of her Young Lucius, Taymor demands a more complex negotiation between the two modes of viewing. Howell's approach asks the audience to understand the effects of the violence upon the child, while Taymor's Young Lucius first observes then becomes complicit in the violence himself.

In addition to their contrasting aesthetic and formal properties, the two films also differ in terms of ideology. Howell foregrounds a deterministic version of history as a cyclical process in which mankind is doomed to repeat the mistakes of the past. As she has explained in an interview, her own son had 'terrible nightmares when he was the age of [Young] Lucius', and her aim was to re-create that childish 'landscape of a dream' through deployment of techniques such as split screens and dissolves (Willems 1987a: 83). Yet this was not to be the fictitious re-creation of a child's overactive imagination but the child's way of processing what he had already witnessed through the mediums of books and television. Howell explains further:

> I suddenly thought if a child watched a TV news bulletin with its catalogue of violence and war, read a book about the fall of Rome to the Goths and then went to bed and dreamed, he would have dreamed a play like this. It is not done as a dream play, because that would wrench the structure, but the boy is palpably there all the time so that, if two people are arguing, he is to be seen behind them watching. You have to find a hook for yourself

and, in this case, the viewer is constantly forced to think – what are we doing to the children?

(Billington 1985: 29)

This is Postman's thesis writ large. The 'secrets' ([1982] 1994: 88) that the seventeenth-century print culture had precluded the child from accessing have now become available to all. The literate twentieth-century child not only reads from a much earlier age than the sixteenth-century child but has access to a multitude of visual mediums, including television. Using this very medium to present the child's dream, Howell thus provides her viewers with a means, however tenuous, however tentative, of escaping a deterministic vision of history and futurity by confronting them with the uncomfortable question: 'what are we doing to the children?' (Billington 1985: 29).

If Howell's nihilistic vision is depressing, it is at least a nihilism that she self-consciously parades and self-consciously questions. After all, framing the action through the eyes of the child, as theatre critic John J. O'Connor observes, 'allows Shakespeare to have his violence while openly questioning it, too' (1985: 30). By unapologetically confronting the viewers with her bleak ending, Howell challenges them not only to look *like* a child but to take action *for* the child and for futurity itself. Laura Mulvey notes in her classic essay 'Visual Pleasure and Narrative Cinema' that 'the voyeuristic-scopophilic look [...] is a crucial part of traditional filmic pleasure' (1975: 17), a pleasure that, as we have seen, Polanski exploited in his film of *Macbeth*. There are, of course, obvious analogies to draw with the boy actor in the early modern playing companies in this respect. As Edel Lamb and other scholars have noted in relation to early modern children's performance, 'The child is often a focal point for erotic desire, and the physical manifestation of the child on stage is not entirely absent from this fantasy' (2009: 51).[13] Central to Mulvey's critical argument is the Lacanian concept of the controlling and fetishistic male gaze and its dominance in Western visual culture, particularly mainstream cinema. The critical paradigm she promotes for analysing the mechanisms of voyeurism and cinematic pleasure is illuminating as a tool for studying Howell's and Taymor's different approaches to the iconography of the child, notably in the opening sequences of their films. Mulvey identifies a paradox in the premise of mainstream narrative film fiction: 'the female image' she argues, constantly endangers the unity of the diegesis by piercing the cinematic illusion as 'an intrusive, static, one-dimensional fetish' (1975: 18). In order to disavow the mediating presence of the camera and maintain the cinematic illusion, the audience is presented with an eroticized image of the female object that 'freezes the look, fixates the spectator and prevents him from achieving any distance from the image in front of him' (1975: 18). It is this very practice of 'fixat[ing] the spectator' through a fetishized image (in this case, the image of the child rather than 'the female image') that, I shall argue, differentiates Taymor's voyeuristic frame-sequence from Howell's more television-friendly 'static, one-dimensional' (Mulvey 1975: 18) and self-consciously artistic opening montage. Howell's film, in other words, foregrounds the act of viewing itself.

As the credits fade in Howell's film, mist clears to reveal a side-on image of a grinning skull facing to the left. The image then dissolves and reforms as a close-up face-on shot of the same skull and then dissolves again to a split screen. This time the skull is on the left of the screen and a frontal close-up of a boy's face appears on the right-hand side. The skull is turned to face the child, as though confronting him with his own mortality. The skull fades, the camera pulls out and the child is absorbed into the opening scene of the film, which has been rearranged to begin with the arrival of Titus into Rome with the bodies of his sons. Throughout this long scene, the child is a silent observer, occasionally assisting, such as when he lights the candles to the memory of the dead Andronici or hands his grandfather a bowl of water to wash his hands, but always watching, always observing. The camera draws attention to the act of viewing by shooting the opening few seconds of the scene from a position directly behind the boy's head, as though the audience is peering over his shoulder, then pulls out to show the child standing silently as witness to the unfolding action. This opening sequence is a reversal of Mulvey's model inasmuch as Howell deliberately presents the child as an 'intrusive, static, one-dimensional fetish', highlighting rather than disavowing the 'mediating presence of the camera' (1975: 18) and encouraging an interrogatory mode of viewing in her audience. Rather than 'fixat[ing] the spectator' with a pleasurable image, the juxtaposition of the skull (the icon of death) and the child (the signifier of life) creates a cognitive dissonance that is distancing rather than absorbing.

The skull is a highly denotive and connotative sign, one that, as Andrew Sofer observes, 'fascinate[s] because of its sheer uncanniness' (2003: 90). On the one hand it is a metonym for mortality, 'charging man' as Carol Chillington Rutter notes, 'to know his end by gazing on his future' (2001: 8). In this respect it undermines the future by insisting on the inevitability of death. The skull is also an iconographic emblem of the theatre, replicated to the point of parody in countless photographic and publicity-related images of both *The Revenger's Tragedy* and *Hamlet*. In Howell's opening sequence, however, it has yet further connotations. By presenting the skull alongside the image of the child, Howell not only foregrounds her theatrical aesthetic through intertextual citation of these early modern revenge tragedies, but also undermines the fetishization and idealization of childhood by associating it with a *memento mori* that denies the child's role as icon of the future and, by extension, denies the existence of futurity itself.

The denial of futurity in this way is, for Lee Edelman, as discussed in the Introduction, tantamount to an act of political subversion because it is a rejection of dominant ideological narratives of compulsory reproduction. Edelman's vision of futurity is as nihilistic as it is subversive. Howell's association of the child with death is comparable in terms of its radical nihilism, but her approach is wider-ranging and more far-reaching in terms of its effect. Unlike Edelman, whose writing is framed through the lens of queer theory, Howell does not speak on behalf of a specific marginalized group. Her film is neither overtly feminist nor ideologically allied to a particular political agenda. It is, rather, a stark commentary on the self-defeating nature of what Sir Francis Bacon called the 'wild justice' of *lex taleonis* – a lawless pursuit of retaliatory violence as relevant today as it was to the Elizabethans ([1625] 1985: 2–3). Indeed, Howell herself has drawn analogies between the classical setting and both Federico Fellini's 1930s Fascist Rome and Northern Ireland in the 1980s (Willems 1987a: 83). She holds the mirror up to a society that is intent on self-destruction by revealing a glimpse of the future through the eyes of a helpless child. In the final instance, both children (Young Lucius and Aaron's baby) in Howell's film are sacrificed at the altar of the self-destructive revenge ethic.

The baby (already dead) is brought on in a coffin and displayed to the gathered Goths and Romans like a sacrificial lamb, while a repetition of the opening sequence featuring Young Lucius and the image of skull closes the film. However, this time Young Lucius's picture morphs into a second skull, and we are left with a split-screen mirror image of the skull both looking at itself and out into the camera, as though mocking viewers with their own mortality. Like Edelman, Howell offers no palliative, no romantic *deus ex machina* to resolve this crisis. However, unlike Edelman, she does not disavow the possibility of searching for an alternative vision by advocating a retreat into a passive oppositional stance. While offering no solution herself, she uses the medium of television – a medium she herself describes as 'incredibly responsible' (2003: 89) – as a means to confront her audience in the intimacy of their own homes with the life-destroying futility of war and to force her viewers into a personal examination of their own consciences, both as participants and as silent observers.

The role of Young Lucius as the audience's proxy is a key element of the fly-killing scene. Although, unlike Taymor, Howell remains faithful to her overall commitment to textual fidelity by leaving the killing of the fly in the hands of Marcus, rather than reassigning to Young Lucius, Howell alternates close-up reaction shots with shots from Young Lucius's perspective to underscore visually the boy's dual role as witness and actor in the play more generally. In the heated exchange between Titus and Marcus immediately following the line 'What dost thou strike at, Marcus, with thy knife?' (3.2.52), the camera closes in on the two brothers, adopting a shot/reverse-shot perspective that emphasizes their antagonistic positions. At Marcus's 'Pardon me, sir, it was a black ill-flavoured fly' (3.2.68), the camera pulls out to a position behind Young Lucius, so that we as spectators are aligned with his point of view. Although we cannot see his features, his reaction is suggestively reflected in the silent terror sketched on the face of Lavinia, who is seated opposite the boy and therefore face-on to the camera. Her open-mouthed horror is thrown into relief by the three guards standing behind her on the edge of the frame. Their faces are covered in masks which, according to Howell, were designed to convey 'a dignity' on the 'passive onlookers' to the unfolding tragic events (Fenwick 1986: 19). However, lacking both eye and mouth holes, these masks do not merely represent what Howell calls the 'blank faces' of the witnesses but also function as doubles for Lavinia, the 'speechless complainer' (3.2.39), and Young Lucius, the impotent witness.

Howell's Titus, played by Trevor Peacock, addresses 'Give me thy knife' (3.2.72) not to Marcus, as is the conventional interpretation, but to the boy. As he does so, the camera closes in on Titus's face, moving directly behind Young Lucius's left shoulder as though to reinforce further the alignment of our optical perspective with that of the boy. However, Young Lucius is not merely an anonymous observer. He becomes an active, albeit reluctant, participant in this scene when Titus forcefully wrests his knife from his hands and waves it threateningly towards him. As the boy turns his head to the left, we catch a brief close-up of his features screwed up in anguish. Temporarily chastened by the child's distress, Titus lowers the knife and, for the first time, the camera cuts to a close-up of Young Lucius, his distraught face registering the fear and horror that we as spectators have been subtly manipulated to imagine thus far. It is, moreover, a face that draws attention to the very act of viewing itself. For this Young Lucius is wearing anachronistic, metal-rimmed spectacles. Like the camera, the spectacles are mediating devices that manipulate vision, foregrounding not only the unreliability and impotence of the human eye but also the videocentric nature of the film medium itself. This short interaction, albeit lasting merely two minutes, thus demonstrates in microcosm Howell's artistic methodology throughout this production. The spatial configuration of the actors, the positioning of the camera, the theatrical use of props as semiotic devices – these elements are all part of an overall design to draw attention to the voyeuristic nature of film, and in particular of television, which is more intimate and immediate in form than the feature film. By drawing attention to the act of voyeurism in this way, Howell's adaptation forces the spectators to confront their own complicity in the violence on display. In Howell's *Titus Andronicus*, the presence of Young Lucius is metonymic of the innocence of childhood itself, which, while providing a morally instructive subject position for the audience, is nonetheless ill-equipped to shoulder the burden of futurity within the social world of the play. It is a world which is intent on self-destruction and in which the ideology of 'reproductive futurism' (Edelman 2004: 3) is markedly absent.

THE BURDEN OF FUTURITY IN *TITUS ANDRONICUS* 115

FIGURE 10 *Edward Hardwicke as Marcus, Paul Davies Prowles as Young Lucius, Trevor Peacock as Titus and unidentified male in* Titus Andronicus, *dir. Jane Howell, 1985. Courtesy The BBC Shakespeare.*

By emphasizing the role of the boy as both impotent witness and reluctant participant, the fly-killing scene also foreshadows the bleak closing sequence. Jane Howell ends her film with a nihilistic vision that is arguably much closer to the self-destructive drive of the revenge tragedy genre in general, and of *Titus Andronicus* in particular, than Taymor's more ambivalent ending. Bleak and uncompromising, Howell's closing sequence leaves the viewers in no doubt as to how they are supposed to read this interpretation of the play. Her Young Lucius is a tearful observer throughout the film, silently directing the audience to see the senseless violence through his innocent eyes. He is not, in contrast to Taymor's Young Lucius, infected by the Andronici's brutal gene but remains a horrified but impotent witness to the very end. Howell's child makes two failed interventions during the film that are not in Shakespeare's original text. When Titus sacrifices Alarbus in Act 1, Scene 1, he silently kneels beside a pleading Tamora and then when Lucius stabs Saturninus in

Act 5, Scene 3, he leaps at his father's neck, begging him to stop. For a film that is otherwise remarkably faithful to the original text, these are significant amendments that work to underscore the impotence, vulnerability and violated 'innocence' of the child. Howell's most radical directorial innovation, however, comes in the final sequence, where the ambivalence of Shakespeare's text is eschewed in favour of clarity and finality. Her presentation of Act 5, Scene 3, consolidates many of the themes introduced earlier in the play. The guards, for instance, bear staffs with effigies of skulls carved into their tips, recalling the image of the skull in the opening frame-sequence. Silent observers wear the blank masks of the impotent witness that were so prominent in the fly-killing scene. The mood is sombre, and the tragicomic extremes are contained within a bleak but naturalistic aesthetic. The camera alternates between tracking shots that move like a roving eye around and among the action, and close-ups on the face of Young Lucius.

At 'behold the child' (5.3.118), Marcus takes a black box from Publius and holds it aloft. He opens the lid for the gathered crowd to see, but it remains tantalizingly obscured to the television audience's view. However, a close-shot of the horrified face of Young Lucius confirms our worst fears. Howell's baby is already dead, and, as Alan Dessen observes, the impact of the baby's death is all the more powerful because Howell (like Taymor after her) chose to employ a real baby for the earlier scenes (1989: 106). The death of this formerly vital baby goes some way towards vindicating the malevolence of Aaron's final words, which he delivers in the knowledge that his baby has already been murdered. It also confronts the audience with the stark realities of the Andronici's merciless brutality. During Lucius's final speech the camera begins with a shot over the shoulder of Young Lucius, who is looking into the open box, the body of the dead baby on full display. It then cuts to Marcus and tracks him as he walks towards the boy and closes the lid. As we hear Lucius's final denunciation of pity, the camera pauses on a close-shot of the boy's weeping face. The final stage direction (written by Jane Howell) in the printed edition of this film script is 'Young Lucius stares into space' (Howell 1986: 88). This gesture of hopelessness is then reaffirmed by Howell's closing sequence of shots. In a visual montage that recalls the opening sequence, the shot of Young Lucius 'star[ing] into space' fades and a split-screen image of two skulls appears. This time there is

FIGURE 11 *Paul Davies Prowles as Young Lucius, in* Titus Andronicus, *dir. Jane Howell, 1985. Courtesy The BBC Shakespeare.*

no counter-image of the boy, just the skull looking at and being confronted by its own image.

In his groundbreaking work on the function of the skull on the Renaissance stage, Sofer explores what he calls the anamorphic 'either/or-ness' of this stage property in performance (2003: 95). According to Sofer's analysis, the skull is simultaneously a literalization of the *memento mori* metaphor and an anthropomorphization as character – a character that refuses to be 'reified into a dead thing' and insists 'on turning others into its props' (2003: 94). By closing her film with a still shot of two skulls in this way, Howell creates what Sofer calls 'a moment of unmetaphoring' (2003: 98), whereby the skull threatens to overwhelm Young Lucius by turning the boy into its prop and thus extinguishing life and all hope for futurity. However, within the ambiguity of this slightly surreal moment lies a glimmer of hope. Although the fate of Aaron's baby is sealed – his tiny body lies motionless inside a coffin, *rigor mortis* having turned his limbs to stiff appendages – the fate of Young Lucius, this ending seems to suggest, lies with the audience. What Howell's symbolic sequence of images in fact equates to is a direct and unequivocal appeal: look *at* the child; look *like* the child; but most importantly, look at what are we doing *to* the child.

A false dawn: Questionable redemptions in Julie Taymor's *Titus* (1999)

Where Howell's film is a 'nightmare' framed through the eyes of the child with some rare moments of (failed) interventions, Taymor's 1999 feature film veers between taking the child's point of view and fixing the camera's gaze on the child, and between distancing the audience by drawing attention to the illusory nature of cinema and using the image of the child-like Mulvey's eroticized female in a manner designed to maintain rather than pierce the cinematic illusion. Her Young Lucius in the opening frame-sequence is the embodiment of Kincaid's fetishized child: a complex and self-contradictory amalgam of innocence, precocity and eroticism (1998: 20). He is also a child immersed in the television culture that, according to Postman and his followers, was responsible for destroying childhood in modern society. Thus both object of and consumer of videocentric media, Taymor's child is a fascinating case study in the interconnected worlds of the child and the moving image and a key figure in terms of understanding how to interpret the overall message of this film. Like Howell, Julie Taymor also uses Young Lucius as a witness with an interpolated opening and closing frame and a considerable enlargement of his role. However, far from being an innocent witness and powerless agent, as in Howell's version, this child is complicit in the violence from the start.

The first few seconds of the opening frame-sequence is momentarily disorientating. An extreme close-up of piercing blue eyes pulls out to reveal a young white-skinned boy's face. It is tantalizingly obscured by a brown paper bag with makeshift holes cut out for the eyes and mouth. A fork with a hotdog sausage appears from the bottom of the frame and the boy takes a bite, his greasy lips protruding through the mouth-hole as he chews vigorously, his gaze fixed upon the television in front of him. The shot then cuts to show the boy standing on a chair at a kitchen table. Plastic toy soldiers, artillery and remote-control vehicles are scattered amid half-eaten food as he begins squirting milk and ketchup across the table and enacting violent encounters with his toys in time to the frantic soundtrack of a violent cartoon playing in the background. The interaction between the violence on the television and the violence enacted by the boy in this scene is, as Peter S. Donaldson observes, a 'well-known dystopia stereotype[s] of the case against children's television watching' (2005: 459). Later in the film, a hyperstimulated Chiron and Demetrius are shown playing video games. They are, as Lehmann, Reynolds and Starks observe, 'boys whose digital mastery of virtual beings is inseparable from their desire to decimate, even as they inseminate, real bodies' (2003: 225). As in the opening sequence, the film here makes the implicit connection between virtual violence and actual violence and the blurred boundaries between the two. Taymor herself has been critical about the effects of technology on children's imagination, stating in an interview that 'sitting in a chair in front of an ugly box when you could be running around in an open space seems regressive' (Snyder n.d.). In the light of this alliance of technology with regression, it is noteworthy that the opening scene is set in a 1950s kitchen and not in a contemporary (1990s) setting. According to Postman's thesis, the 1950s is the very decade in which television began to erode childhood, marking what he calls, in typically apocalyptic terms, 'The Beginning of the End' (1982: 67–80). That Taymor should set the opening scene in the 1950s rather than in the 1990s when she shot the film may be a coincidence, but it is symbolic nonetheless.

As though mimicking the rapidly changing frames of the cartoon flickering at the edge of the shot, the camera cuts rapidly from shot to shot, with close-ups of the boy's face and hands switching to long shots of his whole body as he gets more excited and gradually more aggressive. The walls then begin shaking and an explosion rips through the windows. A large man wearing motorcycle goggles and a First World War helmet ('The Clown' in Taymor's screenplay) bursts in, drags the crying child out from under the table and pulls off his paper-bag mask. The child is then forcibly removed from the 1950s 'television-saturated world of the middle class' (Donaldson 2005: 460) to a Roman amphitheatre and an invisible baying crowd. For Donaldson, the mask 'works to align [the child] with tragic theatre' (Donaldson 2005: 459), while for Rutter it both 'tropes masks military and theatrical' (2007b: 11). These are both valid readings but I think they miss the most crucial symbolic significance of the mask in this scene: it emblematizes the precarious protected world of childhood and the fine line between childhood play and adult violence.[14] With his unmasking, the child, who is revealed to be Young Lucius, graduates from the contained world of imaginary violence to the adult world of real violence. Flung helplessly over the shoulder of the Clown, he is transported, like Alice in Wonderland down a rabbit hole, into the Roman Colosseum, the 'archetypal theatre of cruelty, where violence as entertainment reached its apex' (Taymor 2000: 178). Here, violent play morphs into violent reality; child's play transforms into adult experience; and Postman's prediction of children 'adultified' ([1982] 1994: 126) through exposure to media is played out in front of our eyes.

After entering the Colosseum, the boy is held aloft by the Clown for the cheering crowd in a gesture that anticipates the same Clown holding up Aaron's caged baby in the final scene. The camera moves down and closes in upon the boy. As the Clown turns in a circular motion, displaying Young Lucius like a human prize, the camera rotates in the opposite direction, its focus fixed upon the bewildered face of the child. The boy is then gently set down, the Clown recedes and the crowd is abruptly silenced. What follows is shot as though through the eyes of Young Lucius. He reaches down into the dirt floor of the Colosseum and picks up one of his toy soldiers. Hearing a sound, he turns and is faced with an army of battle-weary soldiers, their faces and bodies covered in dirt, their uniforms an adult-sized replica of the toy version he holds in his hand. A drum strikes up a beat and the soldiers begin marching in time with the rhythm. Their movements are mechanical and jilted as they make their slow progression from all sides of the Colosseum towards the boy at the centre of the arena. The opening credits play out to the sound of their pounding feet. The boy's head whips round and sees, entering from the other side of the auditorium, soldiers bearing the dead bodies of the Andronici sons. He turns again as a cavalcade of 1930s motorcycles advances towards him, followed closely by Titus at the helm of a horse-drawn carriage. The Goth captives are in a wagon behind him and their captured armour and weapons, on display in a plexiglass case mounted on a motorized vehicle, follow closely behind.

The scene is a clash of historical times and places, and there are multiple ways in which it can be read. Rutter is right when she asserts

FIGURE 12 *Osheen Jones as Young Lucius, in* Titus, *dir. Julie Taymor, 1999. Courtesy Clear Blue Sky Productions.*

that this scene is 'a temporal palimpsest' that shows 'the ancient world [...] surviving in our own' (2007b: 14). But what becomes clearer as the film develops is that Taymor's citation of the 'ancient world' is not merely a direct analogy to 'our own' world but one refracted through the ideology and iconography of 1930s Fascism. From the SS-inspired uniforms to the political rallies, ritualized violence and Riefenstahl-inspired military marches, the analogies are clear to see. Indeed, Taymor herself has openly cited the rise of Fascism and the Holocaust as her inspiration. In the 'Director's Notes' to the book *Titus*, for instance, she comments that the setting of Saturninus's and Bassianus's campaign speeches was intended to be a visual evocation of the 'Rome of E.U.R' (2000: 182), and in interviews, she more generally equates the excesses of the play with the rise of the far right in 1930s Europe.[15] When asked whether audiences today struggle to 'understand' the play, she is quoted as saying: 'When people think this is "over the top" they're absolutely wrong. What could be more "over the top" than the Holocaust?' (de Luca and Lindroth 2000: 31).[16]

The groundwork for this evocation of Nazist brutality is clearly laid in the opening frame-sequence. The Colosseum into which the young boy is transported recalls the forty arenas, called *Thingplätze* or *Thingstätten* (assembly places), built during the Weimar Republic to stage the then newly conceived drama, the *Thingspiele* (community theatre).[17] These outdoor theatres accommodated thousands of people and came to stand for Nazi ideals of order, creativity and collective consciousness. At the opening ceremony for the 8,000-seat

Heidelberg *Thingplätz* in 1934, Joseph Goebbels spoke of 'National Socialism in Stone', a 'living, tangible and monumental expression' to 'our concept of life', and compared the new theatres to the ambitious network of Autobahns conceived and built under Hitler in the 1930s (London 2000: 56). The *Thing* plays were intended make spectators feel like participators in the drama through their proximity to the stage, but also were to see themselves, as a nation, reflected in the plays themselves. A similar movement was under way in Italy, inspired by Mussolini's proposal for 'a theatre of masses'.[18] Yet, Taymor's reference to these *völkish* (folk) theatres is not straightforward. By giving the Colosseum audience voice but no body (in the final scene she reverses this practice by filling the auditorium seating with people but silences and freeze-frames them, as I discuss in more detail below) she deconstructs the very ideology of crowd consciousness and participation. The problematical Fascist references are present not merely in the architecture and its present-absent crowd but in the styling of the play's key characters as well. The mechanical, synchronized movements of the marching soldiers recall both the goose-stepping soldiers of the Nazi parades and the onstage marching groups that were a regular feature of the *Thing* plays (London 2000: 67–9). However, far from being youthful exempla of the Nazi ideal, Taymor's soldiers are fatigued, covered in dust and zombie-like in their expressions. In addition, while the entry of Titus on a horse-drawn carriage appears to re-create iconic images of Hitler entering Rome during his historic visit in 1938, it too raises some difficult questions.[19] If Titus represents Fascism, then how does this reconcile with the SS-inspired uniform worn by Saturninus, nemesis of the Andronici? If Titus and Saturninus are on opposing sides, then who represents the anti-Fascist stance?

There are no simple binaries in Taymor's film and, taking inspiration from the ambiguous moralities in Shakespeare's text, she indicts almost everybody in her bleak portrayal of patriarchy, violence and authoritarian ultranationalism. However, the most complex and (albeit unintentionally) flawed symbol of all in this highly referential and multilayered film is the character of Young Lucius. Taymor herself seems undecided about how this character is to be interpreted. On the one hand, she talks about the trajectory of Young Lucius's narrative as a 'counterpoint to Shakespeare's dark tale of vengeance', departing on his own journey towards 'knowledge, wisdom, compassion and choice' and 'the promise of daylight' (2000: 185). On the other hand, she claims in the 'Director's Commentary' of the DVD that she filmed the ending 'without [...] giving an answer or going into horrific, pathetic cliché'. Yet, she continues, in a non-committal, elliptical and circumlocutionary explanation, that 'after such a dark story', she liked 'the idea of this child getting towards the exit, moving out of this coliseum towards a bleak and barren landscape (oh, some water in the distance, potentially) [...] towards, maybe, a sunrise – maybe...' (1999). It is this very ambivalence that problematizes Taymor's conception of Young Lucius as a 'counterpoint' to the 'dark tale of vengeance' and further complicates the already-ambiguous Fascist references in this film. The ending seems to suggest that the boy has attained enlightenment as he walks from the horrors of the Colosseum into a bright sunset, bearing the child of Aaron in his arms. However, it is unclear whether this in fact heralds a new dawn for civilization or a mere continuation of the play's unremitting cycle of violence. Although far less overtly nihilistic than Kurzel's *Macbeth*, and far less directly provocative than Howell's *Titus Andronicus*, the final

FIGURE 13 *Osheen Jones as Young Lucius, in* Titus, *dir. Julie Taymor, 1999. Courtesy Clear Blue Sky Productions.*

sequence betrays an ambivalence that the director herself tried but failed to completely resist and one which has created similar divisions among scholars.

For Richard Burt, Young Lucius represents both a 'child-centred anti-Fascism' and the 'Fascist romanticisation of the child' and thus undermines any attempt at a coherent anti-Fascist message (2001: 98, 83). There is certainly some merit to this argument. The 'abduction' of Young Lucius in the opening sequence, his removal to the Colosseum and his triumphant presentation to the cheering crowd invite comparisons with the 'Fascist romanticisation of the child' that Burt describes. Osheen Jones, moreover, with his fair hair, blue eyes and pale skin, certainly appears to typify the Aryan ideal. As Helen Brocklehurst explains, the racially pure 'constructed' child was an 'embodiment of the [German] state's security needs' and 'a germ-cell of the nation' (2006: 57). These were not, in the words of Joseph Goebbels, 'children at any cost' but 'racially worthy, physically and mentally unaffected children of German families' (Bock 1994: 120). As a metaphor for the future of Nazism, and emblems of Edelman's 'reproductive futurism' (2004: 3), children featured frequently and prominently in political addresses as exemplified in Hitler's speech to the Nationalist Socialist Women's Organization in 1934:

> The programme of our National Socialist movement has in reality but one single point, and that point is the child, that tiny creature which must be born and grow strong and which alone gives meaning to the whole life struggle.
>
> (Noakes and Pridham 1984: 450)

Although Hitler publicly reified the role of the mother, his statements came with careful caveats that revealed more sinister objectives, such as 'children belong to their mothers as at the same moment they belong to me' (Fest 1970: 269). There were multiple incidents of Aryan children being forcibly removed from non-complying German mothers and up to two hundred thousand 'blond and blue-eyed children' were abducted from the occupied territories. The child was the property of the state, a political tool and a resource to be 'propagandized, nationalised and socialized' (Brocklehurst 2006: 66–7); the putative 'cult of motherhood' was in reality, like in the androcentric world of *Titus Andronicus*, 'a cult of fatherhood and masculinity' (Block 1994: 129). The abduction of the 'Aryan' child in the opening sequence of Taymor's *Titus* thus inevitably elicits comparisons with Fascist appropriation of 'racially worthy' children within a masculinist social structure. But as Taymor herself indicates in her stilted attempts to describe Young Lucius's role, this analogy is not as simple as it first appears. Not only does the ambiguous closing sequence problematize a straightforward anti-Fascist reading, as I explain further below; similarly, to reduce the full significance of Young Lucius to one single symbol, the embodiment of the eugenic ideal, is to overlook the multiple ways in which he works as a signifier in this film.

While the opening frame-sequence lasts less than two minutes, it has generated more critical analysis than perhaps any other aspect of Taymor's production.[20] It is surprising, therefore, that more attention has not been focused on the erotic nature of its various images: the sausage and the squirting milk; the atomization of body parts; the burly adult abductor; the boy commodified and exposed to the objectifying gaze of the Colosseum audience. Moreover, although commentators have identified the actor as Osheen Jones, the same boy who played the child-observer in Adrian Noble's 1996 film of *A Midsummer Night's Dream*, nobody to my knowledge has commented on his remarkable likeness to a figure with far wider cultural purchase at the time of the film's release than Jones himself: Macaulay Culkin.[21] In the 1990s, Culkin was a media phenomenon and icon of idealized childhood. Such was his popularity that the film, *Home Alone*, made more than $500 million in 1990 (Kincaid 1998: 116). Like Jones, and the young Keith Chegwin of Polanski's *Macbeth*, he had floppy hair, a skinny body and, to borrow a disconcerting term from Kincaid, a 'kissy-lipped' androgynous face (1992: 369). There are also parallels between *Titus* and Culkin's work. For instance, Michael Jackson's *Black or White* video features Culkin in a two-minute framing narrative that has remarkable similarities to the opening frame-sequence of *Titus*. It begins with a hyperactive Culkin jumping around his bedroom, playing air-guitar to loud rock music. Make-believe then morphs into reality as he drags oversized amplifiers into his parents' living room and produces a real guitar. The camera, meanwhile, in a manner remarkably similar to Taymor's *Titus*, cuts rapidly between close shots of his hands and face and full-body shots. When he plugs the guitar into the amplifier, the windows explode and, in a reversal of the adult–child paradigm of *Titus*, it is the male *adult* (his father) who is violently removed via an ejector-style seat that sends him through the roof of the house. Flying through the air, he eventually lands in a parallel universe. What greets him, however, is not the grim adult version of childhood fantasy play (as in *Titus*) but the fantasy land of Culkin and the 'adult-child' (Postman [1982] 1994: 98–119) Michael Jackson.

Whether consciously or not, Taymor seems to have appropriated the iconography of this short film while reversing the trajectory of its narrative. For, where the child in Michael Jackson's video foregrounds what Ruth M. Goldstein and Edith Zornow have termed the filmic trope of the 'omnipotent tot' who 'saves' the adults through his precocious child-like wisdom (1980: xiv), Young Lucius in Taymor's film is educated out of childishness via the television into the brutal adult world of mutilations, rape and murder. Yet what endures in *Titus*'s intertextual homage to Macaulay Culkin is the fetishized image of Kincaid's 'alluring child'. A ubiquitous figure in the Hollywood mainstream, this child, according to Kincaid's analysis, is an unthreatening, pre-sexual icon of childhood: 'bleached, bourgeois and androgynous' (1998: 20). He is, in other words, an alternative embodiment – the young, androgynous boy equivalent – of Mulvey's female 'erotic spectacle'. Taymor states in her 'Director's Notes' that she wanted to 'allow the adrenaline to rush while the heart and mind are challenged' (2000: 183). Yet, what she in fact created, or re-created, in her highly citational production is a boy so familiar an icon of American cinematic childhood as to appear almost entirely unworthy of note.

As the film progresses and Young Lucius is assimilated further and further into the action, he becomes less of an homage to Culkin and more of a Culkin anti-type who absorbs and reproduces the adult violence he witnesses. Central to this metamorphosis is the fly-killing scene, in which the violent play of the opening scene is actualized in reality. Through careful editing, Taymor places the child at the centre of the action, tracking in a few short shots a shift from child-like artlessness to one of devious and manipulative guile. He morphs, in short, from Kincaid's 'alluring child' (like the angelic Fleance in Polanski's *Macbeth*) into Anne Higonnet's 'knowing child' (more akin to the complicit page in Holmes's *Richard III*). For a play that repeatedly insists on the innocence of childhood, where adults refer to Young Lucius as 'tender' (3.2.48, 50), 'sweet' (5.3.168) and 'made of tears' (3.2.50), this is a significant shift in characterization by Taymor. It is worth noting here that Taymor does not, unlike Howell, depict Young Lucius weeping over the body of his grandfather in Act 5, Scene 3, and his four lines from 'O grandsire, grandsire' to 'My tears will choke me if I open my mouth' (5.3.171–4) are completely excised. This change is further evidence of how the Young Lucius of this film develops as a character and in doing so how far he diverges from the Young Lucius of Shakespeare's text.

From a narrative perspective, the killing of the fly is the point at which Taymor's Young Lucius function as almost exclusively extra-diegetic observer morphs into that of intra-diegetic actor. No longer the liminal subject hovering on the margins of the action – hiding behind pillars, peeking round doors, peering through windows – Young Lucius becomes, through his participation in the fly-killing scene, fully complicit in his grandfather's narrative of revenge. The setting of the fly-killing scene recalls the opening sequence, where the location of the boy's violent play is also, as in this scene, a kitchen table. However, whereas in the former the boy is bathed in the flickering light of the television, his agitated movements accompanied by the frenetic sounds of a violent cartoon, in the latter scene he is framed between Titus and Lavinia, his sudden attack on the fly erupting into their tender exchange with unexpected ferocity. It is the first time within the film (aside from the violent play of the frame-sequence) that Young Lucius has enacted the violence he has, thus far, been merely observing. Far from the tearful boy on the periphery, this Young Lucius takes centre stage, testing the boundaries of his own agency. A tracking shot follows Titus as he rises angrily from his seat. A shot/reverse-shot sequence takes in the face of the crest-fallen boy, before closing in on a low-angle close-up of Titus's face, aligning us, the spectators, with the boy as his grandfather looms threateningly over him (this shot recalls a similar adult–child exchange in the *Black or White* video when George Wendt, playing Macaulay Culkin's father, bears angrily down on the young boy). Again, the camera pauses on the broken expression of the boy before there is another remarkable transformation. After a beat, he raises his chin with a new-found confidence, smirks knowingly and announces with conspiratorial relish: 'It was a black ill-favoured fly / Like to the empress' Moor. Therefore I killed him' (3.2.67–8). He giggles as Titus's mood changes from fury to glee, the moment of tension successfully dissipated. But it is not, I suggest, a 'collapse into childness', where innocence educates evil and playfulness prevails (Rutter 2007b: 19). The crafty, knowing look on Young Lucius's face denies, for me at least, such an idealistic reading. Unlike the Young Lucius of the opening sequence where, snot and tears pouring down his face, he is forcibly removed from the kitchen and held aloft as a powerless prize for the cheering Colosseum crowds, this newly empowered child is a killer in the making, honed in the arts of deceit and dissimulation. The reassignment of the fly-killing episode from Marcus to Young Lucius has profound implications for the final scene and the film's representation of childhood as a problematic emblem of futurity and the subject of lively critical debate.

In the final scene of Shakespeare's text, the fate of the children is a blank to be filled, elided or foregrounded in performance. Marcus orders the gathered Romans and Goths to 'behold the child' (5.3.118), as he or one of his followers holds aloft 'the issue of an irreligious Moor' (5.3.120), but the ultimate fate of the baby, and of Young Lucius, is unexplained. At this point in Taymor's film it is the Clown who lifts up Aaron's baby, still alive but enclosed in a small cage. It is a conscious repetition of the opening sequence when he holds Young Lucius aloft for the invisible, cheering crowds. This time, however, the Colosseum crowds are present but eerily silent. After Lucius's closing speech, the sound of a crying baby interrupts the silence and the camera closes in on Aaron's infant. The door of the cage begins to open, and as the camera pulls out, a wide-eyed Young Lucius is slowly revealed. He looks up to the skies, as the sound of one crying baby merges into countless other crying babies. The shot freezes for a moment before switching to a shot of the boy's back as he walks in slow motion away from the camera towards the archway leading out of the Colosseum, cradling the baby across his shoulder. For a full two minutes, he continues his slow journey towards the outside world, the sound of crying infants having transformed into the more soothing and joyful sound of church bells. As he reaches the archway, the camera begins to follow him out of the Colosseum and finally freezes, the silhouette of the two children bathed in the garishly bright colours of a pixelated and self-evidently artificial sunrise (see Figure 13). For Lisa S. Starks, this final coda functions as a re-gendering of the slasher movie's 'Final Girl' narrative and signifies, however tentatively, the possibility of release and redemption (2002: 136). Drawing on Carol Clover's analysis of gender and the horror genre, Starks argues that Taymor's Young Lucius inverts the conventional paradigm of the surviving female, an androgynous figure standing in as, what Clover terms, the 'congenial double for the adolescent male' in the horror film's male coming-of-age narrative, to take on the maternal, nurturing role himself (Clover 2002: 51). According to this reading, Taymor's film replaces the *phallicized* Final Girl of the slasher film with a *maternalized* male adolescent who is at once, as Lehmann argues, 'Other, mother, and "Final Boy"' (Lehmann 2009: 58).

Despite Starks's and Lehmann's optimistic reading of *Titus*, it is by no means the only way to read this coda. David McCandless compares the ending of Taymor's 1994 off-Broadway stage production with her 1999 film, arguing that the revised ending (in the stage version Young Lucius stared with horror at the tiny coffin of Aaron's baby) creates a 'wish-fulfilment fantasy' that sanctions violence and retribution by releasing the audience from trauma through a Hollywood-style happy ending (2002: 510). Kenneth

FIGURE 14 *Unidentified actor as Aaron's baby, in* Titus, *dir. Julie Taymor, 1999. Courtesy Clear Blue Sky Productions.*

Rothwell agrees that 'one leaves the movie theatre with a sense of relief, where otherwise such calamities might inflict permanent trauma', but also hints at a cynicism inherent in this 'feel-good' movie ending when he states that 'it relieves not only the director but also her audience from facing the pitiless horrors of a holocaust' (he uses a small 'h' here but the analogy is implicit) (2004: 272). When considered within the Nazi-inspired context of Taymor's setting, the image of the Aryan child leading the biracial baby into the future raises troubling questions of its own. For Catherine Silverstone, the hopeful ending 'works to elide the problematical racial politics of [Young Lucius's] paternalistic gesture' (2014: 5). However, I argue that the racial politics are not elided but foregrounded through the Fascist imagery that pervades this film, and the future for the biracial baby seems far from secure. Although the ending has attracted multiple interpretations, by many, such as Kim Fedderson and J. Michael Richardson (2009: 85–6), and Carol Chillington Rutter (2007b: 26), it has been taken at face value for its recuperative and redemptive qualities. By contrast, I believe that what Burt terms the final 'schlocky' (2007: 229) shot of Young Lucius walking out of the Colosseum with the baby in his arms *appears* to offer hope of a new dawn in the hands of this androgynous Final Girl inversion, but its apparent closure is undermined by the ambiguous role of Young Lucius in this adaptation and by the constant presence of what Taymor herself has called a 'ghastly, ghostly history' of racial and sectarian violence (Blumenthal 2007: 229). What has been seen by many as a paternalistic gesture is thus undermined by the racial implications of the Fascistic references, the ambivalent role of the witness, the garishly artificial sunrise and Young Lucius's complicity in the violence he appears to be fleeing. As symbols of 'reproductive futurism' (Edelman 2004: 3), then, Taymor's children offer us a glimpse of a future that is at best questionable and at worst as grimly nihilistic as that depicted in Howell's unequivocal ending.

Conclusion

That Taymor's *Titus* fails to offer a definitive sense of closure is symptomatic of a film that constantly interrogates the role of the audience in the cinematic illusion, demanding that the viewer accepts nothing at face value. Like Shakespeare's play, it toys with blurred boundaries – of gender, genre, race and form – and deconstructs fixed binaries of fiction and reality, good and evil, witness and participant. To ask viewers to invest in a happy ending and accept without question a representation of Edelman's politics of 'reproductive futurism' (2004: 3) is tantamount to asking that they reject the interrogatory mode of viewing the film has been promoting throughout. Although, of the three productions under consideration, Taymor's *Titus* departs furthest from Shakespeare's play in terms of textual emendations, it also, somewhat paradoxically, most closely dramatizes its ambiguities and indeterminacies. Shakespeare asks us to 'behold the child' (5.3.118), but the child is an imperfect signifier. For Marcus, the child (Aaron's son) represents the wrongs inflicted on the Andronici by the 'irreligious Moor, / Chief architect and plotter of these woes' (5.3.120–1). Yet this fails to account for Titus's behaviour in the opening act, where a lack of compassion towards not only Tamora but also his son, Mutius, establishes him as a flawed hero, and in the final scene, where his ruthless killing of Lavinia denies the audience any remaining sense of empathy. The multiple Fascistic references that Taymor employs, as we have seen, do not clearly distinguish victim from perpetrator. Like the oxymoronic 'irreligious piety' (1.1.133), villain and hero are distinctions that collapse under close scrutiny. That the fate of the two children remains ultimately unresolved is thus characteristic of a play that denies its audience an unproblematic viewing experience. If the burden of futurity lies in the hands of Young Lucius and Aaron's baby, then we are left by Taymor with the inevitable conclusion that it is a burden almost impossible to bear, despite the best efforts of her revisionary, if highly questionable, 'happy ending'.

Warner and Howell smoothed over the ambiguities in the play's depiction of the children and their questionable futures with vastly different results. For Warner, Young Lucius and Aaron's baby were marginalized characters who existed merely to support Titus and his patriarchal narrative of revenge. Their lack of agency and authority was reinforced by the fact that they were both self-evidently *not* children. By manifesting Young Lucius as an adolescent soldier and the baby as a lifeless toy, Warner neutralized their power to disrupt the brutal regime of the Andronici and her narrative of revenge tragedy. Unlike the puppet-princes of Ostermeier's *Richard III* and the statuary reincarnation of Mamillius in Wheeldon's ballet, both of whose disruptive presence subverted ideas about teleology, ontology and futurity, the children of Warner's production functioned to reinforce rather than subvert the patriarchal hegemony of the play world. To portray the children as potential conduits out of that world would have diminished the tragic stature of Brian Cox's Titus and destroyed the very foundations upon which Warner built her production. It would, moreover, have raised questions about the agency of the children that she was evidently not concerned with pursuing.

Howell's adaptation used the child as the 'hook' for accessing the 'catalogue of violence' that enfolds in the play by filming its excesses through his eyes (Billington 1985: 29). Like Warner, she does not suggest that Young Lucius and Aaron's baby might offer an alternative future, choosing instead to confront her audience with the life-destroying futility of sectarianism in a frame-sequence that is bleakly nihilistic. The questions that Shakespeare's text leaves unresolved are addressed by Howell with unequivocal finality: Aaron's baby is dead; Young Lucius weeps helplessly over his body; and the skull reappears to confirm the death not only of childhood but of futurity itself. Taymor offers a tentative glimmer of hope in her final sequence but her 'hero' is an ambiguous character – a fetishized Aryan child within a Fascistic frame of reference who is capable of acts of unprovoked violence and manipulative guile. To empower him with the ability to direct the future seems a burden he is ill-equipped to bear. It is a future, moreover, signified by an artificial sunrise that appears to be no more than a mirage. The power to act in Howell's film, on the other hand, lies not with Young Lucius but with the viewers themselves. The future for Young Lucius and Aaron's baby is beyond redemption. By confronting viewers with this uncomfortable truth, Howell forces them to look at themselves and ask, in her own words, 'what are we doing to the children?' (Billington 1985: 29).

In the final chapter I consider *The Winter's Tale*, a play with an equally problematical ending that has, like *Titus Andronicus*, received renewed attention in recent years following a relatively sparse performance history. Recent productions have tended to foreground the ambiguities of Shakespeare's text by focusing on the absent-present role of the child, as in the stage revival by Nicholas Hytner. Like Howell and Taymor, Hytner took the role of the child, Mamillius, and turned him into the audience's proxy by filtering the action through his eyes. By contrast, and breaking with convention, Branagh and Ashford's 2015/16 adaptation tried to impose a 'happy ending' which smoothed over the loss of Mamillius and focused instead on the redemptive qualities of the play. However, like Taymor's *Titus*, the Branagh/Ashford 'happy ending' felt far from unequivocal and ultimately posed more questions than it answered.

4

'No age': Disappearing Childhood in *The Winter's Tale*

The Winter's Tale is undergoing a remarkable revival. A brief glance at the five years between 2012 and 2017 reveals an almost uninterrupted run of productions across the major theatre companies of the UK. Notable examples include Edward Hall's 2012 revival of his 2005 production for Propeller; Lucy Bailey's 2013 production for the RSC; Conrad Nelson's 2015 modern-dress production for Northern Broadsides; the Kenneth Branagh Company's 2015/16 production at the Garrick Theatre; Michael Longhurst's 2015/16 production for Shakespeare's Globe at the Sam Wanamaker Theatre; and Cheek by Jowl's 2016/17 touring production directed by Declan Donnellan. Interest in the play has also crossed artistic genres, with three groundbreaking adaptations in the fields of dance, prose fiction and opera. In addition to Christopher Wheeldon's 2014 ballet version for the Royal Opera House, discussed in the Introduction, Jeanette Winterson published the novel *The Gap of Time: The Winter's Tale Retold* in 2015, and a new three-act opera version written by Ryan Wigglesworth was premiered at the London Coliseum in March 2017. For a play that has often been overlooked by directors and adaptors in the past, it is a remarkable surge of interest that raises the following question: why has *The Winter's Tale* emerged from the periphery to become one of the most revived, adapted and celebrated Shakespearean plays in recent years? The answer, as I argue in this chapter, lies in the character of Mamillius, in his sudden and premature death and in the ways in which that resonates with twenty-first-century audiences facing their own particular crisis of what Neil Postman termed, in his book of that name, 'the disappearance of childhood' (1982).

The last early modern recorded performance of *The Winter's Tale* was in 1634 and revivals during the eighteenth and nineteenth centuries appear to have been spasmodic and irregular with numerous cuts, revisions and adaptations.[1] Two ballads, hybrid versions of Robert Greene's romance *Pandosto; The Triumph of Time* (a source for Shakespeare's *The Winter's Tale*) and Shakespeare's play were printed during the Restoration by pro-Royalist writers, Thomas Jordan (1663) and S. S. Gent (1672), later attributed to Samuel Sheppard. However, as Lori Humphrey Newcomb notes, the material was adapted 'so freely that neither work can be claimed as its primary source' (2002: 143). The play in its original form only began to grow in popularity during the second half of the twentieth century, and the past thirty-five years in particular have seen a slow but incremental increase in new productions at the major theatres of the UK.[2] Although this change in fortune can be partly attributed to audiences' willingness to embrace non-realist theatre, I would like to suggest another explanation that speaks to a wider social concern about childhood. As discussed in Chapter 2, *Macbeth* was a play to which late-twentieth- and early-twenty-first-century directors turned to explore society's conflicted attitude towards children as a contradictory symbol of the vulnerable innocent and the threatening 'other': a figure of hope but also one of despair. I argued that *Macbeth*, with its ambiguous and multifaceted portrayal of childhood, provided the ideal vehicle for exploring changing ideas about what it means to be a child in a society facing an increasingly acute crisis of classification. Although Charlotte Scott calls *The Winter's Tale* 'the culmination of Shakespeare's writing on children' (2018: 140), it is, in the final scenes of reconciliation and redemption, notable for its absence of children. No young boys remain at the end as a silent threat to the play's sense of closure, like Aaron's baby and Young Lucius in *Titus Andronicus*, Fleance in *Macbeth* or Prince Gonzalo, the equivalent of Mamillius in Richard Brome's reinterpretation of *The Winter's Tale, The Queen and Concubine*. There is also a distinct lack of 'parlous' or precocious children, like the pageboy and the two young princes in *Richard III*, Moth in *Love's Labour's Lost,* William in *The Merry Wives of*

Windsor or Macduff's boy in *Macbeth*. Childhood has, by the end of *The Winter's Tale*, quite simply disappeared. Although the play opens with a young boy, Mamillius, and his heavily pregnant mother, Hermione, when the choric figure of Time enters in Act 4, Scene 1, to 'slide / O'er' sixteen years (4.1.5–6), he/she creates a temporal blank. No 'child' between the ages of five and twenty-one – a crucial developmental stage between infancy and adulthood and a slightly elongated version of Neil Postman's definition of childhood – appears in this play.[3] Mamillius has already died while still in petticoats; Florizel, whose birth 'was not full a month' (5.1.117) apart from that of Mamillius, is by now a 21-year-old man; and Perdita, last seen as a baby at the end of Act 3, reappears aged sixteen. Anxieties related to this 'disappeared' age of childhood are echoed throughout the play. Polixenes reminisces about being 'boy eternal' (1.2.65); Leontes wistfully imagines he 'did recoil / Twenty-three years' (1.2.154–5) when looking at his son's face; and Antigonus threatens to neuter his own three daughters before they reach adulthood should Hermione prove false, vowing 'by mine honour, / I'll geld 'em all' (2.1.146–7). At the beginning of Act 3, the Old Shepherd expresses fears about the precocious sexuality and antisocial behaviour of children when he says: 'I would there were no age between ten and / three-and-twenty, or that youth would sleep out the / rest; for there is nothing in the between but getting wenches with child, wronging the ancientry, stealing, / fighting' (3.3.58–62). What Time actualizes in the sixteen-year lacuna at the centre of the play is almost an exact fulfilment of this wish. The age of childhood – the very age over which both Florizel and Perdita 'slide' directly to adulthood; before which Leontes and Polixenes fantasize about returning; and beyond which Mamillius is doomed never to live – becomes the 'no age' of the Old Shepherd's whimsical musing.

One of the reasons for *The Winter's Tale*'s irregular performance history through the eighteenth, nineteenth and twentieth centuries is its stylistic and formal heterogeneity and spatiotemporal dislocations. It is listed under the 'comedies' in the 1623 First Folio, yet the classification of this late play has long confounded commentators. It is a generic hybrid replete with anachronisms, plot reversals, duplications and linguistic complexity. Shakespeare was not averse to setting his action in one place that plays out in real time and conforms to the Aristotelian three unities as *The*

Tempest, which may have been written and performed in the same year as *The Winter's Tale*, attests. The reason for *The Winter's Tale*'s temporal lacunae and disjunctions is quite simply a question of form reflecting matter. 'The carelessness' as Bartholomeusz has observed, 'is quite careful, the disorganisation apparently deliberate' (1982: 6). Time is not merely a crucial element in the play's narrative. It is, as commentators have noted, its fundamental structuring principle and central thematic concern.

Inga-Stina Ewbank's essay 'The Triumph of Time' in *The Winter's Tale* was one of the earliest papers to apply temporal theory to *The Winter's Tale* and remains a seminal work in this field. For Ewbank, the ambivalent representation of Time as both 'Destroyer' and 'Revealer' in the early modern consciousness is pivotal to understanding the play's thematic and structural design. According to this reading, time is a depoliticized and essentialized force under which human agency is subordinated to teleology. *The Winter's Tale*, she asserts, is all about 'what time means and does to man' ([1968] 1983: 114), and the sacrifice of Mamillius is a crucial, if regrettable, stage in the play's overarching atonement-redemption structure. Taking a similar critical perspective that draws on mythopoetic and theurgic emblems to inform his reading, William E. Engel argues that the key to understanding the function of time in *The Winter's Tale* lies in the classical concepts of *Kairos* and *Kronos* and in the early modern emblematic idea of *Temporis filia veritas* (Truth is the daughter of Time), a motto which is quoted on the title page of Shakespeare's principal source material, Robert Greene's *Pandosto; The Triumph of Time* (1588). *Kairos* is a qualitative form of time that signifies an opportune or propitious moment, and, according to Engel, is manifested in the figure of Paulina, who 'patiently manipulates the conditions for actualizing the possibilities of transformative and redemptive art'. *Kronos*, on the other hand, is a quantitative concept of time associated with sequentiality and mortality. It is thus traditionally represented as an old man wielding a scythe. Engel argues that the choric figure of Time that appears in Act 4, Scene 1, and 'collapses the sixteen years of Perdita's childhood' is a benign version of *Kronos*, but that ultimately 'it is the influence of *Kairos* that crowns the restoration and renewal of time with which [the] play concludes'. Through its pattern of death, atonement and renewal, the play enacts in dramatic form the motto *Temporis filia veritas*, and thus, Engel argues, 'truth comes to light in the end' (2013: 71–87).

Although these readings provide an illuminating insight into the overall formal and narrative design of the play, they underestimate a key point famously made by Stanley Cavell: that 'a dead five- or six-year-old boy remains unaccounted for' (2003: 193). In doing so, they overlook a fundamental – if not *the* fundamental – function of time as a classifier of life-stages. At the centre of the play is a young boy who whispers his winter's tale to his mother. However, he dies in Act 3 before his tale has had chance to unfold. Although his age is never explicitly stated, it can be deduced from oblique references in the text. When Leontes meets Florizel in the final act, for instance, he exclaims: 'Were I but twenty-one, / Your father's image is so hit in you, / His very air, that I should call you brother' (5.1.125–7). Taking into account the sixteen-year gap, this suggests that Mamillius, who was the same age as Florizel, would have been five when he died. It is widely agreed among early modern scholars that the progression from boyhood to manhood was conceptualized as a continuum in which the two states were unstable, fluid and interdependent. As Gina Bloom explains, 'Boys are always-already in the process of becoming men and men, by implication, are merely grown-up boys' (2010: 333). Although the boundary between boyhood and manhood was fluid, however, the progression from infancy to boyhood (or from infancy to the 'no age' of childhood) was far more clearly demarcated through the social practice of breeching.

Up until around the age of seven, both genders were dressed in petticoats and spent their time almost exclusively with women, and the word 'child' was a generic classification that signified an early modern perception of all children as gendered feminine. Thomas Elyot's observation 'after that a child is come to seuen yeres of age, I holde it expedient that he be taken from the company of women' is typical of early modern anxieties about separating boy-children from the influence of women in order to inculcate a masculine gender identity (1531: *EEBO* image 25 of 258).[4] The Old Shepherd's musings about whether the baby Perdita is a 'boy or a child' (3.3.69) certainly seems to suggest that Shakespeare considered childhood to be in some way synonymous with femininity. At some point between the ages of five and seven, boys were removed from the female sphere, dressed in breeches and prepared for manhood.[5] At the time of his death, Mamillius thus stands at the cusp of the transition from the unbreeched infant to the breeched boy-child. Childhood is curtailed at the very point at which it becomes gendered and individuated, and the whole period between infancy and adulthood is elided. As we have already seen, this is also a crucial developmental stage in terms of the 'childhood in crisis' debate, and Julie Taymor made allusions to the pernicious effects of television and digital technology in her 1999 film *Titus*, as discussed in Chapter 3. It can surely be no coincidence, then, that the Shakespearean play that most closely enacts the crisis outlined by Postman in 1982 and further defined and debated by childhood scholars in the intervening years – the crisis of 'disappearing childhood' – has enjoyed an unprecedented revival in the past few years.

In this chapter, I consider the different ways in which two productions have responded to this crisis through their treatment of the death of Mamillius and the sixteen-year temporal vacuum in performance. In the first section, I consider the 2001 production by Nicholas Hytner, whose childish adults and precociously adult-like Mamillius seemed to encapsulate in dramatic form the crisis outlined by Postman, Cunningham and others. Using the single-sex public school as a modern-day context for the childhood friendship of the two princes, Hytner provided a framework for understanding and pathologizing Leontes's regressive behaviour, turning Mamillius into an embodied metaphor for Leontes's 'inner child', the *puer aeternus* (eternal boy), who must be destroyed in order to achieve closure, however equivocal that turned out to be. Next, I consider the 2015/16 production by Kenneth Branagh and Rob Ashford in which Mamillius was re-imagined as a sentimentalized Victorian 'wise child' created to save his sister and reverse the moral degeneration of his father. In this reading of the play, his death was presented less as a tragic byproduct of Leontes's jealousy and more as an act of divine intervention – the Shakespearean equivalent of the Dickensian 'dying child' sent 'to indict the adult world' with his death (Grylls 1978: 137). Capitalizing on the late-twentieth- and early-twenty-first-century trend for cultural and literary Victoriana, Branagh/Ashford's *Tale* evoked nostalgia for a mythologized past and what Victorian scholar Kathleen Tillotson calls the 'mysterious simplicities of fairy-tale' ([1954] 1956: 174) in order to secure the survival not only of Perdita but of futurity itself. The crisis of 'disappearing childhood' was at the heart of both of these productions. However, the extent to which they foregrounded or occluded this crisis *as* a crisis had contrasting implications for the final reconciliation scene and therefore the overall tone of their plays. From ambiguous irresolution in Hytner to redemptive sentimentality in Branagh/Ashford, their focus on the erosion of childhood had profound repercussions for the message conveyed by their respective tales and goes some way to explaining why this long-neglected play is now attaining widespread attention.

Healing the 'inner child' in Nicholas Hytner's *The Winter's Tale* (2001)

Nicholas Hytner's 2001 production for the National Theatre approached the 'no age' of childhood from two opposing but interconnected perspectives: the premature child whose accelerated maturation queers the normative child-to-adult telos; and the regressive adult, whose stunted growth, pathologized within a post-Freudian psychological framework, threatens heterosexuality, 'reproductive futurism' (Edelman 2004: 3) and, as a consequence, the very existence of futurity itself. In the first act of the play, Polixenes reminisces about his childhood relationship with Leontes, describing an Edenic time of carefree innocence before the fall into sexual knowledge and, by implication, corruption:

> We were as twinned lambs that did frisk i'th' sun
> And bleat the one at th'other. What we changed
> Was innocence for innocence. We knew not
> The doctrine of ill-doing nor dreamed
> That any did. Had we pursued that life,
> And our weak spirits ne'er been higher reared
> With stronger blood, we should have answered heaven
> Boldly, 'Not guilty,' the imposition cleared
> Hereditary ours.
>
> (1.2.67–74)

The age of innocence for which Polixenes yearns is one that predates breeching and thus also predates heterosexualization and its perceived dangers. As an emblem of childhood innocence, his boyhood friendship with Leontes is eulogized as the epitome of mutual affection and their wives depicted as satanic temptresses.

Mamillius, who has entered with his parents and Polixenes at the beginning of this scene, is present throughout this exchange. As Charlotte Scott notes, 'theatrically this is important' because the images of childhood innocence invoked by Polixenes are symbolically transferred onto Mamillius, and the play thus invites the audience to 'observe him within those terms' (2018: 144–5). But these are adult subject matters discussed in terms unsuitable for children and ultimately result in the death in the child who witnesses too much of adult emotions and fears. Polixenes's imagery in this speech is biblical, specifically referencing the Garden of Eden myth in Genesis, which, as W. Thomas MacCrary notes, projects a 'strange nostalgia men have for a time before women, when they were intimate with their male god and knew no difference, no need, no guilt' (1985: 203). However, Shakespeare's is a queer version of the Fall that is adapted from its Christian context to incorporate ideals of virtuous male friendship as defined in key classical and Renaissance discourses such as Cicero's *De Amicitia* ([45 BC] 2004) and Michel de Montaigne's 'Of Friendship' (1603). There are two men in Polixenes's re-imagined version of the Garden of Eden, and Satan comes in the form of a woman. Hermione reiterates this female-Satan analogy in mock horror, accusing Polixenes of suggesting that she and his wife are devils and challenging him to pursue it further:

> Grace to boot!
> Of this make no conclusion, lest you say
> Your queen and I are devils. Yet go on.
> Th'offenses we have made you do we'll answer –
> If you first sinned with us, and that with us
> You did continue fault, and that you slipped not
> With any but with us.
>
> (1.2.80–6)

It is a challenge which Polixenes declines to meet, yet the accusation is left hanging, with no denial forthcoming from either men. Although Polixenes is the first to frame the boyhood friendship in biblical language, it is presented in a playful exchange with Hermione and, as John Pitcher observes, his 'temporary slipping back to childhood has no consequences for him' (2010: 34). For Leontes, however, the metaphor takes hold in a dangerous and ultimately destructive way.

In his fertile imagination, the temptress does not merely corrupt him with sexual knowledge, thereby forcing his separation from his friend and his ejection from his Edenic world of male-male bonding, but she also corrupts his friend, driving a near-deadly wedge between husband and wife.

Scholars have long debated the extent to which Polixenes's and Leontes's boyhood friendship is based upon a homoerotic attraction and whether Leontes ever succeeds in fully relinquishing childhood ties.[6] Although there are advocates of both sides of the argument, the majority of commentators occupy the middle ground, which can probably be best summarized in Stephen Guy-Bray's analysis that 'Leontes is jealous of his wife because he thinks she has sex with his friend and of his friend because he thinks he has sex with his wife' (2002: 206). I agree that Leontes's jealousy is directed towards both Polixenes and Hermione, but Guy-Bray's analysis suggests a symmetry in the relationships that the text belies. When Leontes articulates his suspicions of infidelity, he places responsibility almost entirely with his wife rather than with his friend. He begins by accusing them both of 'paddling palms and pinching fingers' (1.2.115), but then more explicitly states that it is Hermione who is 'still virginaling / Upon his palm' (1.2.125–6). He accuses her of 'hold[ing] up the neb, the bill, to him' (1.2.182) and linking arms 'with the boldness of a wife' (1.2.183). As his language becomes more sexually explicit, it is the penetrated not the penetrator who is the object of his disgust: 'be it concluded, / No barricado for a belly. Know't; / It will let in and out the enemy / With bag and baggage' (1.2.201–3).

A comparable vocabulary of misogynistic rancour is employed in Shakespeare's *Sonnets*, particularly Sonnet 144, where the Polixenes/Leontes/Hermione relationship is dramatized in compressed form. Here Shakespeare juxtaposes antitheses of evil and purity to place his male (angel) love in opposition to his female (devil) love:

Two loves I have, of comfort and despair,
Which like two spirits do suggest me still:
The better angel is a man right fair,
The worser spirit a woman colored ill
To win me soon to hell my female evil
Tempteth my better angel from my side,
And would corrupt my saint to be a devil,

Wooing his purity with her foul pride.
And whether that my angel be turned fiend
Suspect I may, yet not directly tell;
But being both from me, both to each friend,
I guess one angel in another's hell.
Yet this shall I ne'er know, but live in doubt,
Till my bad angel fire my good one out.[7]

Miltonic language is employed to describe the female temptress, who is here imagined as the fallen angel Satan, seducing the friend and causing his fall from grace. Like Leontes, the speaker uses plosive alliteration, in, for example, 'purity [...] pride' and in the repetition of 'both', to convey his disgust. If we compare Shakespeare's treatment of Leontes's jealousy with his source material, the prose narrative *Pandosto; The Triumph of Time* by Robert Greene (1588), it becomes clear to see how he reconfigures the directions of triangulated desire between the three main characters to reproduce the miniature drama of Sonnet 144. In Greene's narrative, the boyhood relationship is given only passing mention. He describes how, upon meeting at the entrance to the city, Pandosto (Shakespeare's Leontes) and his boyhood friend travel by horseback, 'devising and recounting how, being children, they had passed their youth in friendly pastimes' (1588: *EEBO*, image 4 of 28). The language of a prelapsarian homosocial idyll contaminated by female sexuality, all spoken in the presence of the young Mamillius, is entirely Shakespeare's invention. Greene, moreover, is far more unequivocal in his account of the burgeoning intimacy between Bellaria (Shakespeare's Hermione) and Egistus (Shakespeare's Polixenes). He describes 'such a secret uniting of their affections that the one could not well be without the company of the other' (Greene 1588). Shakespeare's Leontes, on the other hand, is given no such apparent cause for jealousy. Shakespeare thus rearranges his source material to give visual manifestation to Leontes's sexual anxieties: a young boy on the cusp of gendered individuation to remind him of his separation from Polixenes and a pregnant wife to remind him of his fall into (hetero)sexual knowledge. In Hytner's production, it was the destruction of this peculiarly insular and exclusively male domain, the intimations of a same-sex erotic relationship and the submission to heteronormativity that were literally and metaphorically given centre stage.

Hytner's *The Winter's Tale* was a contemporary-dress production in a sophisticated urban setting. The Sicilian court was re-imagined as the private apartment of a modern, informal monarch, while Bohemia became a Glastonbury-style music festival. The lights came up on Act 1 to reveal a chic penthouse apartment with floor-to-ceiling windows looking out onto a hazy city view. Memorabilia from Leontes's and Polixenes's schooldays were scattered among its sleek, monochromatic furniture, the old and the ultra-modern commingling in an eclectic mélange of styles. To the right of the window was an oversized sepia-tinted photograph of the two kings as young schoolboys of a similar age to Mamillius. Tousle-haired and dirty-kneed, the boys were dressed in matching sports kits and holding a rugby ball. Silver-framed photographs of schoolboys also adorned the top of a baby grand piano. A large display cabinet was filled, not with bottles of spirits or expensive-looking glassware as might be expected but with an assortment of sporting trophies and shields, rugby balls, cricket bats, school caps and toys. Childhood in this Sicilian court was clearly a phase to be eternalized and memorialized, while the young boy Mamillius behaved less like a child than a 'pint-sized, hot-housed "performer"' (Rutter 2010: 219) who played Schumann, read books and recited poetry.

Servants hovered discreetly in the shadows carrying trays of drinks and *hors d'œuvres* and a group of dark-suited courtiers stood around a coffee table, looking, as reviewer Susannah Clapp described, 'something like mafiosi, something like public schoolboys' (2001). Leontes was set apart from the group, sitting cross-legged on the floor in an outfit of meticulously pressed stone linen trousers and a preppy v-neck blue sweater. Standing upon the coffee table in the spotlight was Mamillius, dressed as a miniature Father Time in a black cloak complete with white wings and a scythe. He was reciting Sonnet 12:

> When I do count the clock that tells the time,
> And see the brave day sunk in hideous night;
> When I behold the violet past prime,
> And sable curls all silver'd o'er with white;
> When lofty trees I see barren of leaves
> Which erst from heat did canopy the herd,
> And summer's green all girded up in sheaves

> Borne on the bier with white and bristly beard,
> Then of thy beauty do I question make,
> That thou among the wastes of time must go,
> Since sweets and beauties do themselves forsake
> And die as fast as they see others grow;
> > And nothing 'gainst Time's scythe can make defence
> > Save breed, to brave him when he takes thee hence.

The words were eerily prophetic. This little boy was destined to meet 'Time's scythe' before he had grown out of his short trousers. There was also a grim irony in his exhortations to breed as a defence against the depredations of time when Leontes was to be the cause of his only son's untimely death. This was without doubt a particularly apt choice of sonnet in view of the play's preoccupation with the ravages of time and the two men's nostalgic memories of their boyhood friendship (the sonnet is, after all, addressed to a young man and dedicated to the mysterious 'onlie begetter... Mr. W. H.').[8] However, there was an oddly disconcerting disjunction between the content and the delivery. Although he was dressed as a miniature Father Time, Mamillius was quite clearly a little boy (the actors who alternated the role of Mamillius, Liam Hess and Thomas Brown-Lowe were aged around nine at the time of the performance), and the dark, enveloping folds of the costume drew attention to rather than masked the youthfulness of the boy underneath. The wistful sense of yearning and regret conveyed in the words of the sonnet, moreover, felt uncomfortably inappropriate in the high-pitched, stilted voice of a child. This was more than merely childish precociousness. It was as though Mamillius had been unnaturally fast-tracked through his childhood to achieve an impression of maturity in terms of behaviour, dress and intellect that was at odds with his immature physical development. It was, in fact, a dramatic manifestation of Leontes's own psychic 'inner child' and his compensatory 'adultifying' attitude towards his son (Postman [1982] 1994: 126). This is made clear when he says: 'How like, methought, I then was to this kernel / This squash, this gentleman' (1.2.159–60). In the space of one sentence, through the three metaphors 'kernel', 'squash' and 'gentleman', he imaginatively constructs an accelerated growth from infancy to adulthood for his young son. Indeed, the last words Leontes speaks directly to Mamillius in the play are 'thou'rt an honest man' (1.2.209). The Mamillius of Hytner's play, like the Mamillius of Leontes's imagination, was a premature child whose precocious talent and uncannily adult demeanour disrupted normative teleological child-to-adult development and threatened what queer theorist Judith Halberstam calls the 'logic of reproductive temporality' (2005: 4).

When Mamillius solemnly bowed and climbed off the table to the applause of his politely appreciative audience, a large hourglass was revealed in the place where he had been standing. The hourglass is a paradoxical symbol of time. Time passes, denoted by the sand trickling through the narrow bottleneck, but it is the same sand that is constantly recycled. The contradictory aspects of the hourglass – a symbol of both movement and stasis, progress and regression – captured perfectly Hytner's dual approach to childhood in this play. On the one hand, the boy Mamillius would die while still an undeveloped infant. On the other hand, he was already a mature performer, or perhaps more accurately, a performer of maturity, comporting himself with the calm possession of a young man who had left his childhood behind. For Hytner's Leontes and Polixenes, by contrast, childhood represented a time before separation and sexual pollution – a time which, although memorialized in photos and memorabilia, could never in fact be reclaimed. The age separating infancy and adulthood, that crucial period of development, maturation, control and protection, was quite simply a yawning chasm.

As the lights went up on Act 1, Scene 2, Mamillius had changed out of his Father Time costume and was wearing a green sweater and white trousers, like a miniature version of his casually attired father. He was seated at the grand piano, playing a rendition of the opening movement of Schumann's *Kinderszenen* (Scenes from Childhood) Op. 15. This was another telling choice of performance piece that reflected the yearning for lost childhood from the perspective of an adult and yet was performed by a disquietingly adult-like child. Written in 1838, the series of thirty short movements was inspired, according to a letter written by Schumann to his wife Clara, by Clara's remark that the composer sometimes seemed 'like a child' (Jensen 2012: 162). They were thus a musical expression of Schumann's own childish self – a desire to recapture what he can only ever be *like* but will never actually *be* again. When the performance ended, the courtiers clapped politely, and Mamillius gave a stiff bow, walked downstage right and sat down next to a little wagon full of toys. Leontes galloped boyishly across the stage and sat on the floor next to him. The remarkable similarity between the two – the boy dressed like a miniature adult and the man behaving like a playful child – can be seen in Figure 15. After a brief spell of father–son bonding, Leontes picked up a rugby ball from Mamillius's wagon and threw it playfully at Polixenes. They tossed the ball backwards and forwards between them like overgrown schoolboys while Mamillius sat quietly, engrossed in his own world of childish play. He answered his father's questions with a distracted air and was apparently oblivious to the tension building around him. At 'Go play, Mamillius' (1.2.209), his mother tapped him on his shoulder and he obediently loaded his toys into his trolley and wheeled it offstage. This Mamillius was almost automata-like in his movements – distant, unemotional and self-contained. In other words, he was a prematurely 'adultified' child to counterbalance the regressively 'childified' (Postman [1982] 1994: 126) behaviour of his father.

Act 2 was set in an adult games room with a full-size table-tennis table and darts board. A portion of the stage had been sectioned

FIGURE 15 *Alex Jennings as Leontes and Liam Hess as Mamillius, in The Winter's Tale, dir. Nicholas Hytner, 2001. © Catherine Ashmore.*

off with sliding walls to create a room that doubled as Hermione's bedchamber in Act 2, Scene 2, and Mamillius's sickroom in Act 2, Scene 3. Panels opened and closed to offer glimpses of the action within, and when it became Mamillius's sickroom in the following act, lights illuminated the closed-off interior to reveal Leontes at his bedside through the semi-translucent screens. The outer rooms of Martin-Davis's set were dominated with childhood memorabilia that were signifiers of a very specific masculine childhood environment: the English public school. Hytner's multiple rugby balls – a visual synecdoche for a game famously codified in the nineteenth century at Rugby School, one of the first independent schools in Britain – was a particularly evocative signifier of this environment.[9] The traditional single-sex public schools such as Eton, Harrow, Sherborne, Radley and Winchester (five of the original 'Clarendon nine') are among only a few remaining areas in social life in which gender differentiation and masculine privilege still prevail.[10] As psychotherapist Nick Duffell observes in his study of the history, social function and psychological effects of the boarding school system, 'These schools were conceived out of fear of the feminine, and specifically to educate young gentlemen away from the influence of females' ([2000] 2015: 108).[11] In this respect, they are probably the closest modern equivalent to the all-male socialization of boys and young men practised in the schools, universities and Inns of Court of early modern England. Boys are often separated from their mothers and sent away to board at preparatory school from the age of five in a manner analogous with the early modern practice of breeching. The pedagogical ethos and curricula of these schools are, like the early modern education system, originally based on the precepts of classical learning and to some extent this continues today. The teaching of Latin and Greek, what Bruce R. Smith calls 'a code-language that initiated boys into manhood' (1994: 83) in early modern England, reinforced gender hierarchies through language and laid 'the foundation for English patriarchy' (Sasser 2018: 159). Although the gendering of education has largely disappeared in this country, Latin and Greek are still an important part of the curriculum of public schools and it is rugby, rather than the nation's most popular sport football, that continues to dominate their playing fields.[12]

Promoted in the nineteenth century as bastions of fair play, social privilege, empire and sporting prowess, public schools have a reputation for fostering an environment of all-male homosocial, if not homoerotic, bonding. One of the natural results of separating boys from the 'influence of females' (Duffell [2000] 2015: 108) at such a key stage in their sexual and personal development is, according to Duffell, a propensity for same-sex experimentation. He explains as follows:

> It is not surprising [...] that English boarders find themselves in some difficulty with regard to their sexual education and their self-expression as sexual, loving, relational beings. But the libido is not easy to completely repress, thank God. Boarders often have little option but to turn to themselves, or to their own gender – 'blokes resorting to little boys' – for their first experience of sexual contact, as well as for some affectionate physicality.
>
> (Duffell [2000] 2015: 164)

This reputation for homoerotic experimentation has been dramatized and further reinforced in the public psyche through plays such as Julian Mitchell's *Another Country* (1982); films including *If* (1968) and *Dead Poets Society* (1989); and novels such as John Le Carré's *Our Game* (1995). Yet there is a darker side to these institutions, hinted at in Duffell's parenthetical 'blokes resorting to little boys', that has recently come to the fore through personal testaments of bullying, loneliness and both physical and sexual abuse. There are firmly established accounts of whippings and floggings during the nineteenth century at both Eton and Westminster which, as James R. Kincaid has surmised, were 'weak versions of what came later, in terms of severity and sadistic terror' (1992: 253).[13] Similar accounts of physical punishment and education through 'sadistic terror' can be found in early modern writing. John Evelyn, for example, recalls in a diary entry in 1692 how he would not go to Eton because he was 'unreasonably terrified with the report of the severe discipline there' (Evelyn [1692] 1901: 6). More disturbingly, an anonymous 1669 pamphlet accuses schoolmasters of a 'vile way of castigation, wherein our secret parts, which are by nature shameful and not to be uncovered, must be exposed to the immodest eye and filthy blows of the smiter' (Anon 1669: 11). Indeed, as Keith Thomas notes, schooling more generally in the early modern period was likely to be 'a repressive regime, governed autocratically, sustained by corporal punishment and tempered only by the master's mildness, incapacity, or financial dependence upon his pupils (1976: 66–7)'. But what was almost accepted as a commonplace in these earlier texts became a subject of close scrutiny in the late twentieth century, as the work of Nick Duffell demonstrates.

Duffell is probably the most high-profile figure currently involved in organizing support for adults traumatized by their boarding school experiences. However, his initiatives would not have been made possible without a considerable body of work to support him. Extensive research has been conducted in the past few decades into the long-term psychological damage of separating children from their families and educating them in single-sex environments at such a young age – a practice that author-activist Robert Bly, speaking for many detractors of these schools, has provocatively termed 'institutionalized child abandonment'.[14] The issues related to boarding have become so widely recognized that a specialist rhetorical shorthand has emerged to describe its effects, which include terms such as 'boarding school survivors', 'boarding school syndrome' and 'the board generation'.[15] One psychological condition associated with 'boarding school survivors' that has obvious parallels with remembrances of childhood in Hytner's *Winter's Tale* is the conflict between the so-called 'inner parent' and the 'inner child'. This condition was first identified and named by psychiatrist Eric Berne to describe a psychic split between a responsibility to conform to socially expected behavioural norms (the 'inner parent') and a desire to regress to a childish world of dependency and innocence (the 'inner child') (1961). It is a battle that is often won by the 'inner child', resulting in a developmental impasse whereby the subject is trapped in a psychic state of eternal childhood.

Although her reading is informed by queer theory rather than psychoanalysis, Kathryn Bond Stockton makes a similar observation about arrested development in her reading of *The Winter's Tale* when she says that 'Leontes's childhood wish to arrest the clock on his love with Polixenes to live inside that state, to curl up in it, adumbrates a pattern that would emerge as "gay" child suspensions centuries later' (2011: 425). For Stockton, the 'no age' of lost childhood in *The Winter's Tale* is a form of hibernation in which time is suspended and childhood advances 'in stopped motion' (2011: 423). She identifies this as a precursor to the phenomenon of the 'ghostly gay child': the inner child of a 'gay' adult whose development is discontinued at the point of homosexual self-identification or of the 'straight person's "death"'. In other words, this is a child who has grown sideways rather than in a straight (both 'unswerving' and 'heterosexual') progression (2009: 17).[16] Although Hytner's interpretation of *The Winter's Tale* was not as overtly homoerotic as Stockton's reading of the play, his use of the public-school trope was a particularly effective way of placing the two kings' relationship within a contemporary context that operated on many levels. It not only drew parallels with the homosocial, classical education of the early modern boy, but it also hinted at a sexual aspect to the boys' friendship and it gave Leontes's regressive behaviour a psycho-pathological framework, thus making the play resonate for a society which has become increasingly sensitive to the long-term effects of childhood trauma.

Although both men speak about their boyhood friendship in terms that suggest a desire to regress to their 'inner child', it is in fact only Leontes who manifests this desire in his behaviour. As Stockton explains, he 'unconsciously project[s] his feelings for Polixenes onto Hermione – making his own heat for Polixenes supposedly hers' (2011: 424). However, I contend that it is not, as Stockton asserts, so much a '"man crush" (with its roots in boyhood)', as a reciprocal relationship (2011). It is Polixenes, after all, who describes them as 'twinned lambs that did frisk i'th' sun / And bleat the one at th'other' (1.2.66–7). Although Polixenes apparently progresses to adulthood and heterosexualization, however, Leontes keeps the boyhood relationship alive through his 'inner child', as Hytner's production made so clearly manifest. The feelings he has for Polixenes, and displaces onto Hermione, are thus feelings related to his childish past rather than to his adult present. And his 'inner child', which he projects onto Mamillius, can only be metaphorically destroyed through the actual death of his young son. Polixenes's behaviour towards Florizel, on the other hand, is much closer to the typical behavioural patterns of the 'inner parent' in Berne's psychological model. As Duffell explains, the 'inner parent' is 'a distortion of adulthood [...] which is in itself a reaction to the repressed inner child'. It operates 'as a criticising and repressive force' that must 'be repressed or projected out on some other children' (2000: 199–200). In accordance with this analysis, Polixenes projects his 'inner parent' onto his son when he demands that Florizel abandon Perdita or be disinherited:

> If I may ever know thou dost but sigh
> That thou no more shalt see this knack, as never
> I mean thou shalt, we'll bar thee from succession,
> Not hold thee of our blood, no, not our kin,
> Far than Deucalion off. Mark thou my words.
>
> (4.4.432–5)

In Stockton's queer reading of the play, it is Perdita, not Florizel, who is the main casualty of the two kings' lost boyhood friendship. She is, Stockton concludes, 'love-lostness, from [Leontes's] childhood, *as* his child' and her pairing with Florizel is doomed to repeat the "blocked connection" of their fathers' love' (2011: 427). However, Florizel rebels against his father and thus breaks the cycle of the repressed child/oppressive parent dyad, enabling a full reconciliation between father and son in the final act. I suggest that, rather than Florizel or Perdita, the real casualties of what Stockton calls the 'love-lostness' between the two men are in fact Mamillius and Leontes, as the final scenes of Hytner's production made clear.

The boy playing Mamillius returned at the beginning of the second half after the interval as the choric character of Time. It is not uncommon to double the part of Mamillius with another part, whether this be with Perdita (Doran 1998/9; Mendes 2009) or Time (Kahn 1987; Hytner 2001) and in Theatre de Complicité's 1992 adaptation, with Paulina, Time and the Old Shepherd (Arden 1992). Yet Mamillius's reincarnation as Time in Hytner's production was more than a mere case of doubling, as he was wearing the same Father Time costume he had worn when reciting the sonnet in the opening frame-sequence. This boy-as-Time was the ghost of Mamillius, returning to represent the destruction of not only Leontes's child but also, and more crucially, of Leontes's 'inner child'. When the action returned from Bohemia to Sicilia in the final act, Leontes was a far more subdued, sombre and mature version of his earlier self. In the place of the schoolboy photograph of Leontes and Polixenes hung a large black-and-white portrait of an earnest-looking Mamillius, dressed in his school uniform with slicked-down hair and an unsmiling face. His image reminded us of the fate of a little boy who had always been old before his time but from whom time had also been cruelly stolen. In the centre of the stage was a large tomb with writing across the black marble covering, detailing, in accordance with the instructions of Leontes in Act 3, Scene 2, his own culpability in the curtailed childhood of his son, Mamillius. As the lights fell on the final scene, Florizel and Polixenes walked off arm in arm, Hermione and Perdita clung together in an emotional embrace, and Leontes was left to depart on his own. He had finally been able to break the psychic bonds of his 'inner child', but the costs were clear to see. The Leontes at the end of Hytner's *Tale* was a tragic figure brought down by a childhood trauma that destroyed his son, his marriage and his friendship. In a conversation with Royal Ballet choreographer Christopher Wheeldon, Hytner described *The Winter's Tale* as a 'fairly jumbled' play, suggesting that Shakespeare had got 'a little bit lazy' when he came to write it in 1611 (Monahan 2015: 11). By taking the trope of the child and locating it within a context that was legible to a twenty-first-century audience, Hytner not only made sense of the play's 'fairly jumbled' spatiotemporal dislocations, as he saw it, but accounted for the disappearance of Mamillius in a way that spoke to a society increasingly preoccupied with resurrecting the ghosts of childhood trauma and the emotional, social and familial costs involved in confronting and eventually laying them to rest. In the next section, I consider a production by Kenneth Branagh and Rob Ashford which, far from confronting the ghosts of childhood trauma, subsumed them within a narrative of redemption that kept Mamillius firmly within the bounds of the 'sub-tragic' child (Hollindale 2007: 174–91). Not only did they attempt to erase the memory of Mamillius, but they took the crisis of 'disappearing childhood' – both in Shakespeare's *Tale* and in society more generally – and made the crisis itself disappear. On the surface, it was an effective theatrical prestidigitation that smoothed over temporal and dramatic dislocations. However, beneath their comic *Tale* of reconciliation and redemption lay a submerged tale of loss whose silence spoke volumes.

A fairytale for the twenty-first century; or legitimizing child sacrifice in Kenneth Branagh and Rob Ashford's *The Winter's Tale* (2015/16)

> The surrogate victim dies so that the entire community […] can be reborn […] Understanding this process, we can also understand why death should be regarded as the elder sister, not to say the mother and ultimate source, of life itself.
>
> (Girard [1972] 2016: 293)

Capitalizing on the twenty-first-century fashion for Victoriana, Kenneth Branagh and Rob Ashford drew upon a literary tradition of sacrificial children – the 'surrogate victim' of Girard's quotation above – to present their *Tale* as a redemptive narrative with a comic resolution. In their re-imagining of the Sicilian setting as a Victorian domestic drama, Mamillius was presented less as a tragic victim than as a Dickensian 'wise child' – a creature of 'deeper wisdom, finer aesthetic sensitivity and a more profound awareness of enduring moral truths' – upon whose martyr-like death the moral regeneration of his father and the reconciliation of his family depended.[17] Unlike Hytner's Mamillius, who, in his queer prematurity, was disengaged from and seemingly oblivious to the world around him, the Mamillius of this production was a seer-like moral touchstone whose death guaranteed Edelman's 'reproductive futurism' (2004: 3) by restoring Perdita to the family fold. As writers such as Kaplan, Heilmann and Llewellyn, Boehm-Schnitker and Gruss, and Poore have observed, the trend for Victoriana has been gathering momentum over the past four decades and is now evident in many aspects of twenty-first-century Britain, from popular culture in the form of television serializations, novels, films, exhibitions and stage adaptations to the academic arena of dedicated journals, conferences and publications.[18] Although the terms 'Victoriana' and 'neo-Victorianism' encompass a wide range of literary and cultural responses to Victorian themes, Heilmann and Llewellyn have identified two 'prototypical preoccupations': 'loss, mourning, and regeneration' and 'children and the idea of children's stories' (2010: 34). Within the field of childhood studies, moreover, the Victorian period is widely accepted as the period during which, according to John R. Gillis, the 'iconization, ritualization, and mythologization' (2003: 92) of childhood originated: 'The Victorians were the first to make the child a presence in the absence of real children. They supplied Western culture with a plethora of beloved child figures – innocent, pure, timeless' (2003: 84). Framing the Sicilian scenes as a Victorian winter wonderland seen through the eyes of the child thus seemed a remarkably apposite setting for a twenty-first-century *Tale*. It not only participated in and benefitted from a widespread and current cultural phenomenon but also resonated with its dominant themes of loss, regeneration and childhood. In *The Heritage Industry*, Robert Hewison argues that the 'nostalgic impulse is an important agency in adjustment to crisis' (1987: 47). In their evocation of the literary Victorian child, the death of Mamillius thus became, for Branagh and Ashford, an act of 'seamlessly perfect surrogation' (Roach 2009: 131) – Perdita for Mamillius – that revealed anxieties about the status of childhood and its relation to futurity that were perhaps even more telling than the more direct approach of many of their predecessors.[19]

Although Branagh/Ashford's *Tale* opened, like Hytner's production, with an interpolated frame-sequence featuring the boy Mamillius, the tone and context were very different. Where Hytner's Sicilia was a twenty-first-century apartment with clean lines and a monochromatic colour-scheme, Christopher Oram's set for the Branagh/Ashford production was a warm, festive, aestheticized and unironic vision of Victoriana. The curtains rose to reveal a plush, opulent room with heavy crimson drapes enveloping marble columns and receding proscenium arches. This not only gave the stage a feeling of depth but also created a visual frame within which a child's tale might imaginatively unfold. The nineteenth-century architecture of the recently restored Garrick Theatre, with its pale-veined marble, cream and scarlet fabrics and gold-coloured fittings, contributed to the sumptuous Victorian ambience. It provided, moreover, a further frame for the play, giving a sense of a tale-within-a-tale which was particularly suited to this picture-book interpretation of the play. The Christmas setting was symbolically laden with cultural and historical meanings. As a religious festival, it recalled the ultimate Christian symbol of sacrifice and thus prefigured the dramatic sacrifice of the surrogate victim (Girard [1972] 2016: 293), Mamillius. In its more secularized manifestation, with its origins in the nineteenth century, it provided a theatrical sign-system that reinforced the Victoriana theme. As Gillis explains, during the nineteenth century, 'the newly invented, secularized family Christmas was thought of [...] as a moment when adults could reconnect not only with children but also with their own childhoods' (2003: 92). Ever since Saint Nicholas had been reinvented as the avuncular grandfatherly figure of Santa Claus in Clement Clark Moore's 'The Night Before Christmas' (1823), Victorian fathers had begun dressing up as Santa Claus, allowing them to 'enter fully into the world of their children' (2003).[20] It remains to this day a festival with a strong element of sentimentality which began with the Victorians. As Golby and Purdue explain: 'The Victorians installed the belief that Christmas is a time for the celebration of families and for the indulgence of children, and perhaps most interestingly of all, they also built into the festival a nostalgia for Christmas past' (2000: 12). Designing the Sicilian scenes as a picture-book image of Christmas domesticity was thus particularly apposite for a play and a production that was so heavily invested in the symbol of the child and, through Branagh/Ashford's Victorian setting, in exploiting the current vogue for nostalgia. Moreover, the decision to open with Mamillius rather than with the dialogue between Archidamus and Camillo was a natural extension of this child-centric focus.

The frame-sequence was staged as a dialogue between Paulina, played by Judi Dench as a compassionate, wise old sage, and Mamillius, a part rotated between the actors Pierre Atri and Rudi Goodman, aged thirteen and eleven respectively. They first appeared as two faces peering round a curtain at a glittering Christmas tree set in a toboggan-shaped base and surrounded with colourfully wrapped presents. Then, sitting down upon a bench next to the tree, Paulina handed Mamillius a present from the towering pile. As he excitedly tore off the wrapping, the tinkling sound of nursery bells rang out and a single spotlight revealed an adult Perdita, played by Jessie Buckley, singing a sentimental anthem to lost childhood. She was standing on a small round platform upstage right, directing her song downstage towards Mamillius. He was nestled in the crook of Paulina's arm, oblivious to the haunting presence of the sister he would never grow up to meet. Dressed in a pale diaphanous dress, her hair a mass of bouncing curls framing her face, Perdita appeared like an ethereal angel hovering over the set. Paulina turned to Mamillius as the song finished and, pre-empting the words attributed to Hermione in Act 2, Scene 1, said: 'Come, sir, now / I am for you again. Pray you sit by us, / And tell's a tale' (2.1.21–3). The young boy then raised an old cine film reel and announced 'A sad tale's best for winter' (2.1.25). As Paulina closed this interpolated opening frame-sequence with 'give't me in mine ear' (2.1.33) the lights dropped on the stage, allowing Perdita, Mamillius and Paulina to fade away like ghostly apparitions. The members of Leonte's court began advancing towards the stage through the two aisles either side of the auditorium seating, singing a rousing version of 'deck the halls with boughs of holly' and scattering fake snow over the audience. Then, having mounted the stage, they held a curtain around the platform where Perdita had been standing and dropped it to reveal Polixenes, Hermione and Leontes in a three-way embrace. The characters all gathered round a projector screen to watch Mamillius's cine film, a mix of original material featuring child actors and real footage of Alexei Romanov, the only son of Russian Tsar Nicholas II and great-grandson of Queen Victoria (Morrison 2016).[21] The montage of images was designed to depict Polixenes, Leontes and Hermione as young children, however analogies between Mamillius and the Romanov child were impossible to ignore. Like Mamillius, this royal heir was doomed to die young, massacred by the Bolshevik guards in 1918 at the age of fourteen. However, unlike the Tsarevich, whose death signified the end of the Romanov rule in Russia, Mamillius's death functioned as a dramatic means of safeguarding the Sicilian royal line. The ominously foreboding film notwithstanding, the whole opening sequence was an idealized image of Victorian antiquarianism, stage pictorialism and a sensory overload of music, lights and festive cheer that could have come straight from a Hollywood movie.

As Branagh revealed in an interview with the *Telegraph*, the decision to stage *The Winter's Tale* was inspired by his experience directing the 2015 film *Cinderella* for Disney Studios, which employed some of the same creative consultants as *The Winter's Tale* (Hiscock 2015). Kenneth Rothwell has observed that 'Branagh's gift is in knowing how to combine the theatrical with the filmic' (2004: 235), and it was clear to see from its sumptuous staging and orchestral score (composed by Patrick Doyle, who has worked with Branagh on sixteen films to date) that the idea of a

FIGURE 16 *Pierre Atri as Mamillius and Judi Dench as Paulina, in* The Winter's Tale, *dir. Kenneth Branagh and Rob Ashford, 2015/16. Courtesy Johan Persson/ArenaPAL.*

film version of *The Winter's Tale* in the future was, as Branagh himself confirmed, 'very much in his thoughts' when he began working on this production (Hiscock 2015). 'There is a sense of a cinema-like widescreen view from both the stalls and the circles', he observed, 'a beautiful horizontal view that chimes perfectly with the 2:35:1 cinema ratio. As a result our minds were always playing in widescreen […] so the marriage between theatre and film was woven in from the beginning of our plans' (Lollar 2015). His awareness of the widescreen aesthetics of this production was not merely related to future plans for a film version of the play but linked to a more pressing concern: the first ever live theatrical broadcast from the Garrick Theatre and Branagh's first venture into the world of the simulcast. On 26 November 2015, the evening performance of *The Winter's Tale* was broadcast live to 520 cinemas in the UK, taking £1.1 million and surpassing popular film franchise *The Hunger Games: Mockingjay – Part 2* in terms of gross revenue (Barraclough 2015). It was simultaneously screened in more than one hundred cinemas across Europe, with a delayed broadcast to the United States, Australia, Hong Kong, South Africa, China and

Japan. The live feed was captured by seven cameras and featured pre-show interviews, documentaries and a voice-over introduction from Branagh. That a production so invested in nostalgia should employ the latest digital technology to broadcast in this way seems at first glance a paradox. However, as I have already noted, *The Winter's Tale* is a play whose plot is predicated upon spatio-temporal dislocations and thus, from this perspective at least, seems a natural fit for the 'live' and 'not-quite-live' experience of the mediated broadcast. Moreover, framing the narrative through the eyes of the child is a peculiarly cinematic device, as we have seen in films such as Julie Taymor's *Titus* and Adrian Noble's *A Midsummer Night's Dream* (see Chapter 3).

Although Branagh/Ashford's production appeared to be following recent conventions with its opening frame-sequence, it had very different effects.[22] Unlike Hytner's frame-sequence, which foregrounded the absent 'no age' of childhood in the figure of the prematurely aged infant Mamillius dressed as Father Time, Branagh/Ashford used their prologue to collapse temporal difference and signal a comic/romantic resolution. By introducing Perdita at this point, they prefigured the atonement and rebirth of the final scenes and smoothed over the temporal lacuna, mitigating the deficit to be left by the death of Mamillius with a proleptic glimpse of his surrogate in the form of his sister. The prologues inserted into these two productions of *The Winter's Tale* thus established a clear generic divergence in their interpretations: tragedy for Hytner and comedy for the Branagh/Ashford production. By bringing both children onstage for the interpolated prologue, the directors of this Victorian re-imagining visually synthesized the two halves of the play and elided the sixteen-year 'no age' hiatus at its centre. The 'seamlessly perfect surrogation' (Roach 2009: 131) of one child for another, as the prologue made so apparent, enabled Leontes not only to secure but also to extend his succession through the marriage of his daughter Perdita with Florizel, the son of his childhood friend, the King of Bohemia, Polixenes. More significantly, the onstage appearance of both Perdita and Mamillius seemed designed to reassure the audience that in spite of the tragedy to unfold in the first half of the play, the 'innocent babe' (3.2.132) of the Delphic Oracle's prophecy would be found, the surrogation of one child for another would be seamless and comic order would be ultimately restored. The elegiac tone of Perdita's song thus simultaneously prefigured the death of the 'surrogate victim' Mamillius (Girard [1972] 2016: 293) and anticipated Perdita's reunion with the family, drawing a direct correlation between the two events. One was, as this prologue made clear, dependent upon and compensation for the other.

Presenting the death of Mamillius as a spiritually and emotionally edifying experience was consistent with a Victorian literary culture in which, as Victorianist David Grylls explains, 'the spectacle of a child dying... was so relished by those who were fond of children that enjoyment of it was even assumed in the potential participants' (1978: 40). Lee Edelman also turns to the Victorians for a narrative paradigm to illuminate his theory of 'reproductive futurism' (2004: 3). Taking the example of Dickens's *A Christmas Carol*, Edelman explains that Tim, the young son of Bob Cratchit who the reader is led to believe has died, actually 'survives at our expense in a culture that always sustains itself on the threat that he might die' (2004: 48). For Edelman, Tiny Tim represents the 'promise of futurity' (2004: 47), an ideology which is reinforced and sustained by the threat of its destruction. Although Shakespeare's Mamillius does, unlike Tiny Tim, in fact die, a similar process to that described by Edelman could be seen playing out in Branagh/Ashford's staging of this play, which recalled an earlier Dickens novel – *Dombey and Son* (1846–8). In this admonitory tale of paternal cruelty, Dombey Senior invests all his hopes and ambitions for the continuation of his commercial enterprise in his young son Paul, whose development into 'a grown man, the "Son" of the Firm' (1846–8: 97), he attempts to accelerate, while neglecting his older daughter, Florence ('What was a girl' asks the ironic voice of the narrator, 'to Dombey and Son!' [1846–8: 3]). Paul, however, dies while still in his infancy and after a long period of intense and self-absorbed mourning during which Dombey Senior cruelly rejects his daughter's tentative advances, the Dombey family business falls into financial ruin and Florence eventually returns to seek a reconciliation. Like Perdita, Florence is by this time a young woman of marriageable age and Dombey finally sees what he has been blind to all this time: that his daughter's children could continue the family business and that, in the words of Miss Tox, 'Dombey and Son should be a Daughter after all' (1846–8: 241).[23] Crucially, in both Branagh/Ashford's *The Winter's Tale* and Dickens's novel, the death of the boy, which in both texts is tantamount to what Peter Coveney terms 'the psychic murder of a son by his father', is recompensed by the survival of his sister (1967: 140).²⁴ As a result, the 'promise of futurity', as in *A Christmas Carol*, eventually emerges unimpaired.

The influence of Shakespeare on Dickens's writing has been well documented, and scholars have drawn parallels in the treatment of the father-daughter relationship in *Dombey and Son* and *King Lear*.²⁵ However, the similarities between *Dombey and Son* and *The Winter's Tale* have been largely overlooked.²⁶ Yet, when watching Branagh/Ashford's sentimentalized Victorian re-imagining of Shakespeare's *The Winter's Tale*, the correspondences between these two texts – a father blinded by his own selfishness who can only achieve enlightenment through the death of one child and the reconciliation with another, the restoration of patriarchal order through the daughter's marriage and the substitution of one child for another – were impossible to ignore. Both texts even feature a personification of Time that queers teleology by prematurely ageing the child to create the *puer senex* (boy/old-man) motif.²⁷ Little Paul Dombey, moreover, has an otherworldly quality that enables him to see beyond earthly materialities, a quality also brought out in the Branagh/Ashford prologue with the ghostly presence of Perdita, the temporal collision of present and future and the uncannily seer-like narrator-style function of Mamillius. He was the *puer senex*, the child propelled 'into grotesqueries of premature adulthood' to Leontes's *puer aeternus*, the adult with an 'incapacity for growth and refusal to surrender childhood' (Hollindale 2007: 176) and, like Paul Dombey Junior, Mamillius invited the audience to see the narrative through his eyes. The similarity between *Dombey and Son* and the Branagh/Ashford production in particular that was most striking, however, was the apparently seamless surrogation of one child for another. Instead of indulging what Edelman calls the 'pleasurable fantasy of survival' (2004: 45) through the *threat* of a child's death, like *A Christmas Carol*, Branagh/Ashford's *The Winter's Tale* achieved the same 'pleasurable fantasy' by compensating for the *actual* death of one child with the survival of another. By fashioning Mamillius as a Dickensian 'wise child', then, whose death is required to ensure the moral regeneration of his father and, crucially, the survival of his sister, Branagh/Ashford indulged Victorian (and 'neo-Victorian') fantasies of the ideal child – the child who never grows up – without rejecting or negating futurity itself. Thus, Branagh/

Ashford's Mamillius died while still in his infancy, Perdita was restored to the patriarchal order as a young adult and the process of 'growing up' from infant to adult was elided with a Dickensian sleight of hand without compromising Edelman's 'fantasy of survival' (Edelman 2004: 45).

One further threat to the ideology of 'reproductive futurism' (ibid.: 3) that was introduced only to be deftly averted was the suggestion of a same-sex eroticism to the friendship of Polixenes and Leontes. One critic observed that the production gestured towards but didn't quite 'have the courage of its homoerotic hints' (Szalwinska 2015). However, I contend that it was less a case of lack of courage than one of deliberate intent. The opening image of Leontes, Polixenes and Hermione locked in a three-way embrace certainly suggested a complex sexual relationship like the one dramatized in Sonnet 144 (see above). However, any impression of homoeroticism (or indeed heteroeroticism) was almost immediately neutralized by the decidedly asexual and 'buttoned-up' (Hemming 2015) performance of Branagh as the jealous king, Leontes. Even when descending into a barely articulate rage, he maintained tight-lipped control throughout, spitting out the sexually loaded alliterative 'sluiced' (1.2.193), 'slippery' (1.2.271), 'bag and baggage' (1.2.205), 'paddling palms and pinching fingers' (1.2.115) with a puritanical horror. This performance of childish regression, moreover, was thrown into high relief by the erotically charged Bohemian scenes. In an extended song-and-dance routine that was more reminiscent of Rodgers and Hammerstein than Dickens, perky shepherdesses wrapped their legs around the waists of 'strapping bare-chested shepherds' (Szalwinska 2015), and Perdita glowed with rustic sensuality and 'erotic fervour' (Billington 2015). The marked change in tone made the asexual Victorian asceticism of the Sicilian scenes even more notable. For instance, when Leontes eventually reached his jealous climax in Act 1 and curled into a tight foetal position at the front of the stage, Polixenes and a heavily pregnant Hermione were shown skating innocently across a frozen lake in the background. This juxtaposition of madness and serenity was unequivocal in its intention: to show Leontes's sickness to be an infection of the mind rather than a suspicion based in any reality. His was less a performance of sexual jealousy than a desperation to regress to an infantile state of helplessness and to reclaim an unattainable pre-sexual childhood idyll. This was entirely consistent with the idealized Victorian setting, as Dickens scholar Amberyl Malkovich explains:

> The romanticized notions of the Victorian child set children apart from adults and childhood became something to be protected and preserved. Such children were presented as innocent, loving, religious, and, above all, *untouched by human misery and knowledge*. They were examples of mankind before Eve plucked her sinful apple, *and thus a status to which culture and society could never return or attain* (my emphasis).
>
> (2013: 89)

Unlike the public-school setting of Hytner's production, which evoked literary and cultural associations with the homoerotic, the Victorian framework for Branagh's performance capitalized upon a collective cultural nostalgia for domesticity and family values that was firmly rooted in heteronormative, albeit de-eroticized, foundations: heteronormative in terms of a desire to connect with the child and de-eroticized because of a paradoxical desire to connect with one's own childhood. This was a paradox which, as Gillis has observed, had its roots firmly in the Victorian period (2003: 102–3). It was only after the announcement of the death of his son that Branagh's Leontes finally broke free from his regressive behaviour (the desire to connect with his own childhood) and began to behave with the dignity and self-possession that was to signal the onset of enlightenment and atonement (through the ultimate connection with his daughter). The death of Mamillius, like the death of the virtuous Dickensian child, was 'almost indispensable as a moral preservative' for this Victorianized version of Shakespeare's play (Grylls 1978: 136).

Branagh remarked in an interview that he saw *The Winter's Tale* 'very much as a fairytale' (Hiscock 2015), and in keeping with the mid-Victorian trend for the socially responsible and ethically edifying fairytale (Zipes 1989: xix–xx), he gave his own interpretation a moral touchstone (in addition to but closely associated with the 'wise child' Mamillius as the opening scenes made clear) in the figure of Judi Dench. Dench's long and successful stage, television and film career has earned her the admiration and affection of the public and press alike, with epithets such as 'national treasure' and 'cultural icon' regularly applied to her name. Her face, while unremarkable in terms of conventional ideals of beauty, is capable of expressing subtle changes of emotion; her voice has a distinctive husky quality with a tendency to break or catch at key moments; and her acting style conveys an authenticity and generosity of spirit that transmits to both stage and screen audiences. Stanley Wells describes her as 'the best loved English actress since Ellen Terry', explaining that 'her success on stage, like Ellen Terry's, is indivisible from the personality that enables it' (2012: 37). Michael L. Quinn explains this phenomenon of perceived indivisibility of celebrity and role as follows:

> Celebrities, almost by definition, substitute this 'someone' that we seem to know apart from the play. They bring something to the role other than a harmonious blend of features, an overdetermined quality that exceeds the needs of the fiction, and keeps them from disappearing entirely into the acting figure of the drama. Rather, their contribution to the performance is often a kind of collision with the role, sometimes hard to accept, but sometimes, too, loaded with the spectacular energy that an explosive crash can release.
>
> (1990: 155)

In the case of Judi Dench, the 'collision' released the sympathetic rather than the shrewish aspects of the role of Paulina, conveying a sensitivity that softened the overall tragic aspects of this play and gave the production a patina of authority and authenticity. The directors capitalized upon this 'collision' by expanding and doubling her role so that she was an almost constant feature throughout the Sicilian scenes. As well as opening the play with the interpolated prologue by the Christmas tree, she also closed the first half, comforting a devastated Leontes as he limped off the set. She then reappeared in the second half as the character Time, announcing in her reassuringly 'distinctive vocal husk' (Wolf 2015) the sixteen-year temporal 'slide' (4.1.5) and the geographical shift from Sicilia to 'fair Bohemia' (4.1.21). Casting Dench in the dual roles of Paulina and Time enabled the directors to further reinforce the causal connection between the two distinct parts of the play, smoothing over the spatio-temporal disjunctions and seamlessly transferring focus, and the associated promise of futurity, from Mamillius to Perdita. When the action returned to Sicilia after the sensuous festivities of the Bohemian scenes (even the conflict with Polixenes did not significantly threaten the light-hearted tone of this sensuous bucolic interlude), the set had been transformed into an ice-encrusted palace and Leontes into a grey-haired old man, still being supported by Dench's indomitable but compassionate Paulina.

To complement the reassuring presence of Paulina, there was also a visual symmetry to the opening and close of the play that reinforced the sense of continuity and causality. The ending was, in the words of Michael Billington, 'unfashionably [...] unequivocal' (2015) in its romantic/comic sense of closure. Camillo embraced Paulina, Florizel hugged Perdita and in an evocation of the opening sequence, Leontes held one arm around Polixenes and the other around Hermione, clutching them both to him in a tight embrace. There was no place for Mamillius in this final tableau, whether in a sober portrait like the Hytner revival or as a marble statue, like Christopher Wheeldon's ballet. The surrogation of one child for another had been almost perfectly seamless, offering what Poore calls a 'satisfying [...] Dickensian ending' which secured the future through an evocation of the past (2012: 96). In an essay by Russell Jackson printed in the programme for this production, the death of Mamillius is described as 'the collateral damage that accompanies many happy endings' (2015: v). For Jackson, as for Branagh and Ashford, the death of Mamillius was clearly a necessary, if regrettable, casualty in Leontes's path towards redemption. Jackson's essay gave their production choices academic authority, and Victoriana provided a literary context of loss, regeneration and the 'wise child' that legitimized the 'collateral damage' (2015) represented in the death of Mamillius.

In his book-length study *Violence and the Sacred*, from which the epigraph quoted at the beginning of this section is taken, René Girard coins the term 'sacrificeable victims' ([1972] 2016: 4). These are, Girard explains, the victims upon whom society 'seek[s] to deflect [...] the violence that would otherwise be vented on its own members, the people it most desires to protect' ([1972] 2016). In order to qualify as 'sacrificeable', they must not only be indispensable, but, and this is crucial for understanding the process of sacrifice played out in this production, they must 'bear a *resemblance* to the object they replace' ([1972] 2016: 12). In Shakespeare's text,

Leontes looks for resemblance in his son's face when he says: 'Looking on the lines / Of my boy's face, methoughts I did recoil / Twenty-three years, and saw myself unbreeched' (1.2.153–5). In tracing his son's features Leontes sees traces of his own childhood self, a 'copy' stamped from his own facial mould. In this respect, his son stands in as a 'surrogate victim', sacrificed in order that Leontes can be released from his childish attachments. However, Branagh/Ashford took this concept of surrogacy and substitution one step further by adding a further dimension of 'resemblance'. Their interpolated frame-sequence drew direct correlations between Mamillius and Perdita which, as in the case of Dombey Junior and Florence, created an apparently seamless sibling surrogation. Not only did this Mamillius function as a symbolic substitution for the child-self of Leontes's past, but he also provided a 'sacrificeable' surrogate for Perdita, thus securing the union of the two kingdoms and the future succession of Leontes's reign. Mamillius became, in other words, the victim sacrificed in order to protect the integrity of the royal crown. However, somewhat ironically, in the process of securing and sustaining ideologies of Edelman's 'reproductive futurism' (2004: 3), the directors not only legitimized the sacrifice of a child, but in doing so, smoothed over the 'no age' of disappearing childhood represented by his absence.

In addition to the 'wise child' trope and other cultural and literary associations evoked by the Victorian setting outlined above, there were additional crucial contextual and intertextual factors that seemed designed to influence audience expectation, reception and understanding of this production. The first of these was the decision to stage the play in repertory with a double bill of Terence Rattigan plays, *All On Her Own* (1968) and *Harlequinade* (1948). In his study of theatre as a memory machine, Marvin Carlson describes this practice as a form of theatrical ghosting which 'encourag[es] audiences to allow one play or production to enrich the experience of another' (2003: 104). This is achieved by 'gradually building up a structure of interlocking memories as audiences experience each new element of the work haunted by the experience of previous elements' (2003). Branagh and Ashford maximized the potential for theatrical haunting in this way by using an almost identical ensemble cast in both productions. The only major replacement was the veteran celebrity actor: Judi Dench as Paulina in *The Winter's Tale* was replaced with Zoe Wanamaker as Rosemary

Hodge in the dramatic monologue *All On Her Own* and the tipsy theatrical old-timer Dame Maude in *Harlequinade*. Like Dench, Wanamaker has a long and eclectic stage and television history. She has, moreover, close ties with Shakespeare in the cultural imaginary through the tireless endeavours of her late father, Sam Wanamaker, in reconstructing Shakespeare's Globe on the Bankside. Although some fifteen years younger than Dench, she is held in comparable high esteem and affection by theatre audiences and thus was an apposite substitution in the two partner plays.

The Rattigan plays are linked thematically, both to each other and to *The Winter's Tale*, through their central focus on time, loss and nostalgia and their metatheatrical self-awareness. While *All On Her Own* is a bitter-sweet elegy, *Harlequinade* is a slapstick burlesque that celebrates, while also affectionately making fun of, the mechanics of theatre. Branagh exploited his reputation as an over-earnest thespian by playing *Harlequinade*'s Gosport as a flamboyant, pretentious and self-aggrandizing actor-manager. While rehearsing his ageing Romeo opposite a much younger Juliet, for instance, he donned an absurdly ill-fitting wig and jumped skittishly across the stage, posturing and gesticulating like an eighteenth-century tragedian. He was, in short, playing up to the 'luvvie' (Swain 2015) and 'thespily mannered' (Letts 2015) reputation he has acquired among some critics over his career. Where Dench's celebrity reputation coincided rather than collided with the role of Paulina to emphasize the softer aspects of her character, Branagh's rather more ambivalent celebrity status lent his performance as Gosport a gloss of ironic self-parody. This, in turn, gave audience reception of his Leontes a sympathetic and comic context, which de-emphasized the tragic aspects of Shakespeare's generically unstable play.

Kenneth Branagh the celebrity is a complex blend of antagonistic qualities. Both mainstream and anti-establishment, conservative and radical, idol and scapegoat, his reputation has fluctuated back and forth throughout his career. How spectators negotiate between these binaries depends upon their own experience and interpretation of Branagh the man and Branagh the actor, and the extent to which they have been influenced by the vast and contradictory press coverage. Over his long career as a Shakespearean actor/director of stage and screen, his private life has been scrutinized and his professional accomplishments, initially greeted with accolades, have later met with opprobrium. This practice is so well established that it is commonly termed 'Branagh-bashing' and is neatly summarized by Paul Taylor writing in the *Independent*:

> 'Branagh-bashing' had long been a national sport in newspapers, as dependable an activity as those annual bouts of over-hyping Tim Henman. Our cultural preference for self-deprecation and good losers was affronted by this working-class Belfast-born boy from Reading who, having gone through RADA and the RSC, had the temerity to found his own Renaissance Theatre Company at the grand old age of 26, then dare to court comparison with Laurence Olivier by directing and starring in his own movie version of *Henry V* (1989) and then add insult to injury by mounting a charm offensive on Hollywood.
>
> (Taylor 2013b)[28]

In the past few years, there has been a general trend towards a more moderate response to Branagh's life and work, evidenced in the largely positive media reaction to his knighthood in 2012 and to his central role in the 2012 Olympic opening ceremony.[29] However, some critics still indulge in 'Branagh-bashing', as the review by Quentin Letts of Branagh's performance as Leontes exemplifies: 'Sir Ken, with inky whiskers, is thespily mannered, elongating certain syllables, skating over others. Maybe', he adds caustically, 'a little irritating' (2015). Ann Treneman, writing in *The Times*, takes a similarly disdainful tone, remarking that Branagh's performance was 'mystifyingly OTT', adding that she 'felt like calling the emergency services and reporting a severe case of over-acting' (2015), while the *Evening Standard* reviewer termed his Leontes 'over-egged and earnestly elaborate' (Hitchings 2015). Marianka Swain, reviewing his performance as Gosport in *Harlequinade*, asked whether Branagh 'deliberately programme[d] a critique of luvvie foibles as a commentary on his own overwrought "Winter's Tale"' and concluded that Branagh's company 'runs the risk of offering more to its actors than its audiences' (2015). Letts, Hitchings and Treneman can be accused of lazy journalism, but Swain completely misses the point. Branagh's decision to stage *The Winter's Tale* in repertory with a play that parodied his reputation for 'thespily mannered' overacting is clearly intended as a (meta)theatrical riposte to his more severe critics. 'He reminds us', remarks Dominic Cavendish writing in the *Telegraph*, 'that he has a sense of humour' (2015). But his performance went even further than this. It also reminded us (the audience) that theatre is a place of make-believe and a medium for telling a story. Branagh is evidently an extremely self-reflective director and demonstrates self-awareness and thoughtfulness when discussing his artistic methodology. In an interview with *The Stage* online, he made the following comments: 'I've always been interested, I hope not in a self-indulgent way, in performance. In a way, that is partly why writers like Shakespeare and Rattigan in this case also use theatre and performance so regularly as a metaphor for examining what is real in people's lives' (Shenton 2015). This attunement to the performance aspects of theatre was crucial to understanding his production of *The Winter's Tale*. In this context of metaphor and fairytale, Mamillius's death was all-too-easily glozed over. It was the 'collateral damage' (Jackson 2015: v) necessary for and compensated by the reconciliations and, crucially, for the preservation of 'reproductive futurism' (Edelman 2004: 3) at the heart of his redemptive tale.

Although not all of the audience members would have seen both plays (the Shakespeare and the Rattigan double bill), one set of publicity material, including the programme, was produced for the two productions, making it less easy to extricate the joyful, self-parodying, highly metatheatrical mood of the Rattigan plays from their experience of *The Winter's Tale*.[30] The concurrent staging of the two productions seemed in fact to be a deliberate invitation to see them as a whole. In an interview printed at the front of his self-edited version of *The Winter's Tale* script, Branagh is quoted as saying that 'when you do several plays together, I think there is a particular interchange of ideas and support' (2015: xv). While *The Winter's Tale* was inevitably tinged with a degree of sadness, the Rattigan plays emphasized the comedic and fantastical elements of Shakespeare's play. The discovery by Gosport of a grown-up daughter and grandchild, moreover, drew further attention to the comedy (the discovery of Perdita) rather than the tragedy (the loss of Mamillius) of his *Tale*. This was further reinforced when Gosport was depicted holding auditions for his own upcoming production of *The Winter's Tale*. Mistaking his stage-manager's fiancée for an auditionee, he gives what he thinks is an aspiring Perdita a brief synopsis of the plot:

JACK
Oh, Mr. Gosport.
ARTHUR
Yes.
JACK
Could I introduce Miss Langland?
ARTHUR
Oh. How do you do? Have you read *The Winter's Tale*?
JOYCE
Er – no. I'm afraid I haven't.
ARTHUR
Well it's not a difficult part. It's about a girl who's abandoned by her father when she's a baby, and then many years later they meet –

(Rattigan [1948] 2015: 30)

Although this is intended to provide an ironic reflection of Gosport's own 'abandoned' daughter, the way in which it glosses over the death of Mamillius and focuses entirely on the father-daughter relationship is also a remarkably apposite reflection of the Branagh/Ashford production of *The Winter's Tale*. Seeing this unusual pairing as a repertory in dialogue – an 'interchange of ideas' (Rattigan [1948] 2015: xv), in Branagh's own words – thus inevitably diluted, even if it did not entirely eradicate, the absence of Mamillius and the tragic undertones of Shakespeare's play.

There was one further layer of intertextuality which illuminated the intention and effects of pairing the Rattigan/Shakespeare plays in this way. In 1995 Branagh wrote and directed a feature film, *A Midwinter's Tale* (produced and released in the UK and outside of the United States under the title *In the Bleak Midwinter*).[31] Like *Harlequinade*, it is a burlesque comedy about an ill-fated provincial Shakespearean production, in this case *Hamlet*. It is clear to see the thematic overlaps between *Harlequinade* and *A Midwinter's Tale*. However, what is more revealing is the way in which Branagh brought this film into dialogue with his very own film version of *Hamlet* (1996) and what that reveals about his approach to the repertory pairing of the Rattigan/Shakespeare plays. Emma Smith has argued that *A Midwinter's Tale* functioned as 'a scapegoat, diverging what is potentially ridiculous and laughable about the play itself, siphoning off *Hamlet*'s dangerous proximity to comedy, and leaving the film of *Hamlet* as generically pure and serious high art' (2000: 137).[32] Watching the two films side-by-side it is clear to see that the earlier release did indeed function as a comic counterpoint to the latter, purging it of its parodic potential and pre-empting any criticisms of bathetic over-earnestness or self-importance that it might attract. Where Branagh emphasized the *difference* between these two films (different casts, budgets, lengths, genres, shooting styles, etc.), the pairing of *Harlequinade* with *The Winter's Tale* seemed designed to draw attention to their similarities. Moreover, although, as Smith suggests, there are moments in *Hamlet* that veer dangerously into comedic territory, the ending is unequivocally tragic. *The Winter's Tale*, on the other hand, is far more generically unstable and therefore open to interpretation. What the Rattigan plays provided was a comic context for his Shakespearean tale of redemption, and the 'collateral damage' (Jackson 2015: v) of Mamillius's untimely death, in this context, might (perhaps) seem a relatively small price to pay.

Conclusion

For Kenneth Branagh and Rob Ashford, then, the tragedy of Mamillius was obviated by locating the tale in a Victorian setting and thus enabling a representation of childhood that, like the more general trend for Victoriana, was reactionary, nostalgic and an evasion of twenty-first-century cultural and social realities. Like Dickens's Little Nell or Paul Dombey Junior, Mamillius had to be sacrificed before he lost his idealized innocence. It was a production that emphasized the fairytale aspects of Shakespeare's play, and Mamillius was a fundamental and instrumental element of the narrative process, subsumed in his own 'sad tale' (2.1.25) through the seamless surrogation with Perdita. For Hytner, the 'no age' of childhood was recontextualized within a post-boarding-school world of arrested development and regressive psycho-pathological behaviours. Mamillius was less a fully rounded character than the projected 'inner child' of his father, unnaturally, to borrow Postman's terminology, 'adultified' ([1982] 1994: 126), yet simultaneously memorialized as the 'boy eternal' (1.2.65) of his fantasies. For Branagh/Ashford, the theatre was presented as a platform for indulging feelings of nostalgia, sentimentality and childhood fantasies while simultaneously glossing over the modern crisis facing childhood and its sustainability. For Hytner, it was a harsh lesson in the dangers of indulging regressive childish fantasies and reifying nostalgic ideals of childhood innocence and, in the process, of erasing the crucial developmental stage between infancy and adulthood – the 'no age' of childhood itself. Although the directors approached the play from seemingly irreconcilably different positions, they were in fact reflecting the same issues, albeit through different lenses. What these productions revealed was a society intent on indulging in nostalgia, an 'incurable modern condition' which is, as Svetlana Boym suggests, 'a sentiment of loss and displacement' and 'a romance with one's own fantasy' (2001: xiii). *The Winter's Tale* has proved to be a particularly popular vehicle in the past few years for expressing this peculiarly 'modern condition' with Mamillius, the child at the centre of the narrative, as an apposite symbol of 'loss', 'displacement' and adult fantasies.

Conclusion

Performing Childhood: Shakespeare and Beyond

What Kenneth Branagh and Rob Ashford tried to evade in their adaptation of *The Winter's Tale*, Christopher Wheeldon and Nicholas Hytner made unequivocally apparent: that in the final scene of reconciliation and redemption 'a dead five- or six-year-old boy remain[ed] unaccounted for' (Cavell 2003: 193). There was to be no miraculous resurrection for Mamillius, the 'collateral damage' (Jackson 2015: v) of Leontes's actions and a tragic symbol of loss, displacement and nostalgia for an unrecoverable past. The children of Shakespeare's plays are all, in their various forms, symbols of loss. Mamillius represents the ravages of time and the futility of indulging nostalgic fantasies; the children of *Titus Andronicus* are helpless tools of their fathers' self-destructive revenge narratives and symbols of a future doomed to repeat the mistakes of the past; and the dead, imagined and mourned babes of *Richard III* and *Macbeth* symbolize death and destruction on a catastrophic national scale.

In the past few decades, as I have argued throughout this book, Shakespeare's children have been mobilized in performance to signify another type of loss that speaks to a peculiarly postmodern crisis: the loss of childhood itself. Although attitudes towards childhood have fluctuated over history, what makes this present crisis particularly significant is a remarkable convergence of thinking across institutional structures. The technological revolution not only created anxieties about children gaining access to adult knowledge, as argued by Postman, but also exposed them to dangers and temptations beyond the control of their parents in the form of predatory paedophiles, marketing campaigns and cyberbullying. At the same time, advances in technology gave rise to the instantaneous broadcasting of mediated images of children across multiple media platforms, creating emotive visual narratives, emblematized in the Bulger footage, that emphasized both their vulnerability and their potential for evil and, perhaps more crucially, the impossibility of distinguishing between the two. Recent legislative changes have also contributed to this sense of crisis by extending the rights and responsibilities of children while simultaneously extending the age of dependency.

There is a vast body of scholarship addressing the historiography of childhood and what it means to be a child in this era of seismic ideological, technological, legal and attitudinal change. I am certainly not the first to suggest that there is a correlation between technological advances and a widespread 'moral panic' (Cohen 2002: ix–x) regarding our children. However, while some important work has been done on the Shakespearean child in performance, this book is the first consolidated study to consider the performance of childhood specifically in relation to this remarkable set of circumstances. Perhaps inevitably, my research has generated more questions than it has answered and there are areas that are underrepresented in this book. While I did not intentionally set out to write exclusively about male children, for instance, the main focus of my research has been the boy characters. One key area for further scholarship that I would like to explore is the role of the girls, particularly in relation to their fathers or father figures. Research by Jennifer Higginbotham and Deanne Williams has recently expanded our understanding of the significance of Shakespeare's girls in their early modern context. I would like to explore what contemporary manifestations of these characters might reveal about recent trends in attitudes towards gender and childhood. I am thinking principally of Perdita and Leontes in *The Winter's Tale*, Antiochus and his daughter in *Pericles*, Cymbeline and Imogen in *Cymbeline*, Princess Elizabeth and King Richard in *Richard III*, and Prospero and Miranda in *The Tempest*. I believe that there is a study to be written on how questions of chastity, procreation, marriage and incest inform these relationships and how these issues have been represented in contemporary productions of stage and screen.

There is also an obvious bias towards Shakespeare in my project. In recent years, the expansion of scholarship into the work of other early modern playwrights such as John Webster, John Ford, Christopher Marlowe, Thomas Middleton and Ben Jonson has been accompanied by a growing performance history both on stage and on screen. Although scholars such as Pascale Aebischer (2012), Roberta Barker (2007) and Sarah Werner (2001 and 2010) have produced important scholarship that engages with the ways in which these contemporaries of Shakespeare are given a contemporary relevance in modern productions, there is still work to be done on the significance of the child in relation to the current crisis. Three plays that immediately stand out in this regard are John Webster's *The Duchess of Malfi* and *The White Devil* and Christopher Marlowe's *Edward II*. Who can forget the ending to Derek Jarman's film adaptation of *Edward II*? The closing shot of eleven-year-old Jody Graber as Edward III, dressed in his mother's earrings and heels and dancing to Tchaikovsky's 'Dance of the Sugar Plum Fairy' on top of a cage containing Isabella and Mortimer, is one that certainly invites closer analysis.

Although I have limited my scope to four key plays, I have demonstrated how contemporary concerns about childhood are not only reflected in the manifestation of the Shakespearean child in performance, but that the performances themselves have actively contributed to the debate, even if unintentionally or through deliberate evasion. As I have shown, in the work of some directors, notably Roman Polanski, Julie Taymor and more recently, Kenneth Branagh and Rob Ashford, the fetishization of the child is still evident, and at times this has resulted in a manifestation of its more sinister, eroticized shadow. Other productions have subverted idealized images of childhood by substituting the child in performance with surrogates, as in the case of Thomas Ostermeier's production of *Richard III* and Christopher Wheeldon's *The Winter's Tale*, or by juxtaposing 'evil' and 'innocence', as in Michael Boyd's and Justin Kurzel's *Macbeths*. In stagings by Jamie Lloyd and Nicholas Hytner, the death of the child has been mobilized as a symbol for a wider social malaise, bringing into question Edelman's assumptions of the child as emblem of futurity and the very idea of the future as progress. Marjorie Garber's assertion in 1997 that 'there are very few children in Shakespeare's plays' and that they 'are not, by and large, successful characters' (1997: 30) has been dramatically disproved by these examples. If success can be determined by a character's capacity to signify beyond the sum of his/her spoken lines, then all of the children I have studied are, I argue, extremely 'successful' characters that carry considerable figural weight. By focusing my analysis on these particular children, I hope I have provided a critical framework and methodology for further exploring how the oft-overlooked and underestimated child characters of Shakespeare and his contemporaries have reflected and informed debates about what it means to be a child in this current climate of doubt and uncertainty and beyond.

NOTES

Introduction

1. Kenneth MacMillan's version of *Romeo and Juliet* in 1965 was the last full-length Shakespearean adaptation to premiere at the Royal Opera House.
2. I use 'postmodern' here and throughout to refer to the historical period from the last few decades of the twentieth century to the present day.
3. This claim ought to be qualified with an acknowledgment that only a fragment of early modern playtexts remains in circulation today.
4. My appropriation of Geertz's phraseology here is based on his definition of 'thick description' as 'sorting out the structures of signification [...] and determining their social ground and import' (1973: 9). I am using it as a means of differentiating from 'thin description', being description without interpretation, and thus providing a more context-based interpretation which seeks to place what I see in performance within a cultural and intertextual frame of reference.
5. Mulvey's polemical essay has been challenged since its first publication for adopting a narrow feminist perspective that assumes a white, heterosexual, masculine 'gaze' as the dominant ideological structure of narrative cinema. These limitations notwithstanding, her analysis of 'the voyeuristic-scopophilic look' is a useful perspective from which to consider the Shakespearean child as object of the gaze in stage and film productions.
6. For analysis of the postmodern narrative of a 'childhood in crisis', see, for instance, Postman ([1982] 1994); Scraton (1997); Higonnet (1998); Buckingham (2000); Willem and Zuckerman (2003); Jenks (2005); Cunningham (2005, 2006); and Faulkner (2011, 2013).
7. A crucial legislative outcome arising from the debate around the Bulger killers and criminal responsibility was the passing of the 1998 Crime and Disorder Act in England and Wales. This Act granted local authorities more responsibilities for reducing crime and disorder

and, crucially, abolished rebuttable presumption of *doli incapax* (incapable of wrong): the presumption that a child between the years of ten and fourteen is incapable of committing an offence. Although the Act was passed five years after the killing of James Bulger it came 'out of the process of demonisation and the sensationalism created around [it]', and there is still, in 2017, 'little appetite to change' while the case remains in the public consciousness (Phil Scraton cited in Torney 2011). See also Gerry (2017) for arguments in favour of reinstating *doli incapax*.

8   See Kincaid (1992); Rose (1993: 3–4); and Roth (2009: 23–36).

Chapter 1

1   See Blake (1994: 124–5) and Knowles (2014: 146–7) for an analysis of Cibber's changes to the children's roles.
2   See, for instance, Elgot (2015) and Kingsley and Timur (2015).
3   For a full analysis of the representation of the children in Olivier's and Loncraine's films, see Munro (2005b: 161–77).
4   Although *Richard III* was included among the histories in the First Folio, all title pages (Quartos 1–6 and Folio – see bibliography for full details) classify the play as a tragedy. See Smidt's parallel edition of the texts (1969: 28–9).
5   It is common practice in modern productions to cut both Clarence's children and the page. See, for instance, Mendes (1992, 2011); Silbert (2012); Carroll (2012); Lloyd (2014); Ostermeier (2015); and Goold (2016). In Shakespeare's theatre, it was likely that the same child actors would have played both the princes and Clarence's children and the page.
6   In Cibber's adaptation, it is Catesby who introduces Richard to Tyrrel in the absence of the page character. Other directors have since followed suit, reassigning the role to another adult character.
7   Oxford single edition and complete works, Norton Shakespeare, Arden Shakespeare and RSC Shakespeare all follow this convention.
8   I calculated the total line length by counting each line as it appears on *EEBO*.
9   The scenes in which the pageboy appeared were Act 1, Scenes 1 and 3; Act 4, Scenes 2 and 4; Act 5, Scenes 3, 4 and 5.
10 In Russell Jackson's account of this final scene, the page 'hamstrung Richard (at least in some early performances) as he lay on the battle field and then handed his sword to Richmond' (cited in Munro 2005b: 176). The archival recording I viewed in the SBT only

showed the page taking the sword. There was no indication that he had 'hamstrung' Richard, although this would be consistent with the way in which his character was developed in this production.
11 Shakespeare omitted the following elements that were present in the source material: the numerous references to Jane Shore, the Archbishop's persuasion of the Queen to give up the Duke of York and, most significantly, the depiction of the princes' murder.
12 Puppet is defined in the *OED* as follows: 'puppet, **1.** An image of a human being or a person or thing resembling one; **1a** *depreciative*. An idolatrous image, an idol; any material object that is worshipped; **b.** A (typically small) figure representing a human being; a child's doll. Cf. Poppet; **2a.** A model of a person or animal that can be manipulated to mimic natural movement; (originally) a figure with jointed limbs moved from above by strings or wires, a marionette; (subsequently also) a figure supported and moved from below by rods, or a figure made to be fitted over and moved by the hand, finger, etc.; **2b.** A person who impersonates another; an actor, *esp.* an inferior one; **3.** *derogatory*. A person, esp. a woman, whose (esp. gaudy) dress or manner is thought to suggest a lack of substance or individuality.' As Carol Chillington Rutter has observed, Shakespeare's use of the word 'puppet' throughout his plays is invariably derogatory, used as an epithet to reduce women to 'instruments made to do other people's cultural work' (2017: 64).
13 See, for instance, Hobgood (2015) and Williams (2009).
14 For a full analysis of Craig's 'Über-marionette', see Fisher (2009) and Taylor (2014).

Chapter 2

1 See, for instance, Bristol (2000) and Rutter (2004).
2 See Boxer and Quataert (1987: 37) and Callaghan (1992: 369).
3 Both Jonathan Pryce and Sinead Cusack have also provided illuminating insights into their inspirations for the backstory of bereavement that informed their performances as Macbeth and Lady Macbeth respectively. For Cusack, see Rutter (1988: 53–72); for Jonathan Pryce, see Rutter (2007a: 175–6).
4 Archival materials for the 1985 and 1993 Tron Theatre productions of *Macbeth* consist of a programme for the 1993 production and a flier and cast list for the 1985 production, provided courtesy of Glasgow University Archives and limited secondary accounts. Information on the theatre was taken

from the Tron Theatre official website: https://www.tron.co.uk/docs/059_303__historyleaflet2015largeprint_1425563706.pdf (accessed 26 January 2016).
5   Unpublished copy of *Macbeth Possessed* provided by the Tron Theatre.
6   Adrian Noble's 1986 production also featured the three children playing blind man's buff with Macbeth. For Rutter, this was one particularly noteworthy instance of the way in which Noble 'made children equivocal, saturated signs of the equivocations the *Macbeth* text everywhere produces' (2007b: 179).
7   Roman Polanski himself was detained and pleaded guilty to charges of unlawful sexual intercourse with a thirteen-year-old girl in 1977. He fled to Europe, where he remains at time of writing, following a decision to refuse an extradition request by the US legal authorities. For more details, see Harding (2009) and Connolly (2010).
8   Arden Shakespeare Third Series glosses 'cursed' as 'the guilt Banquo feels in recalling the Witches' prophecies for him, or to the prophecies themselves' (2015: 172); Penguin Books edition notes: 'Just before the fatal deed Banquo is reintroduced beside Macbeth to highlight the central distinction between a moral will and a moralizing imagination' (1967: 118). Of course, in Holinshed, one of Shakespeare's sources for the play, Banquo is Macbeth's accomplice in the murder of Duncan.
9   In famous artistic representations of Cupid, such as Raphael's *The Triumph of Galatea* (1512) or Caravaggio's *Amor Vincit Omnia* (1601–2) and *Sleeping Cupid* (1608), the boy is naked with his genitalia on display. While Polanski's Fleance is fully dressed, first in hunting costume and then in full armour (the change occurs between his appearance at the foot of the bed and the shot of him climbing onto the bed), the associations with these famous paintings are clear to see.
10 See in particular Deats (1986) and Williams (2004).

Chapter 3

1   For a full analysis of the authorial debate and discussion of sources and influences, see Bate (2003: 79–92) and Weber (2014).
2   The only amendment Warner made was to translate 'Terras Astraea reliquit' (4.3.4) into English ('the goddess of Justice has left the earth'). See Dessen (1989: 58).
3   See, for instance, Phelan (1993) and, less emphatically, Sontag (1966).

4   Peter Brook's seminal production in 1955 for the RSC marked the relaunch of this play for the modern audience. It was a pared-back production (a total of 650 lines were cut) with stylized violence and a ritualistic aesthetic.
5   After a hiatus following Trevor Nunn's 1966 production of *The Revenger's Tragedy* for the RSC, Di Trevis's 1987 RSC revival was followed by four productions in the 1990s and three since 2010. Following Deborah Warner's revival of *Titus Andronicus*, there were two further productions at the RSC: a production directed by Bill Alexander in 2003 and Yukio Ninagawa's touring production in 2006.
6   One notable instance of this grotesquerie was Brian Cox's Titus entering in Act 5 dressed in a chef's outfit to a chorus whistling 'Heigh-ho' from the animated Disney film of *Snow White and the Seven Dwarfs*.
7   Jonathan Bate makes this observation in *Titus Andronicus* (2003: 204, n. 265). In the recording I viewed in the archives, I can confirm that Cox did indeed laugh for a full ten seconds.
8   See also Belsey: 'No evidence exists of any apprentices in the adult companies under 11 or 12 years old, though it is possible that little boys acted on stage before they were bound' (2005: 61).
9   For analysis of the ways in which material items were used to establish early modern gender, see Fisher (2006).
10 See also Smith (2003: 296–7).
11 *Titus Andronicus: The Movie* (1996); *Titus Andronicus* (1999); *Titus* (1999); and *Titus Andronicus* (2000). See Rothwell (2004: 328–66) for full filmography.
12 In addition to the thirty-six plays of the First Folio, *Pericles, Prince of Tyre*, from the first impression of the Third Folio was also included. *The Two Noble Kinsmen* was omitted because it was decided that it was predominantly John Fletcher's work.
13 See also Bly (2000).
14 For an analysis of child's play as it relates to violence, see Faulkner (2011: 34–43).
15 The campaign speeches appear in Act 1, Scene 1, in Quarto and Folio editions of Shakespeare's play, but are placed directly after the interpolated opening sequence in Taymor's film. The area south of the city centre was originally chosen in the 1930s as the site for the planned 1942 Universal Exposition of Rome to celebrate twenty years of Fascism. The government building in this square was modelled on the Roman Colosseum and is described as 'the prime example of Fascist modernism'. The exposition never materialized due to the Second World War. See Gundle (2011).

16 See also the making of the film documentary on the DVD *Titus: Special Edition* (1999).
17 *Thingspiele* were plays designed during the Weimar Republic to imitate the ancient Nordic-Germanic practice of collective decision-making, thus giving the audience a sense of community, agency and nationhood. For more details, see London (2000: 54–95) and Strobl (2007: 36–88).
18 The theatre of masses movement culminated in a remarkable single performance of a piece entitled *18 BL* (1934), which featured a truck-protagonist which Mussolini described as a symbol of 'the Fascist everyman and everywoman, a humble and heroic soldier' (Schnapp 1996: 33).
19 For details of Hitler's visit to Rome, see Baxa (2010: 135–54).
20 See, for instance, Burt (2001); McCandless (2002); Rutter (2007b); and Donaldson (2005).
21 For discussion of the casting of Osheen Jones, see Rutter (2007b: 14) and Lehmann (2009: 50).

Chapter 4

1 As far as can be ascertained, the play was not staged for over a century after the last recorded court performance in 1634. It was adapted by David Garrick in 1756 under the title *Florizel and Perdita, a Dramatic Pastoral* and later published in London in 1758 under the title *Florizel and Perdita: A Dramatic Pastoral, in Three Acts. Alter'd from The Winter's Tale of Shakespear. By David Garrick. As It Is Performed at the Theatre Royal in Drury-Lane*. It was based on the last two acts of Shakespeare's play. It was revived frequently in this form until the end of the eighteenth century. The play was staged in a form closer to the original text at the major theatres intermittently throughout the nineteenth century and first half of the twentieth century. However, it suffered from numerous cuts and revisions designed to make sense of the generic inconsistencies. See Pitcher (2010: 102–15) and Bate (2009: 132–44).
2 There were two professional productions in the 1970s, eight in the 1980s, eight in the 1990s and seven between 2000 and 2005 (O'Connor and Goodland 2007: 1594–38). For a full analysis of the play in production, see Bartholomeusz (1982); Dunbar (2010); and Tatspaugh (2002).
3 For Postman, this is specifically the age between seven and seventeen. See the Introduction for a full analysis of Postman's argument.

4   See also Higginbotham (2013: 11–12).
5   For a discussion of breeching, particularly as it relates to maternity in *The Winter's Tale*, see Adelman (1992: 7 and 228).
6   See, for instance, Gibbons (1996/7); Johnson (1998); and Stockton (2011). Other early modern scholars have argued that to view the early modern discourse of male-male love as necessarily sexual is to misinterpret the classical discourse of same-sex emotional intimacy (or *amicitia*) that can be homoerotic without necessarily being sexual. See, for instance, Bloom (2010); Masten (1997); Bray (2003); and Tosh (2016).
7   For a bisexual reading of the erotic conflict depicted in Sonnet 144, see Chedgzoy (1997: 106–19).
8   This is the dedication on the title page of the 1609 Quarto. For discussion of the possible identity of 'W.H.', see Duncan-Jones (2010: 63–9). For criticism that assumes the homoeroticism of the sonnets, see Pequigney (1987); Matz (2010: 447–508); and Gil (2006). For a bisexual reading of the sonnets, see Callaghan (2007) and Chedgzoy (1997).
9   Rugby School was founded in 1567 and is one of the original seven English public schools defined by the Public Schools Act 1868. It became co-educational in 1975. In 1845, three Rugby School pupils produced the first written rules of the 'Rugby style of game'. See 'Rugby School' in Gilman, Thurston and Colby (1902) and Anon (2014).
10 There are nine schools that make up what is called 'the Clarendon nine', the first schools to be named 'public schools' under the 1868 Education Reform Act. More than half of these schools are now either partially or fully co-educational. At the time of writing, Eton, Harrow, Sherborne, Radley and Winchester are still single-sex schools.
11 Duffell runs weekend 'boarding school survivor' therapy courses.
12 For a history of the teaching of classical languages and literature and its role in adolescent rites of passage in all-male educational establishments, see Ong (1981) and Enterline (2012).
13 See Anon (1880: 52–4) and Chandos (1984: 221).
14 See, for instance, Duffell (2000: 29–33); Power (2007: 313–20); Schaverien (2004 and 2011); Renton (2017); and Luke (1994). Robert Bly's review is cited in the jacket sleeve of Duffell's *The Making of Them*.
15 There are multiple websites dedicated to 'boarding school syndrome'. These range from forums for discussing the issues to those offering advice for seeking therapy, compensation and for political lobbying. See, for instance, www.boardingschoolsurvivors.

co.uk, www.boardingrecovery.com, www.boardingconcern.org.uk, boardingschoolaction.wordpress.com.

16 See the Introduction for a full discussion of Stockton's thesis.

17 The term 'wise child' is taken from the chapter of that name in Marcus (1965: 54–91). Marcus uses Oliver Twist as the archetype of the Dickensian 'wise child', describing him as 'the incarnation of a moral quality', whose 'disposition and moral character are so unlike everything he has known, so apart from all external influence, that it seems as if he [...] might have come from another world' (80). Zieger calls this Dickensian type the 'aged child' (2009: 144) and Grylls uses the term 'old-fashioned child' to refer to the same phenomenon, which he describes as 'quaint, broody, closer to God, sedate and usually ailing' (1978: 35–6). Angela Carter takes the Dickensian 'wise children' and applies it in ironic fashion in her novel *Wise Children* (1992). The 'children' of the novel are in fact celebrating their seventy-fifth birthday in the opening chapter.

18 The term 'Victoriana' was first used by Ezra Pound in 1918 as a pejorative term (see *OED* 'Victoriana'). More recently, it has been taken up by literary scholars to describe the late-twentieth- and early-twenty-first-century phenomenon of Victorian literary and artistic re-creations, imitations and revisions. Cora Kaplan was one of the first to use the term in this way and defines it thus: 'Today, "Victoriana" might usefully embrace the whole phenomenon, the astonishing range of representations and reproductions for which the Victorian – whether as the origin of late twentieth century modernity, its antithesis, or both at once – is the common referent [...] a kind of conceptual nomad, not so much lost as permanently restless and unsettled' (2007: 3). In the last few years, particularly since the establishment of the online journal *Neo-Victorian Studies* in 2008, 'Neo-Victorian' has become the more widely accepted term within academia ('Neo-Victorianism', oxfordbibliographies.com). See also Heilmann and Llewellyn (2010); Boehm-Schnitker and Gruss (2014); Poore (2012); Joyce (2007). Among the many television adaptations in the past decade, the BBC's serializations of *Cranford* (2007) and *Little Dorrit* (2008) are particularly notable for their global reach. See Bignell and Lacey (2014) and Leggatt and Taddeo (2014); for novels, see, for instance, A. S. Byatt, *Possession: A Romance* (1990) which was a *New York Times* best-seller and recipient of both the Man Booker Prize and the Irish Times-Aer Lingus International Fiction Prize; films include Michael Robert Johnson, Andrew Peckham and Simon Kinberg's *Sherlock Holmes* (2009), which grossed $524 million worldwide; the exhibition 'Victoriana: The Art

of Revival' was held at the Guildhall Gallery, London (2013), and the Victorian 'whodunnit' exhibition, 'The Game's Afoot', was staged at the Madame Tussaud's Theatre in 2016. See, for instance, peer-reviewed online journal, *Neo-Victorian Studies*; a conference titled 'Neo-Victorian Cultures: The Victorians Today' was held at Centre of English and Cultural History, Liverpool John Moores University, in July 2013.
19 The use of the term 'surrogation' in this section refers to Joseph Roach's analysis of the doubling of Mamillius and Perdita as a 'seamlessly perfect surrogation' (2009: 131). The term 'surrogation' in relation to performance is defined by Roach as follows: The 'attempt to fit satisfactory alternates' into 'the cavities created by loss through death or other forms of departure' (1996: 2).
20 First printed as 'A Visit from St Nicholas' on 23 December 1823 in the *Troy Sentinel*, New York, this poem was subsequently published with illustrations by Thomas Nast in the 1860s. These illustrations featured images of Santa Claus in his present form. See Golby and Purdue (2000: 73–5); and Gillis (1996: 103).
21 This information was provided in an email to the author from Nick Morrison of Fiery Angel, the production company that produced Branagh/Ashford's plays at the Garrick Theatre.
22 In addition to Hytner (2001), Wheeldon (2014/16) and Branagh/Ashford (2015/16), other recent productions to introduce a frame-sequence featuring Mamillius include Noble (1992), which opened with 'a solitary Mamillius looking upstage towards a party tableau' (O'Connor and Goodland 2007: 1620), Donnellan (1997–9), in which Mamillius emerged from the frozen tableau of courtiers in the final seconds of the play before being 'ushered gently but firmly away by the figure of Time' (Gardner 1999) and Hall (2005/12), whose Mamillius entered out of the darkness in the final seconds to blow out Leontes's candle.
23 The conceit of one child dying to allow another child to live was also explored in Dickens's 1837 novel, *Oliver Twist*, with the death of the workhouse child in chapter 51. For a full analysis of the treatment of childhood, and in particular child deaths, in Dickens's novels, see Grylls (1978: 132–52) and Coveney (1957: 71–119).
24 Coveney is referring exclusively to *Dombey and Son* in this description, but I argue that it can equally be applied to the death of Mamillius in *The Winter's Tale*.
25 See, for instance, Welsh (1987: 88, 104) and Schlicke (2004: 94).
26 Valerie L. Gager draws some analogies between *Dombey and Son* and *The Winter's Tale* but these are cursory and underdeveloped

(1996: 13–14). David Lee Miller identifies the similarities in the use of the *puer senex* motif but does not explore the similarities in the daughter-son surrogation (2003: 10–22).
27 'Beneath the watching and attentive eyes of Time […] he passed from babyhood to childhood, and became a talking, walking, wondering Dombey' (Dickens [1846–8] 2008: 95).
28 See also White (2005), esp. chapter four, 'Backlash'.
29 Branagh replaced Mark Rylance who withdrew for personal reasons just three weeks before the ceremony. Branagh played the part of the Victorian architect Isambard Kingdom Brunel reciting Caliban's 'The isle is full of noises' speech from *The Tempest* to the accompaniment of Edward Elgar.
30 This was not the case for *Romeo and Juliet*, which was the sixth, and penultimate, production in the Garrick residency. It did not play in repertory with another production and thus a separate set of publicity material was produced exclusively for this play. That Branagh chose to pair *The Winter's* Tale with the Rattigan double bill can be interpreted as a conscious decision based on dramatic rather than pragmatic imperatives.
31 For a full analysis of this film, see Hopkins (2009: 79–104).
32 See also Hatchuel (2004: 74–5).

REFERENCES

Primary works cited (pre-1900)

Anon. (1594), *The True Tragedie of Richard the Third Wherein Is Showne the Death of Edward the Fourth, with the Smothering of the Two Yoong Princes in the Tower: With a Lamentable Ende of Shores Wife, an Example for All Wicked Women. And Lastly, the Coniunction and Ioyning of the Two Noble Houses, Lancaster and Yorke. As It Was Playd by the Queenes Maiesties Players*, London.

Anon. (1669), *The Children's Petition: Or, a Modest Remonstrance of That Intolerable Grievance Our Youth Lies under, in the Accustomed Severities of the School-Discipline of This Nation: Humbly Presented to the Confederation of the Parliament*, London.

Anon. (1880), *Boys and Their Ways: A Book for Boys and about Boys; by One Who Knows Them*, London.

Cibber, Colley (1700), *The Tragical History of King Richard III as It Is Acted at the Theatre Royal*, London.

Elyot, Thomas (1531), *The Boke Named the Gouernour*, London.

Garrick, David (1758), *Florizel and Perdita: A Dramatic Pastoral, in Three Acts. Alter'd from the Winter's Tale of Shakespear. By David Garrick. As It Is Performed at the Theatre Royal in Drury-Lane*, London.

Gent, S. S. (1672), *Fortunes Tennis-Ball, or, the Most Excellent History of Dorastus and Fawnia Rendred in Delightful English Verse and Worthy the Perusal of All Sorts of People/by S.S., Gent*, London.

Greene, Robert (1588), *Pandosto the Triumph of Time. Vvherein Is Discouered by a Pleasant Historie, That although by the Meanes of Sinister Fortune Truth May Be Concealed, yet by Time in Spight of Fortune It Is Most Manifestlie Reuealed. Pleasant for Age to Auoyde Drowsie Thoughtes, Profitable for Youth to Eschue Other Wanton Pastimes, and Bringing to Both a Desired Content. Temporis Filia Veritas. By Robert Greene Maister of Artes in Cambridge*, London.

Hall, Edward (1547), *The Union of the Two Noble and Illustrate Famelies of Lancastre [and] Yorke Beeyng Long in Continual Discension for* the Croune of This Noble Realme with All the Actes Done in Bothe the Tymes of the Princes, Bothe of the One Linage and of the Other, Beginnyng at the Tyme of Kyng Henry the Fowerth, the First Aucthor of This Deuision, and So Successiuely Proceadyng to the Reigne of the High and Prudent Prince Kyng Henry the Eight, the Vndubitate Flower and Very Heire of Both the Sayd Linages, London.

Hazlitt, William (1838), *Characters of Shakespeare's Plays*, 3rd edn, London.

Jordan, Thomas (1663), 'The Jealous Duke, and the Injured Dutchess: a Story', in *A Royal Arbor of Loyal Poesie Consisting of Poems and Songs Digested into Triumph, Elegy, Satyr, Love & Drollery/ Composed by Tho. Jordan*, London.

Montaigne, Michel de (1603), 'Of Friendship', in *The Essayes or Morall, Politike and Millitarie Discourses of Lo: Michaell De Montaigne, Knight of the Noble Order of St. Michaell, and One of the Gentlemen in Ordinary of the French King, Henry the Third His Chamber. The First Booke. First Written by Him in French. And Now Done into English by Him That Hath Inviolably Vowed His Labors to the Aeternitie of Their Honors, Whose Names He Hath Severally Inscribed on These His Consecrated Altares. . . . Iohn Florio*, London.

Moore, Clement Clark (1823), 'A Visit from St Nicholas', *Troy Sentinel*, 23 December: 3.

Shakespeare, William (1594), *The Most Lamentable Romaine Tragedie of Titus Andronicus as It Hath Sundry Times Beene Playde by the Right Honourable the Earle of Pembrooke, the Earle of Darbie, the Earle of Sussex, and the Lorde Chamberlaine Theyr Seruants*, London ('Q1').

Shakespeare, William (1597), *The Tragedy of King Richard the Third Containing, His Treacherous Plots against His Brother Clarence: The Pittiefull Murther of His Iunocent [Sic] Nephewes: His Tyrannicall Vsurpation: With the Whole Course of His Detested Life, and Most Deserued Death. As It Hath Beene Lately Acted by the Right Honourable the Lord Chamberlaine His Seruants*, London ('Q1').

Shakespeare, William (1598), *The Tragedie of King Richard the Third Conteining His Treacherous Plots against His Brother Clarence: The Pitiful Murther of His Innocent Nephewes: His Tyrannicall Vsurpation: With the Whole Course of the Detested Life, and Most Deserued Death. As It Hath Beene Lately Acted by the Right Honourable the Lord Chamberlaine His Seruants. By William Shake-Speare*, London ('Q2').

Shakespeare, William (1600), *The Most Lamentable Romaine Tragedie of Titus Andronicus as It Was Plaide by the Right Honourable the Earle of Darbie, Earl of Pembrooke, and Earl of Sussex Their Seruants*, London ('Q2').

Shakespeare, William (1602), *The Tragedie of King Richard the Third Conteining His Treacherous Plots against His Brother Clarence: The Pittifull Murther of His Innocent Nephewes: His Tyrannicall Vsurpation: With the Whole Course of His Detested Life, and Most Deserued Death. As It Hath Bene Lately Acted by the Right Honourable the Lord Chamberlaine His Seruants. Newly Augmented, by William Shakespeare.* London ('Q3').

Shakespeare, William (1605), *The Tragedie of King Richard the Third Conteining His Treacherous Plots against His Brother Clarence: The Pittifull Murther of His Innocent Nephewes: His Tyrannicall Vsurpation: With the Whole Course of His Detested Life, and Most Deserued Death. As It Hath Bin Lately Acted by the Right Honourable the Lord Chamberlaine His Seruants. Newly Augmented, by William Shake-Speare*, London ('Q4').

Shakespeare, William (1609), *Shake-Speares Sonnets Neuer before Imprinted*, London.

Shakespeare, William (1611), *The Most Lamentable Tragedie of Titus Andronicus as It Hath Sundry Times Beene Plaide by the Kings Maiesties Seruants*, London ('Q3').

Shakespeare, William (1612), *The Tragedie of King Richard the Third Containing His Treacherous Plots against His Brother Clarence: The Pittifull Murther of His Innocent Nephewes: His Tyrannicall Vsurpation: With the Whole Course of His Detested Life, and Most Deserued Death. As It Hath Beene Lately Acted by the Kings Maiesties Seruants. Newly Augmented, by William Shake-Speare*, London ('Q5').

Shakespeare, William (1622), *The Tragedie of King Richard the Third Contayning His Treacherous Plots against His Brother Clarence: The Pittifull Murder of His Innocent Nephewes: His Tyrannicall Vsurpation: With the Whole Course of His Detested Life, and Most Deserued Death. As It Hath Been Lately Acted by the Kings Maiesties Seruants. Newly Augmented. By William Shake-Speare*, London ('Q6').

Shakespeare, William (1623), *The Life and Death of Richard the Third*, in *Mr. Vvilliam Shakespeares Comedies, Histories, & Tragedies Published According to the True Originall Copies*, London ('First Folio').

Shakespeare, William (1623), *Mr. Vvilliam Shakespeares Comedies, Histories, & Tragedies Published According to the True Originall Copies*, London ('First Folio').

Shakespeare, William (1623), *The Tragedie of Macbeth*, in *Mr. Vvilliam Shakespeares Comedies, Histories, & Tragedies Published According to the True Originall Copies*, London ('First Folio').

Shakespeare, William (1623), *The Tragedie of Titus Andronicus*, in *Mr. Vvilliam Shakespeares Comedies, Histories, & Tragedies Published According to the True Originall Copies*, London ('First Folio').

Shakespeare, William (1623), *The Winters Tale*, in *Mr. Vvilliam Shakespeares Comedies, Histories, & Tragedies Published According to the True Originall Copies*, London ('First Folio').

Primary works cited post-1900 and modern editions

All original publication of plays refer to dates of first production, where known.

Bacon, Francis ([1625] 1985), 'Of Revenge', in John Pitcher (ed), *Francis Bacon: The Essays*, Harmondsworth: Penguin, 72–3.
Brome, Richard ([1659] 2010), Lucy Munro (ed), *The Queen and Concubine*. Available online: https://www.dhi.ac.uk/brome/viewOriginal.jsp?play=QC&type=ORIG&act=1 (accessed 14 April 2019).
Byatt, A. S. (1990), *Possession: A Romance*, London: Chatto and Windus.
Carter, Angel (1992), *Wise Children*, London: Vintage.
Cicero ([45 BC] 1941; repr., 2004), H. E. Gould and J. L. Whiteley (eds), *De Amicitia*, Wauconda: Bolchazy-Carducci Publishers.
Dickens, Charles ([1837–9] 1998), *Oliver Twist*, Oxford: Oxford University Press.
Dickens, Charles ([1843] 2008), *A Christmas Carol and Other Christmas Books*, Oxford: Oxford University Press.
Dickens, Charles ([1846–8] 2008), *Dombey and Son*, Oxford: Oxford University Press.
Evelyn, John ([1692] *c*. 1901), William Bray (ed), *The Diary of John Evelyn*, New York and London: M. W. Dunne. Available online: https://archive.org/details/diaryofjohnevely01eveliala/page/n15 (accessed 14 April 2019).
Freud, Sigmund ([1900] 1953–74), *The Interpretation of Dreams*, in James Strachey (ed. and trans.), *Standard Edition of the Complete Psychological Works of Sigmund Freud*, 24 vols, London: Hogarth Press.
Freud, Sigmund ([1919] 2003), David McLintock (trans. and ed), *The Uncanny*, London: Penguin Books.
Le Carré, John (1995), *Our Game*, London: Hodder and Stoughton.
Mitchell, Julian (1982), *Another Country*, Oxford: Amber Lane Press Ltd.
Rattigan, Terence ([1948; 1968] 2015), Kenneth Branagh (ed), *Harlequinade/All on Her Own*, Plays at the Garrick, London: Nick Hern Books.
Shakespeare, William ([*c*. 1593] 1981), Anthony Hammond (ed), *Richard III*, Arden Shakespeare Second Series, London: Arden Shakespeare.
Shakespeare, William ([*c*. 1593] 1986), *Titus Andronicus*, The BBC TV Shakespeare, London: British Broadcasting Corporation.

Shakespeare, William ([*c*. 1593] 2000), John Jowett (ed), *Richard III*, Oxford Shakespeare, Oxford: Oxford University Press.
Shakespeare, William ([1599] 2002), T. W. Craik (ed), *Henry V*, Arden Shakespeare Third Series, London: Arden Shakespeare.
Shakespeare, William ([*c*. 1593] 2003), Jonathan Bate (ed), *Titus Andronicus*, Arden Shakespeare Third Series, London: Arden Shakespeare.
Shakespeare, William ([2006] 2005), *Macbeth*, George Hunter (ed), Penguin Shakespeare, London: Penguin.
Shakespeare, William ([*c*. 1592] 2005), John Jowett and others (eds), *The Oxford Shakespeare: The Complete Works*, 2nd edn, Oxford: Clarendon Press.
Shakespeare, William (2005), Stanley Wells, Gary Taylor, John Jowett and William Montgomery (eds), *The Complete Works, Oxford Shakespeare*, 2nd edn, Oxford: Clarendon Press.
Shakespeare, William ([1599] 2006), Juliet Dusinberre (ed), *As You Like It*, Arden Shakespeare Third Series, London: Arden Shakespeare.
Shakespeare, William ([1611] 2007), J. M. Nosworthy (ed), *Cymbeline*, Arden Shakespeare Third Series, London: Arden Shakespeare.
Shakespeare, William ([*c*. 1592] 2008), Eugene M. Waith (ed), *Titus Andronicus*, Oxford Shakespeare, Oxford: Oxford University Press.
Shakespeare, William ([*c*. 1593] 2009), *Richard III*, Arden Shakespeare Third Series, ed. James R. Siemon, London: Arden Shakespeare.
Shakespeare, William ([1610–11] 2009), Jonathan Bate and Eric Rasmussen (eds), *The Winter's Tale*, RSC Shakespeare, Basingstoke: Macmillan.
Shakespeare, William ([1610–11] 2010), John Pitcher (ed), *The Winter's Tale*, Arden Shakespeare Third Series, London: Arden Shakespeare.
Shakespeare, William ([1599–1602] 2014), Ann Thompson and Neil Taylor (eds), *Hamlet*, Arden Shakespeare Third Series, London: Arden Shakespeare.
Shakespeare, William ([1610–11] 2015), Kenneth Branagh (ed), *The Winter's Tale*, Plays at the Garrick, London: Nick Hern Books.
Shakespeare, William ([1606] 2015), Sandra Clark and Pamela Mason (eds), *Macbeth*, Arden Shakespeare Third Series, London: Arden Shakespeare.
Shakespeare, William (2016), Stephen Greenblatt, Suzanne Gossett, Jean E. Howard, Katherine Eisam Maus, Gordon McMullan (eds), *The Norton Shakespeare: Essential Plays. The Sonnets*, 3rd edn, New York and London: W. W. Norton.
Shakespeare, William and George Wilkins ([1608–9] 2004), Suzanne Gossett (ed), *Pericles*, Arden Shakespeare Third Series, London: Arden Shakespeare.
Winterson, Jeanette (2015), *The Gap of Time: The Winter's Tale Retold*, London: Hogarth.

Secondary works cited

Adelman, Janet (1992), *Suffocating Mothers: Fantasies of Maternal Origin in Shakespeare's Plays, Hamlet to The Tempest*, Abingdon: Routledge.
Aebischer, Pascale (2002), 'Women Filming Rape in Shakespeare's *Titus Andronicus*: Jane Howell and Julie Taymor', *Études Anglaises*, 55 (2): 136–47.
Aebischer, Pascale (2004), *Shakespeare's Violated Bodies: Stage and Screen Performance*, Cambridge: Cambridge University Press.
Aebischer, Pascale and Kathryn Prince, eds (2012), *Performing Early Modern Drama Today*, Cambridge: Cambridge University Press.
Anon. (1993), 'The Evil and the Innocent', *Daily Mail*, 25 November: 1.
Anon. (2014), 'Six Ways the Town of Rugby Helped Change the World', *BBC*, 1 February. Available online: https://www.bbc.co.uk/news/uk-england-coventry-warwickshire-25946757 (accessed 16 April 2019).
Barker, Roberta (2007), *Early Modern Tragedy: Gender and Performance, 1984–2000*, Basingstoke: Palgrave Macmillan.
Barraclough, Leo (2015), 'Kenneth Branagh's Production of "Winter's Tale" Tops U.K. Movie Box Office', *Variety*, 27 November. Available online: https://variety.com/2015/film/global/kenneth-branagh-winters-tale-u-k-movie-box-office-1201649357/ (accessed 16 April 2019).
Bartholomeusz, Dennis (1982), *'The Winter's Tale' in Performance in England and America 1611–1976*, Cambridge: Cambridge University Press.
Bassett, Kate (1999), 'Lost Child of Lady Macbeth', *Telegraph*, 20 October. Available online: https://www.telegraph.co.uk/culture/4718704/Lost-child-of-Lady-Macbeth.html (accessed 16 April 2019).
Bate, Jonathan (1993), *Shakespeare and Ovid*, Oxford: Oxford University Press.
Bate, Jonathan (2003), Introduction to *Titus Andronicus*, Arden Shakespeare Third Series, 1–121, London: Arden Shakespeare.
Bate, Jonathan (2009), '*The Winter's Tale* in Performance: The RSC and Beyond', in *The Winter's Tale*, RSC Shakespeare, 132–80, Basingstoke: Macmillan.
Baxa, Paul (2010), *Roads and Ruins: The Symbolic Landscape of Fascist Rome*, Toronto: University of Toronto Press.
Belsey, Catherine (2005), 'Shakespeare's Little Boys: Theatrical Apprenticeship and the Construction of Childhood', in Brian Reynolds and William N. West (eds), *Rematerializing Shakespeare: Authority and Representation on the Early Modern Stage*, 53–72, Basingstoke: Palgrave Macmillan.

Belsey, Catherine (2007), 'Little Princes: Shakespeare's Royal Children', in Kate Chedgzoy, Suzanne Greenhalgh and Robert Shaughnessy (eds), *Shakespeare and Childhood*, 32–48, Cambridge, Cambridge University Press.

Berne, Eric (1961), *Transactional Analysis in Psychotherapy: A Systematic Individual and Social Psychiatry*, London: Souvenir Press.

Bignell, Jonathan and Stephen Lacey (2014), *British Television Drama Past Present and Future*, Basingstoke: Palgrave Macmillan.

Billington, Michael (1985), 'Shaping a Gory Classic for TV', *New York Times*, 14 April: 29.

Billington, Michael (1987), 'Review of *Titus Andronicus*', *Guardian*, in *London Theatre Record*, 7 (10): 637.

Billington, Michael (2015), 'The Winter's Tale Review – Kenneth Branagh and Judi Dench Offer Intriguing Touches', *Guardian*, 8 November. Available online: https://www.theguardian.com/culture/2015/nov/08/the-winters-tale-review-kenneth-branagh-and-judi-dench-garrick (accessed 16 April 2019).

Blake, Ann (1994), 'Shakespeare's Roles for Children: A Stage History', *Theatre Notebook*, 48: 122–37.

Block, Gisela (1994), 'Antinatalism, Maternity and Paternity in National Socialist Racism', in David F. Crew (ed), *Nazism and German Society*, 110–40, London: Routledge.

Bloom, Gina (2010), '"Boy Eternal": Aging, Games, and Masculinity in *The Winter's Tale*', *English Literary Renaissance*, 40 (3): 329–56.

Blumenthal, Eileen, Julie Taymor, Antonio Monda (2007), *Playing with Fire*, 3rd edn, New York: Abrams.

Bly, Mary (2000), *Queer Virgins and Virgin Queans on the Early Modern Stage*, Oxford: Oxford University Press.

Boehm-Schnitker, Nadine and Susanne Gruss (2014), *Neo-Victorian Literature and Culture: Immersions and Revisitations*, London: Routledge.

Boenisch, Peter M. and Thomas Ostermeier (2016), *The Theatre of Thomas Ostermeier*, London: Routledge.

Boxer, Marilyn J. and Jean H. Quataert, eds (1987), *Connecting Spheres: Women in the Western World: 1500 to the Present*, Oxford: Oxford University Press.

Boyd, Michael (2014), email to the author, 27 August.

Boym, Svetlana (2001), *The Future of Nostalgia*, New York: Basic Books.

Bradley, A. C. ([1904] 1919), *Shakespearean Tragedy: Lectures on Hamlet, Othello, King Lear, Macbeth*, 2nd edn, London: Macmillan.

Bray, Alan (2003), *The Friend*, Chicago: The University of Chicago Press.

Bristol, Michael (2000), 'How Many Children Did She Have?', in John J. Joughin (ed), *Philosophical Shakespeares*, 18–33, London: Routledge.

Brocklehurst, Helen (2006), *Who's Afraid of Children? Children, Conflict and International Relations*, Farnham: Ashgate.

Brooks, Cleanth (1947), 'The Naked Babe and the Cloak of Manliness', in *The Well Wrought Urn: Studies in the Structure of Poetry*, 21–46, New York: Harcourt, Brace and Co.

Brooks, Libby (2006), *The Story of Childhood: Growing Up in Modern Britain*, London, Bloomsbury Publishing Ltd.

Brown, Georgina (2013), 'Review of *Macbeth*', *Mail on Sunday*, in *Theatre Record*, 33: 143.

Brown, John Russell (2012), *The Routledge Companion to Actors*, Abingdon: Routledge.

Brown, Sarah Annes and Catherine Silverstone, eds (2007), *Tragedy in Transition*, Oxford: Blackwell.

Buchanan, Judith (2017), '*The Winter's Tale*'s Spectral Endings: Death, Dance and Doubling', in Sarah Hatchuel and Nathalie Vienne-Guerrin (eds), *Shakespeare on Screen: The Tempest and Late Romances*, 110–32, Cambridge: Cambridge University Press.

Buckingham, David (2000), *After the Death of Childhood: Growing Up in the Age of Electronic Media*, Oxford: Blackwell Publishing.

Burnett, Mark Thornton and Ramona Wray, eds (2000), *Shakespeare, Film, Fin de Siècle*, Basingstoke: Macmillan Press.

Burt, Richard (2001), 'Shakespeare and the Holocaust: Julie Taymor's Titus Is Beautiful, or Shakesploi Meets the Camp', *Colby Quarterly*, 37 (1): 78–106.

Butler, Judith (2009), *Frames of War: When Is Life Grievable?*, London: Verso.

Callaghan, Dympna (1992), 'Wicked Women in *Macbeth*: A Study of Power, Ideology, and the Production of Motherhood', in Mario A. Di Cesare (ed), *Reconsidering the Renaissance: Papers from the Twenty-First Conference*, 355–69, New York: Medieval and Renaissance Texts and Studies.

Callaghan, Dympna (2007), *Shakespeare's Sonnets*, Oxford: Blackwell.

Callens, Johan, ed (2004), *The Wooster Group and Its Traditions*, Brussels: Peter Lang Publishing.

Campana, Joseph (2011), 'Shakespeare's Children', *Literature Compass*, 8: 1–14.

Cappelle, Laura (2015), 'Avignon's Nude Direction for Shakespeare', *Financial Times*, 17 July. Available online: https://www.ft.com/content/0474a8c4-2aea-11e5-acfb-cbd2e1c81cca (accessed 16 April 2019).

Carlson, Marvin (2003), *The Haunted Stage: The Theatre as Memory Machine*, Michigan: The University of Michigan Press.

Cavell, Stanley (2003), *Disowning Knowledge in Seven Plays of Shakespeare*, Cambridge: Cambridge University Press.

Cavendish, Dominic (2015), 'Harlequinade/All On Her Own, Garrick Theatre, Review: "Farcical Froth"', *Telegraph*, 10 November. Available online: https://www.telegraph.co.uk/theatre/what-to-see/harlequinade-garrick-theatre-review/ (accessed 16 April 2019).

Chandos, John (1984), *Boys Together: English Public Schools, 1800–1864*, New Haven: Yale University Press.

Chapple, Freda and Chief Kattenbelt, eds (2006), *Intermediality in Theatre and Performance*, Amsterdam and New York: Rodopi.

Chedgzoy, Kate (1997), '"Two Loves I Have": Shakespeare and Bisexuality', in Phoebe Davidson, Jo Eadie, Clare Hemmings, Ann Kaloski and Merl Storr (eds), *The Bisexual Imaginary: Representation, Identity and Desire*, 106–19, London: Cassel.

Chedgzoy, Kate, Suzanne Greenhalgh and Robert Shaughnessy, eds (2007), *Shakespeare and Childhood*, Cambridge: Cambridge University Press.

Clapp, Susannah (2001), 'Review of *The Winter's Tale*', *Observer*, in *Theatre Record*, 12 (11): 675.

Clover, Carol, J. (2002), *Men, Women and Chain Saws: Gender in the Modern Horror Film*, Princeton: Princeton University Press.

Cohen, Stanley (2002), *Folk Devils and Moral Panics: The Creation of the Mods and Rockers*, 3rd edn, London: Routledge.

Collin, Robbie (2015), 'Macbeth Review: "Fassbender Was Born for This"', *Telegraph*, 19 October. Available online: https://www.telegraph.co.uk/film/macbeth/review/ (accessed 16 April 2019).

Connolly, Kate (2010), 'Roman Polanski Freed from House Arrest', *Guardian*, 12 July. Available online: https://www.theguardian.com/film/2010/jul/12/romanpolanski-switzerland (accessed 16 April 2019).

Coveney, Michael (1987), 'Review of *Titus Andronicus*', *Financial Times*, in *London Theatre Record*, 7 (10): 636.

Coveney, Peter (1957), *Poor Monkey: The Child in Literature*, London: Rockliff.

Coveney, Peter (1967), *The Image of Childhood*, London: Peregrine.

Cox, Brian (1993), '*Titus Andronicus*', in Russell Jackson and Robert Smallwood (eds), *Players of Shakespeare 3*, 174–88, Cambridge: Cambridge University Press.

Craig, Edward Gordon ([1911] 2009), 'The Actor and the Über-Marionette', in *On the Art of Theatre*, 27–48, London: Routledge.

Crew, David F., ed (1994), *Nazism and German Society*, London: Routledge.

Crompton, Sarah (2014), 'Review of *The Winter's Tale*', *Telegraph*, 11 April. Available online: https://www.telegraph.co.uk/culture/music/classicalcdreviews/10759738/The-Winters-Tale-Royal-Ballet-Covent-Garden-review.html (accessed 16 April 2019).

Croteau, Melissa and Carolyn Jess-Cooke, eds (2009), *Apocalyptic Shakespeare: Essays on Visions of Chaos and Revelation in Recent Film Adaptations*, Jefferson: McFarland.
Cunningham, Hugh (2005), *Children and Childhood in Western Society since 1500*, Harlow: Pearson Education Limited.
Cunningham, Hugh (2006), *The Invention of Childhood*, London: BBC Books.
Davis, Lloyd, ed (2003), *Shakespeare Matters: History, Teaching, Performance*, London: Associated University Presses.
Deats, Sara M. (1986), 'Polanski's *Macbeth*: A Contemporary Tragedy', *Popular Culture Association in the South*, 9 (1): 84–93.
Dessen, Alan C. (1989), *Titus Andronicus: Shakespeare in Performance*, Manchester: Manchester University Press.
Dinshaw, Carolyn, Lee Edelman, Roderick A. Ferguson, Carla Freccero, Elizabeth Freeman, Judith Halberstam, Annamarie Jagose, Christopher S. Nealon and Tan Hoang Nguyen (2007), 'Theorizing Queer Temporalities: A Roundtable Discussion', *GLQ: A Journal of Lesbian and Gay Studies*, 13 (2–3): 177–95.
Donaldson, Peter, S. (2005), 'Game Space/Tragic Space: Julie Taymor's *Titus*', in Barbara Hodgdon and W. B. Worthen (eds), *A Companion to Shakespeare and Performance*, 457–77, Oxford: Wiley-Blackwell.
Draper, John, W. (1939), 'Falstaff's Robin and Other Pages', *Studies in Philology*, 36: 476–90.
Duffell, Nick (2000), 'Gender Difference and the Boarding School', *Self and Society*, 28 (3): 29–33.
Duffell, Nick ([2000] 2015), *The Making of Them: The British Attitude to Children and the Boarding School System*, London: Lone Arrow Press.
Dunbar, Judith, ed (2010), *Shakespeare in Performance: The Winter's Tale*, Manchester: Manchester University Press.
Duncan-Jones, Katherine, ed (2010), *Shakespeare's Sonnets*, Arden Shakespeare Third Series, rev. edn, London: Methuen.
Edelman, Lee (2004), *No Future: Queer Theory and the Death Drive*, Durham: Duke University Press.
Elgot, Jessica (2015), 'Family of Syrian Boy Washed Up on Beach Were Trying to Reach Canada', *Guardian*, 3 September. Available online: https://www.theguardian.com/world/2015/sep/03/refugee-crisis-syrian-boy-washed-up-on-beach-turkey-trying-to-reach-canada (accessed 16 April 2019).
Engel, William E. (2013), '*The Winter's Tale*: Kinetic Emblems and Memory Images in *The Winter's Tale*', in Andrew J. Power and Rory Loughnane (eds), *Late Shakespeare 1608–1613*, 71–87, Cambridge: Cambridge University Press.
Enterline, Lynn (2012), *Shakespeare's Schoolroom: Rhetoric, Discipline, Emotion*, Philadelphia: University of Pennsylvania Press.

Escolme, Bridget (2013), 'Costume, Disguise, and Self-Display', in Farah Karim-Cooper and Tiffany Stern (eds), *Shakespeare's Theatres and the Effects of Performance*, 118–40, London: Bloomsbury.
Escolme, Bridget (2014), *Emotional Excess on the Shakespearean Stage: Passion's Slaves*, London: Bloomsbury.
Estrin, Barbara, L. (1985), *The Raven and the Lark: Lost Children in Literature of the English Renaissance*, London: Associated University Presses.
Ewbank, Inga-Stina ([1968] 1983), 'The Triumph of Time in *The Winter's Tale*', in Kenneth Muir (ed), *Shakespeare: The Winter's Tale, A Casebook*, 98–115, London: Macmillan.
Faulkner, Joanne (2011), *The Importance of Being Innocent: Why We Worry about Children*, Cambridge: Cambridge University Press.
Faulkner, Joanne (2013), 'Vulnerability of "Virtual" Subjects: Childhood, Memory, and Crisis in the Cultural Value of Innocence', *SubStance*, 42 (3): 127–47.
Fedderson, Kim and J. Michael Richardson (2009), 'Liberty's Taken, or How "Captive Women May Be Cleansed and Used": Julie Taymor's *Titus* and 9/11', in Melissa Croteau and Carolyn Jess-Cooke (eds), *Apocalyptic Shakespeare: Essays on Visions of Chaos and Revelation in Recent Film Adaptations*, 70–89, Jefferson: McFarland.
Fenwick, Henry (1978), 'Transatlantic Row Breaks over the BBC's Most Ambitious Drama Series', *Telegraph Sunday Magazine*, 24 September: 22–31.
Fenwick, Henry (1986), 'The Production', in *Titus Andronicus: The BBC TV Shakespeare*, 17–27, London: British Broadcasting Corporation.
Fest, Joachim C. (1970), *The Face of the Third Reich: Portraits of Nazi Leadership*, trans. by Michael Bullock, London: Weidenfeld and Nicolson.
Fisher, James (2009), '"An Idealist": The Legacy of Edward Gordon Craig's Formative Productions, 1900–1903', *Theatre Arts Journal*, 1 (1). Available online: https://taj.tau.ac.il/index.php/current-issue/2-issues/1-2009/5-an-idealist-the-legacy-of-edward-g-craigs-formative-productions-1900-1903 (accessed 17 April 2019).
Fisher, Will (2006), *Materializing Gender in Early Modern English Literature and Culture*, Cambridge: Cambridge University Press.
Gager, Valerie L. (1996), *Shakespeare and Dickens: The Dynamics of Influence*, Cambridge: Cambridge University Press.
Garber, Marjorie (1997), *Coming of Age in Shakespeare*, London: Routledge.
Garber, Marjorie (2002), 'Descanting on Deformity: *Richard III* and the Shape of History', in R. J. C. Watt (ed), *Shakespeare's History Plays*, 62–75, London: Pearson.

Garber, Marjorie (2008), *Shakespeare and Modern Culture*, New York: Pantheon Books.
Garber, Marjorie (1987), *Shakespeare's Ghost Writers: Literature as Uncanny Causality*, London: Routledge.
Gardner, Lyn (1999), 'Ghosts in the Works', *Guardian*, 8 May. Available online: https://www.theguardian.com/books/1999/may/08/books.guardianreview4 (accessed 14 July 2019).
Geertz, Clifford (1973), *The Interpretation of Cultures*, New York: Basic Books.
Gerry, Felicity (2017), 'Should England and Wales Bring Back Doli Incapax?', *Criminal Law and Justice Weekly*, 12. Available online: https://www.lexisnexis.com/uk/legal/results/enhdisplayunit.do?level=2&linkValue=0&docViewState=normToc (accessed 19 May 2019).
Gibbons, Brian (1996/7), 'Doubles and likenesses-with-a-difference: *The Comedy of Errors* and *The Winter's Tale*', *Connotations*, 6: 19–40.
Gil, Daniel Juan (2006), *Before Intimacy: Asocial Sexuality in Early Modern England*, Minneapolis: University of Minnesota Press.
Gillis, John, R. (1996), *A World of Their Own Making: Myth, Ritual, and the Quest for Family Values*, Cambridge: Harvard University Press.
Gillis, John, R. (2003), 'The Birth of the Virtual Child: A Victorian Progeny', in Willem Koops and Michael Zuckerman (eds), *Beyond the Century of the Child: Cultural History and Developmental Psychology*, 82–95, Philadelphia: University of Pennsylvania Press.
Gilman, D. C., H. T. Thurston, F. M. Colby, eds (1902), *New International Encyclopedia*, 1st edn, New York: Dodd, Mead and Co.
Girard, René ([1972] 2016), *Violence and the Sacred*, trans. by Patrick Gregory, London: Bloomsbury.
Golby, John and A. W. Purdue (2000), *The Making of Modern Christmas*, Stroud: The History Press Ltd.
Goldstein, Ruth M. and Edith Zornow (1980), *The Screen Image of Youth: Movies about Children and Adolescents*, London: Scarecrow Press.
Goodman, Henry (2007), 'King Richard III', in Robert Smallwood (ed), *Players of Shakespeare 6: Essays in the Performance of Shakespeare's History Plays*, 198–218, Cambridge: Cambridge University Press.
Gore, Will (2017), 'Now Charlie Gard's Parents Have Ended Their Court Case, We Should Ask Why His Case Became the Media Circus It Did', *Independent*, 24 July. Available online: https://www.independent.co.uk/voices/charlie-gard-court-case-ruling-became-media-circus-a7857841.html (accessed 17 April 2019).
Gray, John (2015), *The Soul of the Marionette: A Short Enquiry into Human Freedom*, London: Penguin.
Gross, Kenneth (2011), *Puppet: An Essay on Uncanny Life*, Chicago and London: The University of Chicago Press.
Gross, Kenneth, ed (2012), *On Dolls*, London: Notting Hill Editions.

Grylls, David (1978), *Guardians and Angels: Parents and Children in Nineteenth-Century Literature*, London: Faber and Faber.

Gundle, Stephen (2011), '10 of the Best 20th-Century Landmarks in Rome', *Guardian*, 13 July. Available online: https://www.theguardian.com/travel/2011/jul/13/top-10-historical-landmarks-rome (accessed 17 April 2019).

Guy-Bray, Stephen (2002), *Homoerotic Space: Poetics of Loss in Renaissance Literature*, Toronto: University of Toronto Press.

Halberstam, Judith (2005), *In a Queer Time and Place: Transgender Bodies, Subcultural Lives*, New York: New York University Press.

Hammond, Antony (1981), Introduction to *King Richard III*, Arden Shakespeare Second Series, 1–119, London: Methuen.

Harding, Kate (2009), 'Reminder: Roman Polanski Raped a Child', *Salon*, 28 September. Available online: https://www.salon.com/2009/09/28/polanski_arrest/ (accessed 18 April 2019).

Harris, Jonathan Gil (2009), *Untimely Matter in the Time of Shakespeare*, Philadelphia: University of Pennsylvania Press.

Hart, Christopher (2011), 'Macbeth, RST', *The Sunday Times*, 1 May: 19.

Hatchuel, Sarah (2004), *Shakespeare from Stage to Screen*, Cambridge: Cambridge University Press.

Hatchuel, Sarah and Nathalie Vienne-Guerrin, eds (2005), *Shakespeare on Screen: Richard III*, 161–77, Rouen: Publications de l'Universite de Rouen.

Hatchuel, Sarah and Nathalie Vienne-Guerrin, eds (2017), *Shakespeare on Screen: The Tempest and Late Romances*, Cambridge: Cambridge University Press.

Heijes, Coen (2012), 'Review of *Macbeth*', *Theatre Journal*, 64 (2): 102–5.

Heilmann, Ann and Mark Llewellyn (2010), *Neo-Victorianism: The Victorians in the Twenty-First Century, 1999–2009*, Basingstoke: Palgrave Macmillan.

Hemming, Sarah (2015), 'Review of *The Winter's Tale*', *Financial Times*, 9 November. Available online: https://www-ft-com.libproxy.kcl.ac.uk/content/b0bd9e46-86df-11e5-9f8c-a8d619fa707c (accessed 17 April 2019).

Hewison, Robert (1987), *The Heritage Industry: Britain in a Climate of Decline*, London: Methuen.

Hickling, Alfred (2011), 'Review of *Macbeth*', *Guardian*, 13 May. Available online: https://www.theguardian.com/stage/2011/may/13/macbeth-everyman-liverpool-review (accessed 17 April 2019).

Higginbotham, Jennifer (2013), *The Girlhood of Shakespeare's Sisters: Gender, Transgression, Adolescence*, Edinburgh: Edinburgh University Press.

Higonnet, Anne (1998), *Pictures of Innocence: The History and Crisis of Ideal Childhood*, London: Thames and Hudson.

Hiscock, John (2015), 'Kenneth Branagh: Cinderella Made Me Weep', *Telegraph*, 27 March. Available online: https://www.telegraph.co.uk/film/cinderella/kenneth-branagh-interview/ (accessed 17 April 2019).

Hitchings, Henry (2015), 'The Winter's Tale/All On Her Own & Harlequinade, Review: Radiant Dame Judi Dench Is Majestivally Authoritative in Wintry Tale', *Evening Standard*, 9 November. Available online: https://www.standard.co.uk/go/london/theatre/the-winter-s-taleall-on-her-own-harlequinade-theatre-review-radiant-dame-judi-dench-is-majestically-a3109961.html (accessed 17 April 2019).

Hobgood, Allison P. (2015), 'Teeth before Eyes: Impairment and Invisibility in Shakespeare's *Richard III*', in Sujata Iyengar (ed), *Disability, Health and Happiness in the Shakespearean Body*, 23–40, London: Routledge.

Hodgdon, Barbara and W. B. Worthen, eds (2005), *A Companion to Shakespeare and Performance*, Oxford: Wiley-Blackwell.

Hollindale, Peter (2007), 'Tragedy and Childhood', in Sarah Annes Brown and Catherine Silverstone (eds), *Tragedy in Transition*, 174–91, Oxford: Blackwell.

Hopkins, Lisa (2009), *Relocating Shakespeare and Austen on Screen*, Basingstoke: Palgrave Macmillan.

Howell, Jane (1986), 'Notes' to the text, in William Shakespeare, *Titus Andronicus*, The BBC TV Shakespeare, 32–88, London: British Broadcasting Corporation.

Hoyle, Martin (1985), 'Macbeth and Macbeth Possessed/Glasgow', *Financial Times*, 22 April.

Hurren, Kenneth (1987), 'Review of *Titus Andronicus*', *Mail on Sunday*, in *London Theatre Record*, 7 (10): 635.

Jackson, Russell (2015), '"It is required you do awake your faith...": Shakespeare's "Old Tale"', in Kenneth Branagh (ed), *The Winter's Tale*, v–ix, London: Nick Hern Books.

Jackson, Russell and Robert Smallwood, eds (1993), *Players of Shakespeare 3*, Cambridge: Cambridge University Press.

Jauss, Hans Robert (1982), *Towards an Aesthetic of Literary Reception*, trans. Timothy Bahti, Minneapolis: University of Minnesota Press.

Jenks, Chris (2005), *Childhood*, 2nd edn, Abingdon: Routledge.

Jensen, Eric Frederic (2012), *Schumann*, Oxford: Oxford University Press.

Johns, Geoffrey, A. (2015), 'A "Grievous Burthen": *Richard III* and the Legacy of Monstrous Birth', in Sujata Iyengar (ed), *Disability, Health and Happiness in the Shakespearean Body*, 41–57, London: Routledge.

Joyce, Simon, *The Victorians in the Rearview Mirror*, Ohio: Ohio University Press, 2007.

Johnson, Nora (1998), 'Ganymedes and Kings: Staging Male Homosexual Desire in *The Winter's Tale*', *Shakespeare Survey*, 26: 187–217.

Kaplan, Cora (2007), *Victoriana: Histories, Fictions, Criticism*, Columbia: Columbia University Press.
Kathman, David (2005), 'How Old Were Shakespeare's Boy Actors?', *Shakespeare Survey*, 58: 220–46.
Kincaid, James R. (1998), *Erotic Innocence: The Culture of Child Molesting*, Durham and London: Duke University Press.
Kincaid, James R. (1992), *Child-Loving: The Erotic Child and Victorian Culture*, London: Routledge.
Kingsley, Patrick and Safak Timur (2015), 'Stories of 2015: How Alan Kurdi's Death Changed the World', *Guardian*, 31 December. Available online: https://www.theguardian.com/world/2015/dec/31/alan-kurdi-death-canada-refugee-policy-syria-boy-beach-turkey-photo (accessed 17 April 2019).
Kirwan, Peter (2015), '*Macbeth* @ Hyde Park Cinema, Leeds', *Bardathon*, 5 October. Available online: http://blogs.nottingham.ac.uk/bardathon/2015/10/05/macbeth-hyde-park-cinema-leeds/ (accessed 17 April 2019).
Kliman, Bernice (1995), *Shakespeare in Performance: Macbeth*, Manchester: Manchester University Press.
Knight, G. Wilson (1949), *The Wheel of Fire: Interpretations of Shakespearean Tragedy*, Oxford: Oxford University Press.
Knights, L. C. ([1932] 1946), 'How Many Children Had Lady Macbeth? An Essay in the Theory and Practice of Shakespeare Criticism', in *Explorations: Essays in Criticism Mainly on the Literature of the Seventeenth Century*, 1–39, London: Chatto and Windus.
Knowles, Katie (2014), *Shakespeare's Boys: A Cultural History*, Basingstoke: Palgrave Macmillan.
Koops, Willem and Michael Zuckerman, eds (2003), *Beyond the Century of the Child: Cultural History and Developmental Psychology*, Philadelphia: University of Pennsylvania Press.
Lamb, Edel (2009), *Performing Childhood in the Early Modern Theatre: The Children's Playing Companies, 1599–1613*, Basingstoke: Palgrave Macmillan.
Lawhorn, Mark (2007), Appendix 1: 'Children in Shakespeare's Plays: An Annotated Checklist', in Kate Chedgzoy, Suzanne Greenhalgh and Robert Shaughnessy (eds), *Shakespeare and Childhood*, 233–49, Cambridge: Cambridge University Press.
Leavis, F. R. (1932), 'The Literary Mind', *Scrutiny*, 1.
Lebeau, Vicky (2008), *Childhood and Cinema*, London: Reaktion Books.
Leggatt, James and Julie Taddeo, eds (2014), *Upstairs and Downstairs: British Costume Drama Television from the Forsyte Saga to Downton Abbey*, Lanham: Rowman & Littlefield.
Lehmann, Courtney (2009), 'Apocalyptic Paternalism, Family Values, and the War of the Cinemas; or, How Shakespeare Became Posthuman',

in Melissa Croteau and Carolyn Jess-Cooke (eds), *Apocalyptic Shakespeare: Essays on Visions of Chaos and Revelation in Recent Film Adaptations*, 47–69, Jefferson: McFarland and Company.

Lehmann, Courtney, Bryan Reynolds and Lisa Starks (2003), 'The Spectacle of Suffering in Taymor's *Titus*', in Bryan Reynolds (ed), *Performing Transversally: Reimagining Shakespeare and the Critical Future*, 215–43, Basingstoke: Palgrave Macmillan.

Letts, Quentin (2015), 'Dame Judi's Voice Brings a Glow to This Winter's Tale', *Daily Mail*, 9 November. Available online: https://www.dailymail.co.uk/tvshowbiz/article-3309718/Dame-Judi-s-voice-brings-glow-Winter-s-Tale-says-Quentin-Letts.html (accessed 15 April 2019).

Lollar, Kate (2015), 'Interview with Kenneth Branagh', *Bender/Helper Impact*, November. Available online: http://www.branaghcompendium.com/kb_wt_interview_november2015.html (accessed 18 April 2019).

London, John, ed (2000), *Theatre under the Nazis*, Manchester: Manchester University Press.

Luca, Maria de and Mary Lindroth (2000), 'Mayhem, Madness, Method: An Interview with Julie Taymor', *Cineaste*, 25 (3): 28–31.

Luke, Colin (1994), *Forty Minutes: The Making of Them*, London: Mosaic Pictures for the BBC.

MacCrary, W. Thomas (1985), *Friends and Lovers: The Phenomenology of Desire in Shakespearean Comedy*, New York: Columbia University Press.

Madelaine, Richard (2003), 'Material Boys: Apprenticeship and the Boy Actors' Shakespearean Roles', in Lloyd Davis (ed), *Shakespeare Matters: History, Teaching, Performance*, 225–32, London: Associated University Presses.

Malkovich, Amberyl (2013), *Charles Dickens and the Victorian Child: Romanticizing and Socializing the Imperfect Child*, Abingdon: Routledge.

Marcus, Steven (1965), *Dickens from Pickwick to Dombey*, New York: Chatto and Windus.

Masten, Jeffrey (1997), *Textual Intercourse: Collaboration, Authorship, and Sexualities in Renaissance Drama*, Cambridge: Cambridge University Press.

Matz, Robert (2010), 'The Scandal of Shakespeare's Sonnets', *ELH*, 77 (2): 447–508.

McCandless, David (2002), 'A Tale of Two *Tituses*: Julie Taymor's Vision on Stage and Screen', *Shakespeare Quarterly*, 53 (4): 487–511.

McDonald, Russ (2006), *Shakespeare's Late Style*, Cambridge: Cambridge University Press.

McMillan, Joyce (1993), 'Plays for Today', *Guardian*, 4 May: A6.

McMillan, Joyce (2016), '*Richard III* Performance Is a Study in Evil', *Scotsman*, 18 August. Available online: https://www.scotsman.com/

lifestyle-2-15039/culture/edinburgh-festivals/richard-iii-performance-is-a-study-in-evil-1-4206232 (accessed 18 April 2019).

Menon, Madhavi, ed (2011), *Shakesqueer: A Queer Companion to the Complete Works of Shakespeare*, Durham and London: Duke University Press.

Merchant, Meolwyn (1959), *Shakespeare and the Artist*, Oxford: Oxford University Press.

Miller, David Lee (2003), *Dreams of the Burning Child: Sacrificial Sons and the Father's Witness*, Ithaca: Cornell University Press.

Monahan, Mark (2015), 'A Tale of Two Kingdoms', in Christopher Wheeldon's *The Winter's Tale* programme: 11–14.

Monahan, Mark (2016), '*The Winter's Tale* Is a Classic of Modern Ballet – Review', *Telegraph*, 14 April. Available online: https://www.telegraph.co.uk/dance/what-to-see/the-winters-tale-royal-ballet-covent-garden-review/ (accessed 18 April 2019).

Morrison, Nick (2016), email to the author, 19 September.

Morse, Margaret (1998), *Virtualities: Television, Media Art, and Cyberculture*, Bloomington: Indiana University Press.

Mulvey, Laura (1975), 'Visual Pleasure and Narrative Cinema', *Screen*, 16 (3): 6–18.

Muñoz, José Esteban (2009), *Cruising Utopia: The Then and There of Queer Futurity*, New York: New York University Press.

Munro, Lucy (2005a), *Children of the Queen's Revels: A Jacobean Theatre Repertory*, Cambridge: Cambridge University Press.

Munro, Lucy (2005b), '"Little Apes and Tender Babes": Children in Three Film Versions of *Richard III*', in Sarah Hatchuel and Nathalie Vienne-Guerin (eds), *Shakespeare on Screen: Richard III*, 161–77, Rouen: Publications de l'Universite de Rouen.

Nathan, John (2013), *Jewish Chronicle*, 'Review: *Macbeth*', 28 February. Available online: https://www.thejc.com/culture/theatre/review-macbeth-1.42329 (accessed 18 April 2019).

Newcomb, Humphrey Lori (2002), *Reading Popular Romance in Early Modern England*, New York: Columbia University Press.

Noakes, J. and G. Pridham, eds (1984), *Nazism: 1919–1945, State, Economy and Society 1933–1939*, 3 vols, Exeter: Exeter University Press.

Norman, Neil (2016), 'The Royal Ballet's *The Winter's Tale* Review – Outstanding', *The Stage*, 13 April. Available online: https://www.thestage.co.uk/reviews/2016/the-royal-ballets-the-winters-tale-review-outstanding/ (accessed 18 April 2019).

O'Connor, John J. (1985), 'TV Weekend; *Titus Andronicus* in Shakespeare Series', *New York Times*, 19 April: 30.

O'Connor, John O. and Katherine Goodland (2007), *A Directory of Shakespeare in Performance: 1970–2005*, Basingstoke: Palgrave Macmillan.

Ong, Walter J. (1981), *Fighting for Life: Contest, Sexuality, and Consciousness*, Ithaca: Cornell University Press.

Orgel, Stephen (1996), *Impersonations: The Performance of Gender in Shakespeare's England*, Cambridge: Cambridge University Press.

Osborne, Charles (1987), 'Review of *Titus Andronicus*', *Telegraph*, in *London Theatre Record*, 7 (10): 636.

Packard, Bethany (2013), '*Richard III*'s Baby Teeth', *Renaissance Drama*, 41: 107–29.

Parker-Starbuck, Jennifer (2004), 'Framing the Fragments: The Wooster Group's Use of Technology', in Johan Callens (ed), *The Wooster Group and Its Traditions*, 215–31, Brussels: Peter Lang Publishing.

Pearson, Joseph (2015), 'Celebrating Evil: *Richard III* at the Schaubühne: A Conversation with Thomas Ostermeier', *Schaubühne* website, 29 January. Available online: http://www.schaubuehne.de/en/blog/celebrating-evil-richard-iii-at-the-schaubuehne.html (accessed 20 May 2019).

Pequigney, Joseph (1987), *Such Is My Love: Study of Shakespeare's Sonnets*, Chicago: University of Chicago Press.

Peter, John (1987), 'Taming the Text with Intelligence', *Sunday Times*, 13 September.

Peter, John (1993), 'Review of *Macbeth*', *The Sunday Times*, in *Theatre Record*, 13 (10): 573.

Phelan, Peggy (1993), *Unmarked: The Politics of Performance*, London: Routledge.

Pitcher, John (2010), 'Introduction', in *The Winter's Tale*, Arden Shakespeare Third Series, London: Bloomsbury Publishing.

Polanski, Roman (1984), *Roman*, London: Heinemann.

Poore, Benjamin (2012), *Heritage, Nostalgia and Modern British Theatre: Staging the Victorians*, Basingstoke: Palgrave Macmillan.

Postman, Neil ([1982] 1994), *The Disappearance of Childhood*, New York: Vintage Books.

Power, Andrew J. and Rory Loughnane, eds (2013), *Late Shakespeare 1608–1613*, Cambridge: Cambridge University Press.

Power, Annie (2007), 'Discussion of Trauma at the Threshold: The Impact of Boarding School on Attachment in Young Children', *Attachment: New Directions in Psychotherapy and Relational Psychoanalysis*, 1.

Purves, Libby (2011), 'Torn between Terror and Rage – A Macbeth That Moves the Heart, *The Times*, 27 April, 'Arts and Sports': 6.

Purves, Libby (2013), 'Macbeth Trafalgar Studios, SW1', *The Times*, 25 February, 'Arts and Sports': 10.

Quinn, Michael L. (1990), 'Celebrity and the Semiotics of Acting', *NLQ*, 6: 154–61.

Rackin, Phyllis (1986), 'Temporality, Anachronism, and Presence in Shakespeare's English Histories', *Renaissance Drama*, 17: 101–23.
Renton, Alex (2017), *Stiff Upper Lip: Secrets Crimes and the Schooling of a Ruling Class*, London: Weidenfeld and Nicolson.
Reynolds, Bryan, ed (2003), *Performing Transversally: Reimagining Shakespeare and the Critical Future*, Basingstoke: Palgrave Macmillan.
Reynolds, Brian and William N. West, eds (2005), *Rematerializing Shakespeare: Authority and Representation on the Early Modern Stage*, Basingstoke: Palgrave Macmillan.
Ridout, Nicholas (2006), *Stage Fright, Animals and Other Theatrical Problems*, Cambridge: Cambridge University Press.
Rissik, Andrew (1987), 'Review of *Titus Andronicus*', *Independent*, in *London Theatre Record*, 7.10: 635.
Roach, Joseph (1996), *Cities of the Dead: Circum-Atlantic Performance*, New York: Columbia University Press.
Roach, Joseph (2009), '"Unpath'd Waters, Undream'd Shores": Herbert Blau, Performing Doubles, and the Makeup of Memory in *The Winter's Tale*', *Modern Language Quarterly*, 70 (1): 117–31.
Rose, Jacqueline (1993), *The Case of Peter Pan: Or the Impossibility of Children's Fiction*, Philadelphia: Pennsylvania University Press.
Rosenberg, Marvin (1974), 'Lady Macbeth's Indispensable Child', *Educational Theatre Journal*, 26: 14–19.
Rosenberg, Marvin (1978), *The Masks of Macbeth*, Berkeley: University of California Press.
Roth, Christine (2009), 'Looking through the Spyglass: Lewis Carroll, James Barrie, and the Empire of Childhood', in Christopher Hollingsworth (ed), *Alice beyond Wonderland: Essays for the Twenty-First Century*, 23–36, Iowa: University of Iowa Press.
Rothwell, Kenneth (1973), 'Roman Polanski's *Macbeth*: Golgotha Triumphant', *Literature/Film Quarterly*, 1: 71–5.
Rothwell, Kenneth (2004), *A History of Shakespeare on Screen: A Century of Film and Television*, 2nd edn, Cambridge: Cambridge University Press.
Royster, Francesca T. (2000), 'White-Limed Walls: Whiteness and Gothic Extremism in Shakespeare's *Titus Andronicus*', *Shakespeare Quarterly*, 51.4: 432–57.
Rutter, Carol (1988), *Clamorous Voices: Shakespeare's Women Today*, London: The Women's Press.
Rutter, Carol Chillington (2001), *Enter the Body: Women and Representation on Shakespeare's Stage*, Abingdon: Routledge.
Rutter, Carol Chillington (2004), 'Remind Me: How Many Children Had Lady Macbeth?', *Shakespeare Survey*, 57: 38–53.
Rutter, Carol Chillington (2007a), 'Looking Like a Child – or – Titus: The Comedy', *Shakespeare Survey*: 1–26.

Rutter, Carol Chillington (2007b), *Shakespeare and Child's Play: Performing Lost Boys on Stage and Screen*, Abingdon: Routledge.

Rutter, Carol Chillington (2010), '"A World Ransomed, or One Destroyed": English *Tales* at the Millennium', in Judith Dunbar (ed), *Shakespeare in Performance: The Winter's Tale*, 213–42, Manchester: Manchester University Press.

Rutter, Carol Chillington (2012), 'Shakespeare Performances in England (and Wales) 2011', *Shakespeare Survey*, 65: 445–83.

Rutter, Carol Chillington (2017), 'Shakespeare for Dummies: Or, "See the Puppets Dallying"', in James Bulman (ed), *The Oxford Handbook of Shakespeare and Performance*, 64–86, Oxford: Oxford University Press.

Sahoo, Narottam (2003), 'Puppetry: The Perfect Medium for Edutainment and S&T Communication, *Current Science*, 84 (8): 976–77.

Sasser, M. Tyler (2018), 'Moth and the Pedagogical Ideal in Love's Labour's Lost', in Jennifer Higginbotham and Mark Albert Johnston (eds), *Queering Childhood in Early Modern English Drama and Culture*, 153–70, Basingstoke: Palgrave Macmillan.

Schaverien, Joy (2004), 'Boarding School: The Trauma of the "Privileged" Child', *Journal of Analytical Psychology*, 4: 683–705.

Schaverien, Joy (2011), 'Boarding School Syndrome: Broken Attachments a Hidden Trauma', *British Journal of Psychotherapy*, 27: Available online: https://onlinelibrary.wiley.com/doi/10.1111/j.1752-0118.2011.01229.x (accessed 19 April 2019).

Schlicke, Paul (2004), 'Dickens and Shakespeare', *The Japan Branch of the Dickens Fellowship* 27: 84–98. Available online: http://www.dickens.jp/archive/general/g-schlicke.pdf (accessed 19 April 2019).

Schnapp, Jeffrey T. (1996), *Staging Fascism: 18 BL and the Theater of Masses For Masses*, Stanford: Stanford University Press.

Scott, Charlotte (2018), *The Child in Shakespeare*, Oxford: Oxford University Press.

Scraton, Phil, ed (1997), *Childhood in Crisis?*, London: Routledge.

Senelick, Laurence (2000), *The Changing Room: Sex, Drag and Theatre*, London: Routledge.

Shenton, Mark (2015), 'I Have Unfinished Business with Romeo and Juliet', *The Stage*, 1 November. Available online: https://www.thestage.co.uk/features/interviews/2015/kenneth-branagh-i-have-unfinished-business-with-romeo-and-juliet/ (accessed 19 April 2019).

Sher, Anthony (2009), *Beside Myself: An Actor's Life*, London: Nick Hern Books.

Silverstone, Catherine (2014), *Shakespeare, Trauma and Contemporary Performance*, Abingdon: Routledge.

Smallwood, Robert, ed (2007), *Players of Shakespeare 6: Essays in the Performance of Shakespeare's History Plays*, Cambridge: Cambridge University Press.

Smidt, Kristian (1969), *The Tragedy of King Richard the Third: Parallel Texts of the First Quarto and the First Folio with Variants of the Early Quartos*, New York: Humanities Press.

Smith, Bruce R. (1994), *Homosexual Desire in Shakespeare's England: A Cultural Poetics*, Chicago: University of Chicago Press.

Smith, Emma (2000), 'Branagh's *In the Bleak Midwinter* and *Hamlet*', in Mark Thornton Burnett and Ramona Wray (eds), *Shakespeare, Film, Fin de Siècle*, 137–46, Basingstoke: Macmillan Press.

Smith, Emma (2013), *Macbeth: Language and Writing*, London: Bloomsbury.

Smith, Emma (2019), *This Is Shakespeare*, London: Pelican.

Smith, Ian (2003), '*Titus Andronicus*: A Time for Race and Revenge', in Richard Dutton and Jean E. Howard (eds), *A Companion to Shakespeare's Works: The Tragedies*, 284–302, Oxford: Blackwell.

Snyder, Joel (n.d.), 'Sharing the Story Within: An Interview with Julie Taymor'. Available online: https://www.uv.es/~fores/programa/snyder_taymor.html (accessed 13 April 2019).

Sofer, Andrew (2003), *The Stage Life of Props*, Michigan: University of Michigan Press.

Sontag, Susan (1966), 'Film and Theatre', *The Tulane Drama Review*, 11 (1): 24–37.

Spencer, Charles (2011), 'Review of *Macbeth*', *Telegraph*, 26 April. Available online: https://www.telegraph.co.uk/culture/theatre/theatre-reviews/8475694/Macbeth-RSC-Stratford-upon-Avon-review.html (accessed 19 April 2019).

Spencer, Charles (2013), 'James McAvoy in Macbeth, Trafalgar Studios', *Telegraph*, 23 February. Available online: https://www.telegraph.co.uk/culture/theatre/theatre-reviews/9888291/James-McAvoy-in-Macbeth-Trafalgar-Studios-review.html (accessed 19 April 2019).

Stambollouian, Edward (2013), 'Tethered to the Text', in Jamie Lloyd's *Macbeth* programme.

Stambollouian, Edward (2014), email to the author, 26 June.

Stanavage, Liberty and Paxton Hehmeyer, eds (2012), *Titus Out of Joint: Reading the Fragmented Titus Andronicus*, Newcastle upon Tyne: Cambridge Scholars Publishing.

Starks, Lisa S. (2002), 'Cinema of Cruelty: Powers of Horror in Julie Taymor's *Titus*', in Lisa S. Starks and Courtney Lehmann (eds), *The Reel Shakespeare: Alternative Cinema and Theory*, 121–41, London: Associated University Presses.

Starks, Lisa S. and Courtney Lehmann, eds (2002), *The Reel Shakespeare: Alternative Cinema and Theory*, London: Associated University Presses.

States, Bert O. (1985), *Great Reckonings in Little Rooms: On the Phenomenology of Theatre*, Berkeley: University of California Press.
Steedman, Carolyn (1995), *Strange Dislocations: Childhood and the Idea of Human Interiority 1780–1930*, London: Virago.
Stockton, Kathryn Bond (2009), *The Queer Child or Growing Sideways in the Twentieth Century*, Durham: Duke University Press.
Stockton, Kathryn Bond (2011), 'Lost, or "Exit, Pursued by a Bear": Causing Queer Children on Shakespeare's TV', in Madhavi Menon (ed), *Shakesqueer: A Queer Companion to the Complete Works of Shakespeare*, 421–8, Durham and London: Duke University Press.
Strobl, Gerwin (2007), *The Swastika and the Stage: German Theatre and Society, 1933–1945*, Cambridge: Cambridge University Press.
Swain, Marianka (2015), 'The Winter's Tale, Garrick Theatre, Review: "Ripe with Operatic Excess"', *Ham&High*, 13 November. Available online: https://www.hamhigh.co.uk/etcetera/theatre/the-winter-s-tale-garrick-theatre-review-ripe-with-operatic-excess-1-4308776 (accessed 19 April 2019).
Szalwinska, Maxie (2015), 'A Bang and a Wimple: Branagh's Rep Season Starts with a Flourish as Judi Dench Wows in The Winter's Tale', *The Sunday Times*, 15 November: 20.
Tatspaugh, Patricia E. (2002), *The Winter's Tale*, Shakespeare at Stratford Series, London: Arden Shakespeare.
Taylor, James, R. (2014), 'The Shadow Puppets of Elsinore: Edward Gorgon Craig and the Cranach Press Hamlet', *Theatre Design and Technology*, 50 (3): 40–55.
Taylor, Neil (1994), 'Two Types of Television Shakespeare', in Andrew Davies and Stanley Wells (eds), *Shakespeare and the Moving Image: The Plays on Film and Television*, 86–98, Cambridge: Cambridge University Press.
Taylor, Paul (2013a), 'Review: Macbeth Starring James McAvoy, Trafalgar Studio 1, London', *Independent*, 23 February. Available online: https://www.independent.co.uk/arts-entertainment/theatre-dance/reviews/review-macbeth-starring-james-mcavoy-trafalgar-studio-1-london-8506690.html (accessed 19 April 2019).
Taylor, Paul (2013b), 'The Man Who Would Be King: Kenneth Branagh Makes a Long-Awaited Return to Shakespeare', *Independent*, 26 June. Available online: https://www.independent.co.uk/arts-entertainment/theatre-dance/features/the-man-who-would-be-king-kenneth-branagh-makes-a-long-awaited-return-to-shakespeare-8675491.html (accessed 19 April 2019).
Taymor, Julie (2000), *Titus: The Illustrated Screenplay*, New York: Newmarket Press.
Thomas, Keith (1976), *Rule and Misrule in the Schools of Early Modern England*, Reading: University of Reading.

Tillotson, Kathleen ([1954] 1956), *Novels of the Eighteen-Forties*, Oxford: Oxford University Press.

Torney, Kathryn (2011), 'The Case Which Changed the Face of Youth Justice', *thedetail*, 8 May. Available online: http://www.thedetail.tv/articles/the-case-which-changed-the-face-of-youth-justice (accessed 10 May 2019).

Tosh, Will (2016), *Male Friendship and Testimonies of Love in Shakespeare's England*, London: Palgrave Macmillan.

Treneman, Ann (2015), 'Review of *The Winter's Tale*', *The Times*, 9 November. Available online: https://www.thetimes.co.uk/article/the-winters-tale-at-garrick-wc2-p5lfbj8h9rr (accessed 19 April 2019).

Tribble, Evelyn (2009), 'Marlowe's Boy Actor', *Shakespeare Bulletin*, 27 (1): 5–17.

Ue, Tom (2016), 'Review of Shakespeare's *Macbeth*', *Shakespeare*, 12 (4): 465–7.

Unjieng, Philip Cu (2016), 'Shakespeare's Masterpiece by Another Name', *The Philippine Star*, 25 January. Available online: https://www.philstar.com/entertainment/2016/01/24/1545928/shakespeares-masterpiece-another-name (accessed 19 April 2019).

Wagner, Matthew D. (2012), *Shakespeare, Theatre, and Time*, Routledge Advances in Theatre and Performance Studies Series, Abingdon: Routledge.

Wagner, Meike (2006), 'Of Other Bodies: The Intermedial Gaze in the Theatre', in Freda Chapple and Chiel Kattenbelt (eds), *Intermediality in Theatre and Performance*, 125–36, Amsterdam and New York: Rodopi, 2006.

Weber, William W. (2014), 'Shakespeare After All?: The Authorship of *Titus Andronicus* 4.1 Reconsidered', *Shakespeare Survey*, 67: 69–84.

Wells, Stanley (1989), 'Shakespeare Performances in London and Stratford-upon-Avon, 1986–7', *Shakespeare Survey*, 41: 159–82.

Wells, Stanley (2012), 'Judi Dench', in John Russell Brown (ed), *The Routledge Companion to Actors' Shakespeare*, 27–39, Abingdon: Routledge.

Welsh, Alexander (1987), *From Copyright to Copperfield: The Identity of Dickens*, Massachusetts: Harvard University Press.

Werner, Sarah (2001), *Shakespeare and Feminist Performance: Ideology on Stage*, London: Routledge.

Werner, Sarah, ed (2010), *New Directions in Renaissance Drama and Performance Studies*, Basingstoke: Palgrave Macmillan.

White, Mark (2005), *Kenneth Branagh*, London: Faber and Faber.

Willems, Michèle (1987a), *Shakespeare à la television*, Rouen: Publications de L'Université de Rouen.

Willems, Michèle (1987b), 'Verbal-Visual, Verbal-Pictorial or Textual-Televisual? Reflections on the BBC Shakespeare Series', *Shakespeare Survey*, 39: 91–111.
Williams, Deanne (2004), 'Mick Jagger *Macbeth*', *Shakespeare Survey*, 57: 145–58.
Williams, Deanne (2014), *Shakespeare and the Performance of Girlhood*, Basingstoke: Palgrave Macmillan.
Williams, Katherine Schaap (2009), 'Enabling Richard: The Rhetoric of Disability, *Richard III*', *Disability Studies Quarterly*, 29 (4). Online article: http://www.dsq-sds.org/article/view/997.
Witmore, Michael (2007), *Pretty Creatures: Children and Fiction in the English Renaissance*, Ithaca: Cornell University Press.
Wolf, Matt (2015), 'Review: "The Winter's Tale," "Harlequinade" and "The Moderate Soprano"', *New York Times*, 19 November. Available online: https://www.nytimes.com/2015/11/20/arts/international/review-the-winters-tale-harlequinade-and-the-moderate-soprano.html (accessed 19 April 2019).
Worthen, W. B. (1994), 'Of Actors and Automata: Hieroglyphics of Modernism', *Journal of Dramatic Theory and Criticism*, 9 (1): 3–20.
Zieger, Susan (2009), 'Dickens's Queer Children', *Literature Interpretation Theory*, 20 (1–2): 141–57.
Zipes, Jack (1989), *Victorian Fairy Tales: The Revolt of the Fairies and Elves*, Abingdon: Routledge.

Stage productions, television broadcasts and films

Dates given are dates of first production, not publication.

Branagh, Kenneth, *In the Bleak Midwinter* (1995), [film] dir. Kenneth Branagh, UK: Sony Pictures Classics.
Craig, Peter and Danny Strong, *The Hunger Games: Mockingjay – Part 2* (2015), [film] dir. Francis Lawrence, USA: Lionsgate Films.
Davies, Andrew, *Little Dorrit* (2008), [television series] dir. Adam Smith, Dearbhla Walsh and Diarmuid Lawrence, UK: BBC.
Delves, Stuart, *Macbeth Possessed* (1985), dir. Stuart Delves, Tron Theatre, Glasgow.
Hughes, John, *Home Alone* (1990), [film] dir. Chris Columbus, USA: Twentieth Century Fox.
Johnson, Michael Robert, Andrew Peckham and Simon Kinberg, *Holmes* (2009), [film] dir. Guy Ritchie, USA: Warner Bros.

Marlowe, Christopher, *Edward II* (1991), [film] dir. Derek Jarman, UK: Working Title Films.
Middleton, Thomas (1987/8), *The Revenger's Tragedy*, dir. Di Trevis, The Swan Theatre, Stratford-upon-Avon.
Rattigan, Terence, *All On Her Own* (2015/16), dir. Kenneth Branagh and Rob Ashford, Garrick Theatre, London.
Rattigan, Terence, *Harlequinade* (2015/16), dir. Kenneth Branagh and Rob Ashford, Garrick Theatre, London.
Schulman, Tom, *Dead Poets Society* (1989), [film] dir. Peter Weir, USA: Buena Vista.
Sears, Ted and others, *Snow White and the Seven Dwarfs* (1937), dir. David Hand and others, US: RKO Radio Pictures.
Shakespeare, William, *Hamlet* (1996), [film] dir. Kenneth Branagh, US/UK: Columbia Pictures.
Shakespeare, William, *Hamlet* (2006), dir. Elizabeth LeCompte for The Wooster Group, touring.
Shakespeare, William, *Henry V* (1989), [film] dir. Kenneth Branagh, US/UK: The Samuel Goldwyn Company and Curzon Film Distributors.
Shakespeare, William, *Macbeth* (1936), dir. Orson Welles, Lafayette Theatre, Adelphi Theatre.
Shakespeare, William, *Macbeth* (1948), [film] dir. Orson Welles, US: Republic Pictures.
Shakespeare, William, *Macbeth* (1971), [film] dir. Roman Polanski, US: Columbia Pictures.
Shakespeare, William, *Macbeth* (1986), dir. Adrian Noble, Royal Shakespeare Theatre, Stratford-upon-Avon.
Shakespeare, William, *Macbeth* (1995), dir. Philip Frank, Crucible, Sheffield.
Shakespeare, William, *Macbeth* (1999), dir. Gregory Doran, Swan Theatre, Stratford-upon-Avon.
Shakespeare, William, *Macbeth* (2004), dir. Andrew Hilton, Tobacco Factory, Bristol.
Shakespeare, William, *Macbeth* (2004), dir. Dominic Cooke, Royal Shakespeare Theatre, Stratford-upon-Avon.
Shakespeare, William, *Macbeth* (2005), dir. John Caird, Almeida Theatre, London.
Shakespeare, William, *Macbeth* (2011), dir. Gemma Bodinetz, Everyman Theatre, Liverpool.
Shakespeare, William, *Macbeth* (2012), dir. Daniel Evans, Crucible, Sheffield.
Shakespeare, William, *Macbeth* (2013), dir. Jamie Lloyd, Trafalgar Studios, London.
Shakespeare, William, *Macbeth* (2015), [film] dir. Justin Kurzel, UK: StudioCanal.

Shakespeare, William, *A Midsummer Night's Dream* (1996), [film] dir. Adrian Noble, UK: FilmFour.
Shakespeare, William, *Richard III* (1992), dir. Sam Mendes, The Other Place, Stratford-upon-Avon.
Shakespeare, William, *Richard III* (1955), [film] dir. Laurence Olivier, UK: London Films.
Shakespeare, William, *Richard III* (1995), [film] dir. Richard Loncraine, US: United Artists.
Shakespeare, William, *Richard III* (2003), dir. Sean Holmes, Royal Shakespeare Theatre, Stratford-upon-Avon.
Shakespeare, William, *Richard III* (2011), dir. Sam Mendes, The Old Vic, London.
Shakespeare, William, *Richard III* (2012), dir. Roxana Silbert, Swan Theatre, Stratford-upon-Avon.
Shakespeare, William, *Richard III* (2012), dir. Tim Carroll, Shakespeare's Globe, London.
Shakespeare, William, *Richard III* (2014), dir. Jamie Lloyd, Trafalgar Studios, London.
Shakespeare, William, *Richard III* (2015), dir. Thomas Ostermeier, Avignon Festival, Avignon, France.
Shakespeare, William, *Richard III* (2016), dir. Rupert Goold, Almeida Theatre, London
Shakespeare, William, *Romeo and Juliet* (2016), dir. Kenneth Branagh and Rob Ashford, Garrick Theatre, London.
Shakespeare, William, *Titus* (1999), [film] dir. Julie Taymor, US: Fox Searchlight Pictures.
Shakespeare, William, *Titus Andronicus* (1955), dir. Peter Brook, Shakespeare Memorial Theatre, Stratford-upon-Avon.
Shakespeare, William, *Titus Andronicus* (1985) [television film] dir. Jane Howell, UK: BBC.
Shakespeare, William, *Titus Andronicus: The Movie* (1996), [film] dir. Lorn Richey, US: Lorn Richey Productions.
Shakespeare, William, *Titus Andronicus* (1999), [film] dir. Christopher Dunne, US: Joe Redner Film & Productions.
Shakespeare, William, *Titus Andronicus* (2000), [film] dir. Richard Griffin, US: South Main Street Productions.
Shakespeare, William, *Titus Andronicus* (2001–2), dir. Xavier Leret, Edinburgh and on tour.
Shakespeare, William, *Titus Andronicus* (2003), dir. Bill Alexander, Royal Shakespeare Theatre, Stratford-upon-Avon.
Shakespeare, William, *Titus Andronicus* (2006), dir. Yukio Ninagawa, Royal Shakespeare Theatre, Stratford-upon-Avon.
Shakespeare, William, *Titus Andronicus* (2006 and 2014), dir. Lucy Bailey, Shakespeare's Globe, London.

Shakespeare, William, *Titus Andronicus* (2007), dir. Gale Edwards, Lansburgh Theatre, Washington.
Shakespeare, William, *Titus Andronicus* (2013), dir. Michael Fentiman, Swan Theatre, Stratford-upon-Avon.
Shakespeare, William, *The Winter's Tale* (1987), dir. Michael Kahn, The Shakespeare Theatre, Washington.
Shakespeare, William, *The Winter's Tale* (1992), dir. Annabel Arden for Theatre de Complicité, Lyric Hammersmith, London and touring.
Shakespeare, William, *The Winter's Tale* (1997–99), dir. Declan Donnellan for Maly Drama Theatre, St. Petersburg and touring.
Shakespeare, William, *The Winter's Tale* (1998/9). dir. Gregory Doran, Royal Shakespeare Theatre, Stratford-upon-Avon, transferring to the Barbican, London.
Shakespeare, William, *The Winter's Tale* (2001), dir. Nicholas Hytner, National Theatre, London.
Shakespeare, William, *The Winter's Tale* (2005 and 2012), dir. Edward Hall for Propeller, touring.
Shakespeare, William, *The Winter's Tale* (2009), dir. Sam Mendes, The Old Vic, London and touring.
Shakespeare, William, *The Winter's Tale* (2013), dir. Lucy Bailey, Royal Shakespeare Theatre, Stratford-upon-Avon.
Shakespeare, William, *The Winter's Tale* (2014 and 2016), [ballet] choreographer and dir. Christopher Wheeldon, Royal Opera House, London.
Shakespeare, William, *The Winter's Tale* (2015), dir. Conrad Nelson, Viaduct Theatre, Halifax.
Shakespeare, William, *The Winter's Tale* (2015/16), dir. Kenneth Branagh and Rob Ashford, Garrick Theatre, London.
Shakespeare, William, *The Winter's Tale* (2015/16), dir. Michael Longhurst, Sam Wanamaker Theatre, London.
Shakespeare, William, *The Winter's Tale* (2017), [opera] composer Ryan Wigglesworth, dir. Rory Kinnear, London Coliseum.
Shakespeare, William, *The Winter's Tale* (2016/17), dir. Declan Donnellan, Barbican Theatre, London and touring.
Sherwin, David, *If* (1968) [film] dir. Lindsay Anderson, UK: Paramount British Pictures.
Tally, Ted, *The Silence of the Lambs* (1991), dir. Jonathan Demme, US: Orion Pictures.
Tarantino, Quentin, *Kill Bill Vols 1 and 2* (2003, 2004), dir. Quentin Tarantino, US: Miramax Films.
Tarantino, Quentin, *Reservoir Dogs* (1992), dir. Quentin Tarantino, US: Miramax Films.
Tarantino, Quentin, *True Romance* (1993), dir. Tony Scott, US: Warner Bros Pictures.

Thomas, Heidi, *Cranford* (2007), [television series] dir. Simon Curtis and Steve Hudson, UK: BBC.
Weitz, Chris, *Cinderella* (2015), [film] dir. Kenneth Branagh, US: Walt Disney Studios.

Music and artwork

Caravaggio (1601–2), *Amor Vincit Omnia*.
Caravaggio (1608), *Sleeping Cupid*.
Da Messina, Antonello (1476), *L'Annunciata*.
Jackson, Michael (1991), *Black or White*, Epic Records.
Raphael (1512), *The Triumph of Galatea*.
Schumann, Robert (1838), *Kinderszenen* (Scenes from Childhood) Op. 15.

Exhibitions and conferences

'The Game's Afoot' (2016), Madame Tussaud's Theatre.
'Neo-Victorian Cultures: The Victorians Today' (July 2013), Centre of English and Cultural History, Liverpool John Moores University.
'Victoriana: The Art of Revival' (2013), the Guildhall Gallery, London.

INDEX

aborted pregnancy 66. *See also* miscarriage
absence 3, 6, 20, 40, 42, 50, 60, 136, 156, 167, 171
actor/actors 9, 10, 17, 19, 24–53, 59–60, 67, 69–76, 84, 88, 95, 99, 102–7, 110, 113–14, 125, 127, 146, 157–8, 167, 168–9
adapt/adaptation 1, 3, 5–6, 9–11, 15, 17–20, 23–4, 26, 31, 39, 45, 57–8, 73–6, 87, 90, 95–6, 106–8, 114, 130, 132–3, 135–6, 142, 153, 155, 175, 177
adolescence 95, 103–4, 107, 129, 131
adult-child 31, 36, 56, 126–7. *See also* childish adult; regressive/regression
adulthood 7, 11, 13, 17, 36, 56, 137, 140, 146–7, 152, 162, 173
adultified 120, 148, 172. *See also* childified
adults 11, 13, 15, 23, 30, 32, 37, 42, 50, 52–3, 80, 82, 103, 126, 140, 151, 157, 164
Aebischer, Pascale 177
Shakespeare's Violated Bodies: Stage and Screen Performance 98

aestheticizing/aestheticization 26, 97–8, 101, 156
agency 5, 14–15, 19, 42, 51, 53, 56, 76, 90, 106, 127, 131–2, 138, 156. *See also* subjectivity
animatronic 4, 106. *See also* artificiality; prop-baby; puppet
Annis, Francesca 60, 75, 82
apprentices/apprenticeship 28, 103
Arden, Annabel 153
artificiality 3–5, 19, 43–7, 54, 105–7, 130, 132. *See also* animatronic; prop-baby; puppet
Aryan ideal 124–5, 130, 132
Ashford, Rob 9, 12, 15, 20, 133, 140–1, 154–73, 175–8
atonement 138, 160, 164
Atri, Pierre 157
audience 3–5, 20–1, 24–5, 31, 37, 44–5, 47–9, 51–2, 59–60, 63, 70, 74, 78–9, 95, 97–9, 101, 103–5, 107–9, 111, 113–18, 121–2, 125, 129–32, 136, 142, 147, 154, 158, 160, 162, 165, 167–70. *See also* viewer
Auslander, Philip 96
Avignon Festival 40, 43

baby 4–5, 18–19, 25, 33, 58, 60–5, 76–7, 85, 88, 94–6, 99–101, 104–7, 112–13, 116–17, 120, 128–32, 136–9

Bacon, Francis 112
Bailey, Lucy 97, 135
Barker, Roberta 177
Barraclough, Leo 159
Bartholomeusz, Dennis 138
Bate, Jonathan 97, 100
BBC Television Shakespeare 95–6, 107–8
Belsey, Catherine 27, 103
Berne, Eric 151
Billington, Michael 99, 102, 110, 132, 163, 166
binaries 56, 102, 122, 131, 168
Bloom, Gina 139
Bly, Robert 151
Bodinetz, Gemma 61
Boehm-Schnitker, Nadine 155
Bonelli, Federico 4
boy-children 139
Boyd, Michael 19, 58, 67–75, 77, 84, 91, 177
boyhood 3, 139, 141–4, 146, 152–3
Boym, Svetlana 173
Bradley, A. C. 59–60
Branagh, Kenneth 9, 12, 15, 20, 88, 133, 140–1, 154–73, 175, 177
breeching 139, 141, 149
Bristol, Michael 60–1
Brocklehurst, Helen 124
Brome, Richard 136
Brooks, Cleanth 60
Brooks, Libby 15–16
brother 34, 68, 76, 100–2, 113, 139. *See also* sibling
Brown-Lowe, Thomas 146
Buckley, Jessie 157
Bulger, James 14, 16, 25, 69, 74, 90, 176
Burt, Richard 124, 130
Butler, Judith 26, 42

Caird, John 90
Campana, Joseph 5
Carlson, Marvin 167
Carré, John Le 150
Carroll, Tim 25
Cavell, Stanley 5, 20, 139, 175
Cavendish, Dominic 170
celebrity 165–8
chastity 176
Chedgzoy, Kate 8
Chegwin, Keith 78, 125
childhood
  and ambiguity 77, 96, 106, 117
  crisis in 5–7, 11, 14–21, 58, 91, 95, 107, 113, 136, 140, 154, 156, 173, 175–7
  de-idealizing childhood 5, 18, 26
  disappearing childhood 20, 91, 135–73
  erosion of 14, 141
  fetishizing childhood 10–13, 18, 50, 58, 77–8, 83, 86, 110–12, 118, 126, 132, 177
  idealizing childhood 18, 23, 30, 32–3, 40, 56, 78, 99–100, 112, 125, 158, 172, 177
  metaphors of 7–8, 10, 59, 60, 65, 91, 124, 140, 146, 152
childified 148. *See also* adultified
childish adult 140, 147. *See also* adult-child; regressive/regression
childlessness 18, 58–67. *See also* infertility
childness 58, 128
children
  adult-child 31, 36, 126–7
  adultified children 120, 148, 172
  alien child 16, 51, 57, 91
  anti-child 26–39, 56
  child-soldier 84
  child-victim 23, 31, 39
  child-witches 69–74, 84, 89, 90

as commodities 50, 52, 99, 125
complicit child 29–31, 37, 49, 109, 118, 126–7, 130
dead child 5, 40, 70, 87
de-corporealized child 42, 53
dying child 140
as erotico-fetishized objects 11, 83
evil/innocent child 68–70, 73–4, 81–2, 90–1, 131, 176–7
hypothetical child 59, 62–3, 91
as an icon 23, 25, 84, 91, 93, 107, 110, 112, 125–6, 156
inner child 27, 140–54, 172
innocent child 11, 15–17, 24, 33–4, 39–55, 75
Janus-faced child 20, 57–91
knowing child 17–18, 36–9, 49, 80, 126–8
as objects of adult fantasies 56, 100, 162, 172–3, 175
omnipotent tot 126
as 'other' 11, 16, 57, 136
over-determined child 3, 31, 57
premature child 141, 147, 148, 160, 162
sub-tragic child 90, 154
as surrogate victim 155, 157, 161, 167
as symbols/signifiers 7, 8, 10, 12, 17–18, 24, 26–7, 31, 34, 37–9, 42, 50, 58, 60, 61, 64, 67–8, 73–4, 77–8, 80, 82, 85–6, 88, 90–1, 93–4, 96, 100, 104, 107, 112, 122, 125, 130–1, 136, 142, 147, 157, 167, 173, 175, 177
tragic child 17, 90
wise child 20, 140, 155, 162, 164, 166–7
as witness 17, 31–2, 86, 95, 108, 111, 113–18, 126, 130–1, 142

Christmas 156–7, 165
Cibber, Colley 24, 26
Cicero 142
cinema 3–4, 23, 74–5, 78, 84–6, 95–7, 107–11, 118, 126, 130, 159–60
Clapp, Susannah 145
closure 76, 102, 130, 136, 140, 166
coda 76, 81, 128–9
coffin 113, 117, 129
Cohen, Stanley 15, 176
collateral damage 166, 170, 172, 175
Collin, Robbie 77, 88
comedy 43, 97, 160, 170–1
compulsory reproduction 112
Cooke, Dominic 90
corporeality 40, 42, 46, 50, 93
corpse 40, 47, 54, 68, 82, 88, 93, 104
Cotillard, Marion 75, 77
Coveney, Michael 99
Coveney, Peter 161
Cox, Brian 19, 97–9, 102, 132
Craig, Edward Gordon 51–5. *See also* Über-marionette
cross-gender casting 24
Crowley, Bob 5
Culkin, Macaulay 125–7
Cunningham, Hugh 14, 16, 21, 57, 72, 90, 140
Cusack, Sinead 60

Delves, Stuart 68–9
Dench, Judi 157, 164–8
Dessen, Alan 116
destruction/self-destruction 12, 74, 91, 112, 114, 144, 153, 161, 175
determinism/deterministic 54, 107, 109–10
deus ex machina 113

devil 142–3
Dickens, Charles
   A Christmas Carol 161–2
   Dombey and Son 161–2, 167, 172
   Old Curiosity Shop, The 172
disability 44–8
disability studies 47–8
displacement 173, 175
Donaldson, Peter S. 119
Donnellan, Declan 135
doppelgänger 26, 34, 36, 38
Doran, Gregory 61, 63, 90, 153
doubling 6–7, 10, 19, 26, 28, 32, 53, 58, 69–70, 75, 84, 90, 153, 165
Doyle, Patrick 88
Draper, John W. 38
Duffell, Nick 149–51, 152–3
dystopia 18, 62, 91, 119

Edelman, Lee 10–13, 18, 27, 54, 56, 62, 74, 90, 112–14, 124, 130–1, 141, 155, 161–3, 167, 170, 177
eden/edenic 141–3. *See also* prelapsarian
Eidinger, Lars 45–8
Elyot, Thomas 139
Engel, William E. 138
Escolme, Bridget 25, 44, 97–8
Estrin, Barbara L. 36
ethnicity 75, 105
Evans, Daniel 61
evasion 20, 172, 177
Evelyn, John 150
Ewbank, Inga-Stina 138
existentialism 18, 58–67

fairytale 155–72
fall, the 46, 141–4
family/familial 1, 7, 62, 65, 86, 101–4, 107–8, 154–7, 161, 164

fascism 9, 121–4
Fassbender, Michael 77, 86
Father Time 145–7, 153, 160
Faulkner, Joanna 40
Fedderson, Kim 130
Fellini, Federico 112
Fentiman, Michael 97
Fenwick, Henry 100, 108, 113
final girl narrative 128
First Folio 100, 137
Ford, John 177
Foy, Claire 65–6
frame; frame-sequence 6, 76–7, 84, 86, 95, 107–8, 111, 113, 116, 118–27, 132, 153, 156–60, 167
Franks, Philip 61
Freud, Sigmund 59, 141
   'The Uncanny' 36, 38, 73
futility 94, 113, 132, 175
futurity 12–13, 18–20, 27, 38, 42, 54–8, 65, 74, 76, 91, 93–133, 140–1, 156, 161–2, 166, 177

Garber, Marjorie 5–6, 27, 48, 53, 177–8
Garrick Theatre 135, 156, 159
gaze 5, 10, 42, 44, 47, 50, 56, 84, 91, 109–10, 118, 125. *See also* scopophilia; voyeurism
gender 7–8, 10, 24–5, 105, 128–9, 131, 139–40, 144, 149–50, 176
genre 6, 23, 48, 93–4, 96–7, 104–5, 108, 115, 129, 131, 135, 137, 139, 160, 168, 172
Gent, S. S. 136
Gilley, Jeremy 102–3
Gillis, John R. 156–7, 164
Girard, René 155, 157, 161, 166
girl-children 24, 46, 67, 86, 89, 99, 105, 176
Goebbels, Joseph 122, 124

Golby, John 157
Goodland, Katherine 61, 71
Goodman, Henry 31, 34–6
Goodman, Rudi 157
Gore, Will 25
Graber, Jody 177
Gray, John 55
Greenan, Scot 88–9
Greene, Robert 136, 138, 144
Greenhalgh, Suzanne 8
grief 25, 32, 61, 63, 66
grievability 26, 42
Gross, Kenneth 46–7
Gruss, Susanne 155
Grylls, David 140, 161, 164
Guy-Bray, Stephen 143

Halberstam, Judith 12, 147
Hall, Edward (chronicler) 29
Hall, Edward (director) 135
Hammond, Anthony 28, 38
Harris, Lochlann 88
haunting 157, 167
Hazlitt, William 23, 39–40, 42, 51, 55
Heilmann, Ann 155
Hemming, Sarah 163
Hess, Liam 146, 148
heteronormativity 12–13, 144, 164
heterosexual/heterosexualization 141, 152
Hewison, Robert 156
Higginbotham, Jennifer 8, 105, 176
Higonnet, Anne 10, 37, 46, 50, 126
Hilton, Andrew 61
Hiscock, John 158–9, 164
historiography 48, 54, 176
Hitchings, Henry 169
Hitler, Adolf 122, 124
Hollindale, Peter 90, 154, 162
Holmes, Sean 13, 15, 18, 26–39, 56, 76, 103, 126
homoerotic 82, 143, 150, 152, 163–4

homosexual 152
homosocial 144, 150, 152
Howell, Jane 19, 95–6, 100–1, 107–18, 123, 127, 130–2
Hoyle, Martin 69–70
Hytner, Nicholas 13, 20, 132, 140–56, 160, 164, 166, 172–3, 175, 177

ideology 74, 108–9, 114, 121–2, 161, 163
infants/infancy 6–7, 17, 105, 128, 137, 139–40, 146–7, 161, 163, 173
infertility. *See* childlessness
inner child 27, 140–54, 172
inner parent 151–3

Jackson, Michael 125–6
Jackson, Russell 166, 170, 172, 175
Jarman, Derek 177
Jauss, Hans Robert 48
Johns, Geoffrey 47–8
Jones, Osheen 121, 123–5
Jonson, Ben 177
Jordan, Thomas 136
Jowett, David 34–5

Kahn, Michael 153
Kane, Sarah 43, 97
Kaplan, Cora 155
Kathman, David 103
Kelly, Jude 61
Kincaid, James R. 10–13, 16, 43, 46, 83
  Child-Loving: The Erotic Child and Victorian Culture 8, 50, 82, 150
  Erotic Innocence: The Culture of Child Molesting 10–11, 46, 78, 118, 126
Kirwan, Peter 86
Knight, G. Wilson 59

INDEX

Knights, L. C. 59
Knowles, Katie 8, 27, 81–2
Kurzel, Justin 75–91, 123, 177

Lacan, Jacques 110
Lamb, Edel 110
Lawhorn, Mark 17, 27, 38
Leavis, F. R. 59
Lebeau, Vicky 109
legislation 24
Lehmann, Courtney 119, 129
Letts, Quentin 168–9
liminal/liminality 109, 127
livecast 4, 43, 49. *See also* simulcast
Llewellyn, Mark 155
Lloyd, Jamie 18, 25, 58–67, 74, 87, 91, 177
Loncraine, Richard 25
loss 20, 30, 60–7, 85–6, 88, 100, 133, 154–6, 166, 168, 170–1, 173, 175. *See also* mourning

McAvoy, James 65–6
McCandless, David 129
MacCrary, Thomas W. 142
McDonald, Russ 86, 90
McKinley, Mairead 61
McMillan, Joyce 43, 70
Madelaine, Richard 28, 38
Malkovich, Amberyl 164
manipulation 45, 49, 53–4, 65, 73, 82, 84, 99, 106, 114, 126, 132, 138
marginalization 12, 19, 28, 95–107, 112, 127, 131
Marlowe, Christopher 177
masculinity 125
masks 69, 113, 116, 119
maternity 7, 94, 101. *See also* motherhood
mediating/mediatized 42–4, 47, 52, 69, 111, 114, 160, 176

memories/memorialize 3, 7, 16, 36, 86, 88, 145–7, 167, 172
Mendes, Sam 56, 153
Merchant, Meolwyn 23
metatheatre 43, 48, 69, 105, 168, 170
Middleton, Thomas 177
  The Revenger's Tragedy 96
Midwinter's Tale, A 171
miscarriage 66. *See also* aborted pregnancy
Mitchell, Julian 150
Monahan, Mark 3, 154
Montaigne, Michel de 142
Moore, Clement Clark 157
moral panic 15, 176
Morrison, Nick 158
motherhood 60, 124. *See also* maternity
mourning 25, 156, 161. *See also* loss
Mulvey, Laura 10, 110–11, 118, 126
Munro, Lucy 103

Nathan, John 65
nationalism 122
Nazism 121–4, 130
Nelson, Conrad 135
neo-Victorianism 155, 162
Newcomb, Lori Humphrey 136
Nicholas II, Tsar 158
nihilism/nihilistic 12, 42, 55, 67, 76–7, 110, 112, 115, 123, 130, 132
Noble, Adrian 60–3, 103, 125, 160
Norman, Neil 3
nostalgia 7, 20, 32, 140, 142, 146, 156–7, 160, 164, 168, 172–3, 175

obfuscation 15, 94
O'Connor, John 61, 71
O'Connor, John J. 110
Olivier, Laurence 25, 47, 169
ontology 5, 132

Oram, Christopher 156
Orgel, Stephen 24
Osborne, Charles 99, 103
Ostermeier, Thomas 26, 28, 39–56, 71, 131, 171
Ovid 97

Packard, Bethany 28, 33, 38
paedophilia/paedophile 82, 176
pageboys 17–18, 26–39, 49, 76, 88, 136
Parker, Joe 1
Parker-Starbuck, Jennifer 44
parody 45, 66, 81, 112, 168, 170
paternity 105
pathos 24–5, 77, 84, 102. *See also* pity
patriarchy 95, 106, 122, 131, 132, 149, 162–3
Peacock, Trevor 114–15
pederasty 83
Peter, John 71, 96
phenomenology 9–10, 50, 72
Piper, Tom 71
pity 80, 84, 90, 93–4, 101, 116. *See also* pathos
Polanski, Roman 9, 12, 19, 38, 58, 74–91, 110, 125–6, 177
Poore, Benjamin 155, 166
Postman, Neil 5, 16–17, 21, 31, 36, 39, 110, 118–20, 126, 136–7, 140, 146, 148, 172, 176
postmodern/postmodernity 5–7, 11–12, 14–18, 21, 43, 72, 90, 108, 175
pregnancy 7, 66, 78, 137, 144, 163. *See also* maternity
prelapsarian 144. *See also* eden/edenic
prematurity 136, 141, 147–8, 155, 160, 162
prepubescence 76
presexual 126, 163
procreation 60, 176

promptbooks 9, 104–5
prop-baby 19, 105. *See also* animatronic; artificiality; puppet
proxy 30, 95, 108, 113, 132
psychoanalytic studies 151
psycho-pathology 152
public schools 140, 145–54, 164
Puer aeternus 140, 162
Puer senex 17, 162
puppet 18, 39–56, 71, 131. *See also* animatronic; artificiality; prop-baby
Purdue, A. W. 157
Purves, Libby 65, 71

queer theory 12–13, 112, 147, 151–3
Quinn, Michael L. 165

Rattigan, Terence 167–72
Ravenhill, Mark 43, 97
rebirth 160
reconciliation 20, 136, 141, 153–5, 161–2, 170, 175
redemption 20, 118–33, 136, 138, 154, 166, 172, 175
regeneration 74, 155–6, 162, 166
regressive/regression 36, 119, 140–1, 147–8, 152, 163–4, 172–3. *See also* adult-child; childish adult
reincarnation 5–6, 10, 68, 106, 131, 153
reproductive futurism 12–13, 54, 62, 74, 90, 114, 124, 130–1, 141, 155, 161, 163, 167, 170
resurrection 1, 3, 175
revenants 68, 75. *See also* supernatural
revenge tragedy 96–7, 115, 131. *See also* tragedy
Richardson, J. Michael 130
Ridout, Nicholas 10, 51–2, 103

Ritter, Sonia 98
Roach, Joseph 156, 160
Romanov, Alexei 158
Rosenberg, Marvin 62–4
Roth, Christine 16
Rothwell, Kenneth 83, 130, 158
Royal Shakespeare Theatre 34
Royster, Francesca T. 106
rugby 145, 148–9
Rutter, Carol Chillington 8, 21
  Clamorous Voices: Shakespeare's Women Today 60
  Enter the Body: Women and Representation on Shakespeare's Stage 112
  'Looking Like a Child – or – Titus: The Comedy' 27, 58, 61–2, 89–90
  'Remind Me: How Many Children Had Lady Macbeth?' 60
  Shakespeare and Child's Play: Performing Lost Boys on Stage and Screen 119–21, 128, 130
  'Shakespeare for Dummies: Or, "See the Puppets Dallying"' 40, 42
  'Shakespeare Performances in England (and Wales) 2011' 72
  '"A World Ransomed, or One Destroyed": English Tales at the Millennium' 145

sacrifice/sacrificial 112, 115, 138, 155–72
Saint Nicholas 157
same-sex desire 144, 150, 163
Sam Wanamaker Theatre 135
Satan 141–2, 144
scapegoat 168, 171
Schumann, Robert 145, 147
scopophilia 42, 50, 52, 56, 78, 82–4, 91, 110. *See also* gaze; voyeurism
Scott, Charlotte 8, 17, 30, 136, 142
self-determination 15, 51
self-expression 15, 98, 150
Seneca 94, 97
Senelick, Laurence 24–5
sentimentalize/sentimentality 18, 20, 24–5, 32, 39, 42, 77, 86, 140–1, 157, 162, 173
Shakespeare, William
  Cymbeline 176
  Hamlet 44, 59, 112, 171–2
  King Henry IV, Part 2 27
  King Henry V 27, 84, 88, 169
  King Lear 162
  Love's Labour's Lost 17–18, 27, 136
  Macbeth 9, 12, 15, 17–20, 38–9, 57–91, 103, 110, 123, 125–6, 136–7, 175, 177
  Merry Wives of Windsor, The 17–18, 136
  Pericles 176
  Richard III 13, 15, 17–18, 20, 23–56, 71, 76, 84, 91, 103, 126, 131, 136, 175–7
  Sonnet 12 145–6
  Sonnet 144 143–4, 153, 163
  Tempest, The 137–8, 176
  Titus Andronicus 10, 15, 17–20, 91, 93–133, 136, 175
  Winter's Tale, The 1–7, 9, 12–13, 15, 17–18, 20, 58, 72, 84, 91, 106, 132, 135–73, 175–7
Shakespeare's Globe Theatre 135, 168
Shaughnessy, Robert 7–8
Shenton, Mark 170
Sheppard, Samuel 136

Sher, Anthony 61
siblings 78
Silbert, Roxanna 25
Silverstone, Catherine 130
simulation 66, 109
simulcast 5, 9, 159. *See also* livecast
sinthomosexual 12
sister 20, 32, 101, 140, 155, 157, 160, 162. *See also* sibling
skull 111–13, 116–17, 132
Smith, Bruce R. 149
Smith, Emma 25, 64, 171–2
Sofer, Andrew 106, 112, 117
Spencer, Charles 65, 72
Stambollouian, Edward 64–5, 67
Starks, Lisa S. 119, 128–9
States, Bert O. 10, 50–1, 103
statue 1–5, 19–20, 40, 106, 166
Steedman, Carolyn 24
Stockton, Kathryn Bond 10–11, 13, 50, 151–3
subjectivity 10, 42, 52. *See also* agency
supernatural 19, 58, 63, 68–9, 74, 84. *See also* revenants
surrogation 1–7, 156, 160, 162, 166–7, 172
Swain, Marianka 169
Swan Theatre 61, 95–6
Szalwinska, Maxie 163

Tarantino, Quentin 97
Taylor, Neil 108
Taylor, Paul 67, 169
Taymor, Julie 9, 12, 19, 93–133, 140, 160, 177
Tchaikovsky, Pyotr Ilyich 177
technology 16, 42–4, 95, 119, 140, 160, 176
teleology 26, 56, 132, 138, 162
temporality 5, 9–11, 13–14, 19, 32, 44, 53, 56, 58, 68–9, 71, 121, 137, 138, 140, 147, 154, 160, 162, 165. *See also* temporal studies
temporal studies 138. *See also* temporality
Terry, Ellen 52, 165
Theatre de Complicité 153
Thingspiele 121–2
Third Ear Band 83
Thomas, Keith 150–1
Trafalgar Transformed 60
tragedy 3, 20, 26, 43, 58, 60–1, 63–6, 78, 90, 97, 99, 160, 170, 172. *See also* revenge tragedy
tragicomedy 97, 102, 116
Treneman, Ann 169
Trevis, Di 96
Tribble, Evelyn 28, 38
Tron Theatre 67–8, 70–1, 73

Über-marionette 51–3. *See also* Craig, Edward Gordon
uncanny 7, 36–8, 46, 53, 73–4
Unjieng, Philip Cu 86

victim/victimhood 17, 23–4, 26, 28, 30–1, 39, 42, 70–1, 74, 77–8, 80, 90, 131, 155, 157, 161, 166–7
Victoriana 140, 155–7, 166, 172
video games 119
viewer 97, 109–10, 113, 115, 130–2. *See also* audience
voyeurism 44, 110, 114. *See also* gaze; scopophilia

Wagner, Matthew D. 14, 56
Wagner, Mieke 42, 47, 54
Walter, Harriet 61
Wanamaker, Sam 168
Wanamaker, Zoe 167–8

Warner, Deborah 10, 19, 94–107, 131–2
Watson, Edward 2, 4
Webster, John 177
Welles, Orson 73
Wells, Stanley 102, 162, 165
Wendt, George 127
Werner, Sarah 177
Wheeldon, Christopher 1–7, 13, 19–20, 40, 72, 106, 131, 135, 154, 166, 175, 177
Wigglesworth, Ryan 135
Williams, Deanne 8, 60, 77, 82–3, 176
Williams, Katherine Schaap 48
Winterson, Jeanette 135
Witmore, Michael 8, 18
Wolf, Matt 165
Wooster Group 44
Worthen, W. B. 52
Wynn, Rob 32, 103

Zipes, Jack 164